Changing Pedagogy
Analysing ELT Teachers in China

Also available from Continuum

Educational Attainment and Society, Nigel Kettley

Analysing Underachievement in Schools, Emma Smith

Teacher Development, Qing Gu

Changing Pedagogy

Analysing ELT Teachers in China

Xin-min Zheng and Chris Davison

continuum
LONDON • NEW YORK

Continuum International Publishing Group

The Tower Building
11 York Road
London
SE1 7NX

80 Maiden Lane
Suite 704
New York
NY 10038

www.continuumbooks.com

British Library Cataloguing-in-Publication Data
A catalogue record for this book is available from the British Library.

ISBN-10: 0-8264-8876-5 (hardcover)
ISBN-13: 978-0-8264-8876-3

Library of Congress Cataloging-in-Publication Data
Zheng, Xin-min.
  Changing pedagogy / Xin-min Zheng and Christine Davison.
    p. cm.
  Includes bibliographical references.
  ISBN-13: 978-0-8264-8876-3
  ISBN-10: 0-8264-8876-5
  1. English language—Study and teaching—Chinese speakers.   2. English language—Study and teaching—China.   3. Second language acquisition—China.   4. English language—Globalization.   I. Davison, Christine.   II. Title.
  PE1130.C4Z54   2008
  428.0071′251—dc22
  2007028670

Typeset by RefineCatch Limited, Bungay, Suffolk
Printed and bound in Great Britain by Biddles Ltd, King's Lynn, Norfolk

Contents

Figures

Tables

Foreword

Changing Pedagogy is an important addition to the second language teaching literature. It provides a grounded account of curriculum change in the largest educational system in the world, that of the People's Republic of China. What makes it of interest well beyond the Chinese context, however, is the lucid explication of concepts critical to language education, including *curriculum*, *methodology* and *pedagogy*.

The concept of 'curriculum' is a large and messy one which is susceptible to a wide range of interpretations. The traditional way of looking at curriculum was to see it as a blueprint setting out all of the planned learning experiences for a specified group of learners (what I have elsewhere called 'the curriculum as plan'). More recently, it has been acknowledged that an adequate understanding of curriculum must include not just what was intended, but also what actually happened at the level of classroom action (the implemented curriculum) along with what was actually learned (the realized curriculum).

> [Curriculum involves] all elements and processes in the planning, implementation and evaluation of learning programs. *Curriculum* includes **syllabus design** (selecting sequencing and justifying content), **methodology** (selecting and sequencing learning tasks and activities), and **evaluation**.
>
> (Nunan, 1999: 305)

One very useful task that the authors have performed is to tease out the distinction between *methodology* and *pedagogy* – two concepts that are sometimes used interchangeably, and often confused. Methodology is defined as 'an external and generalized theory for practice' which encompasses 'the study of the nature of language skills and procedures for teaching them, the study of preparation of lesson plans, materials and textbooks for teaching language skills, the evaluation and comparison of language teaching methods . . . and the practices, procedures and principles themselves'.

Pedagogy, in contrast, is focused on the teacher. It is concerned with the teacher's 'personal construct of teaching beliefs, attitudes, and practices that encompasses all aspects of a teacher's identity'. It is therefore internal to the teaching–learning process. As it sees teaching–learning from the teacher's perspective, and seeks to describe the preparation, delivery and evaluation of the curriculum as plan in terms of teachers' beliefs and practices, it helps us to understand the complex interrelationships between the intended curriculum (the curriculum as plan) and the implemented curriculum.

In the body of the book, the authors contrast a theoretical framework for explicating pedagogical innovation and change with the professional realities of three teachers. These three case studies explore the forces that shape and transform teachers' beliefs and practices, and how, in turn, the beliefs and practices transform the intended curriculum into the implemented curriculum. While generalization is beyond the reach of case study research, insight is not. This book is infused with insights into the nature of curriculum, the nature of pedagogy and the nature of change, and deserves to be widely read by all those with an interest in curriculum development, implementation and evaluation.

David Nunan
Professor of Applied Linguistics and Director of the English Centre
The University of Hong Kong

Acknowledgements

The publication of this book would not have been possible without the guidance and support of a large number of people. First and foremost we would like to express our appreciation to the three anonymous teachers and their students without which this book would not have been possible. We also owe a great debt of gratitude to Bob Adamson, who in many ways was the catalyst for this project, and whose many suggestions helped enormously in shaping and polishing the original material. We also wish to thank our friends, colleagues and graduate students in Hong Kong and Fuzhou who assisted in multiple ways during the process of collecting and developing the material for publication. We deeply appreciate their contributions. We would also like to acknowledge the support and patience of our editorial team at Continuum, in particular Anthony Haynes, Alexandra Webster, Ruth Stimson and Karolin Thomas who shepherded the manuscript into the final production stages. Financial support for the final editorial process was provided by the Education Faculty of the University of Hong Kong. Last, but not least, our love and gratitude to our families for their understanding and support, in particular Zhilin Zhu and Dan Zheng.

Chapter 1

Introduction

1.1 The purpose of this book

This book aims to explore the nature of the implemented English language curriculum, with a particular focus on the pedagogy of the secondary school, often called middle school, teachers in the People's Republic of China (PRC). The book is not so concerned with the effectiveness of the implementation, nor what methods would enhance this effectiveness. Rather, it will examine the effects of the newly implemented English curriculum on English language teaching (ELT) in the secondary classroom, in particular how teachers in different situations with different backgrounds and motives approach the implementation of the curriculum, how they make decisions about what and how to teach, and the extent to which they adapt the promoted methods in their individual teaching environments. In other words, this book focuses on how the teacher becomes the decision-maker and how the promoted methods and implemented pedagogy interact with each other and affect each other in the situated Chinese context.

This book adopts the conceptual framework used by Adamson (1998),[1] who analysed reforms in the English language curriculum for junior secondary schools in China at two levels, that is, the process and the product. Adamson's study focused on the intended curriculum and its relationship to resources and syllabuses. In contrast, this book focuses on the implemented curriculum and the relationship between curriculum and teaching materials, teachers' lesson planning and teaching acts. The scope of this book is shown in Figure 1.1.

According to Snyder *et al.* (1992), there are three main approaches to the study of curriculum implementation: fidelity, mutual adaptation and enactment approaches (see Table 1.1). If adopting a fidelity perspective, the researcher's chief focus and concern would be to measure the degree to which a particular innovation is implemented as planned, and to identify the factors that facilitate or hinder implementation as planned. On the other hand, from an enactment perspective, the researcher would approach curriculum as educational experiences jointly created by students and the teacher. In this situation, curriculum knowledge is a personal construct and the teacher acts as

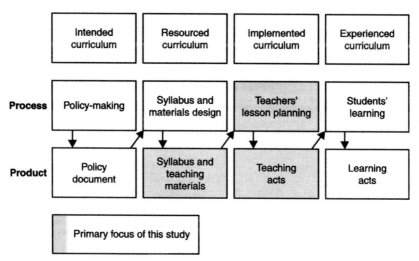

Figure 1.1 The scope of this study (adapted from Adamson and Davison, 2003: 31)

a curriculum developer who together with his or her students grows ever more competent in constructing positive educational experiences. This kind of curriculum implementation and personal developmental change process demands the understanding and acceptance of the subjective realities of the players undergoing the change process.

In contrast, mutual adaptation focuses on the interaction and adaptation between teachers and the curriculum rather than on the unilateral practice. The taught curriculum is by no means the direct implementation of the planned curriculum. The curriculum is mediated and transformed by the teachers' beliefs and their personal pedagogical knowledge, and by their decisions about what to teach and how to teach, themselves shaped by a variety of internal and external factors.

This book frames its study of the implemented pedagogy of three secondary school ELT teachers in the PRC through the theoretical framework of mutual adaptation, assuming that what is most significant and interesting is the way in which individual teachers modify and adapt the planned curriculum to fit their particular teaching environments. As China's latest ELT curriculum is now in the process of being implemented, we believe that it is critical to understand the implementation of policy in practical contexts rather than merely to measure the level of success of the innovation.

As indicated above, this book is essentially exploratory and sociocultural in orientation. We collected much descriptive, classroom-based data to explore the complexity of the teachers' implemented pedagogy, looking in particular for what might be missing or inadequately portrayed in the literature, in order

Table 1.1 Three approaches to curriculum implementation research (adapted from Snyder *et al.*, 1992)

Approach	Research focus
Fidelity perspective	Studies the degree of implementation of an innovation in terms of the extent to which actual use of the innovation corresponds to intended use and determines factors which facilitate and inhibit such implementation.
Mutual adaptation	Studies how the innovation is adapted during the implementation process rather than measuring the degree to which the innovation is implemented as planned.
Curriculum enactment	Studies the implementation and adaptation of proposed curriculum and how curriculum is shaped through the evolving constructs of teachers and students.

to understand the teachers' pedagogy in its fullest possible complexity (Glesne and Peshkin, 1992). Three main data collection techniques, namely, semi-structured interviews, videotaped lesson observation and documentary analysis of the three case study informants' lesson plans and teaching logs, were used to examine Chinese teachers' pedagogical beliefs and practices. The case studies were undertaken in three secondary schools in Fujian province, on the eastern seaboard of the PRC, a mid-range province in terms of economic development and educational development.

This book contributes to our knowledge about the act of teaching, at the same time enhancing our understanding of ELT pedagogic change and the implementation of curriculum in the PRC, assisting teacher educators and publishers in providing teacher support, and providing curriculum planners with information to help design future curricular reforms.

1.2 China and English language teaching (ELT) today

At the beginning of the twenty-first century, China's growing economic, military and political stability have gained recognition internationally (Hsu, 2000). As China increasingly opens up to the world, its unique role in the context of economic globalization becomes even more pronounced, best captured in its 2001 accession to the World Trade Organization (WTO), as well as in Beijing's successful bid to host the 2008 Olympic Games and Shanghai's successful bid for the 2010 World Exposition (Lam, 2002). Not surprisingly,

English has increased dramatically in terms of popularity. English, Zhang (2005: 14) argues, 'creates a new national image for China, projecting a more efficient government of an increasingly open society that welcomes changes as China is eager to import technology, attract foreign investments, and adopt international practice'. English proficiency is also seen as the precondition for a range of socioeconomic and educational opportunities, including university admission and graduation, postgraduate study, study abroad, recruitment to foreign companies or joint ventures, and promotion to higher professional ranks (Hu, 2002; Ng and Tang, 1997). In fact, those with an English language higher proficiency are paid more (Li, 2003), with a national salary survey in 2002 finding that workers who could speak English (or another foreign language) fluently had an average annual income of 53,378 yuan, whereas those workers with a medium or low English proficiency averaged only 31,211 to 38,898 yuan. Due to this close connection between income level, social status and education opportunities, English, not surprisingly, has gained great status in the PRC.

Like the economy, English language learning in China in the new century has also been marked by a transition from liberation to globalization (Bolton, 2002). The Chinese government and Ministry of Education (MOE) appeal to English language teaching at different levels, i.e. primary, secondary and tertiary schools, to reform their curricula, teaching methods, teacher education and teacher professional development, and assessment system, in order to nurture more people who can command better English in listening, speaking, reading and writing. Thus, they can meet the challenging situations in the era of economic globalization (Shu, 2004).

In response to these changes, the State Education Development Commission (SEDC), a central government department, has promulgated a series of educational policies determining the goals, curricula, course books and even the teaching methods throughout the country (Liao, 2000). New textbooks and new teaching methods, such as communicative language teaching and task-based learning, are being strongly promoted in the PRC (Anderson, 1993; Cortazzi and Jin, 1996; Liao, 2000; Liu and Adamson, 1999). These highly centralized initiatives represent a strong top-down intervention in teachers' practices (Yu, 2001). However, Markee (1997) is just one of many researchers from various parts of the world who highlight the limitations of power-coercive approaches to change implementation, which do not lead to long-lasting, self-sustaining innovation.

In China such curriculum change may pose great challenges for teachers: 'striking at the core of learned skills and beliefs and conceptions of education, and creating doubts about purposes, sense of competence, and self-concept' (Fullan with Stiegelbauer, 1991: 45). The influence of the Confucian idea that teachers are knowledge holders, hence favouring teacher-centred, book-centred, grammar-translation methods, albeit with an emphasis on deep understanding and repetitive learning (Anderson, 1993), and the fairly traditional conceptions of language and language learning means that teachers may feel confused or uncertain, their daily routines and practices now perceived as inadequate or outdated. This uncertainty is exacerbated by external pressures, in particular the backwash effects of the high stakes Matriculation English Test (MET) (Cheng, 2005; Gao and Watkins, 2001; Zheng and Adamson, 2003). At the same time, teachers have to deal with many problems in their teaching contexts, such as large class sizes, limited instruction time, inadequate English language proficiency, a shortage of materials, a rigid top-down school culture, unrealistic demands from educational authorities, a lack of resources to support change and rising parental expectations (Anderson, 1993; Hu, 2002; Wu, 2001).

Apart from the attention it receives within the educational system, English is also becoming 'big business' in the wider community (Wang, 2001). The cover story of the December 2001 issue of *Yanzhou Zhoukan* traced such development, citing examples like the New Oriental tuition centres and Li Yang's multi-million Crazy English programme, in which learners may be taught in classes of a few thousand per class, a practice which has attracted much controversy (Bolton, 2003; Shen and Gao, 2004). There are many other similar commercial enterprises, particularly in the coastal cities, which further enhances the status and profile of English teaching, but paradoxically, creates even more pressure on English teachers and their students.

1.3 The historical context

Demand for English language teaching is not a recent phenomenon in China, but its history has been somewhat tumultuous, reflecting the PRC's own see-sawing attitudes to the West. In order to provide the necessary background for readers, these fluctuations and their impact on English language curriculum innovation and change are briefly reviewed, looking first at English teaching during the period of Soviet influence, then at what has been called the First Renaissance (Adamson, 2001; Lam, 2002), followed by the Cultural Revolution and finally, the opening up to the outside world.

1.3.1 The Soviet influence

In this period, English was unpopular in the PRC because of political isolation. Many Western countries did not recognize the PRC, and the economic embargo, most notably by the USA, which blocked its own trade with China, had a negative impact on ELT. In contrast, the special relationship between China and the USSR led to Russian replacing English as the favoured language in schools. Learning Russian was more pragmatic as the Soviet Union was treated as the 'Big Brother' and thousands of Soviet experts worked in all areas of life in China. Many short-term Russian programmes were launched to help teachers of English to become teachers of Russian. In August 1950, the Ministry of Education issued the 'Provisional Teaching Plan of Middle Schools (draft)', which stipulated that every secondary school should teach either Russian or English. The Anti-Rightist Movement and the Great Leap Forward, which took place in 1957, further weakened English teaching and learning in the PRC. As English became increasingly associated with imperialism, fewer people were willing to learn it. It was seen merely as a vehicle to acquire scientific and technological knowledge from the Western world, and hence had a very low official status.

1.3.2 The First Renaissance

In the early 1960s, a tense ideological conflict arose between China and the USSR, which led to a deterioration in the relationship between the two countries. With the change of political atmosphere, English overcame the period of Russian dominance. At the same time, the government adopted a more practical policy towards the national economy and focused less attention on political education. English was treated as a very useful vehicle to achieve modernization and an important medium to communicate with the outside world. Thus, English was once again emphasized in schools. This changing situation challenged the existing teaching materials and teaching methods. Dissatisfaction over the Russian-style textbooks and the prevailing spoon-feeding method of teaching grew, and there was a widespread desire to discard or at least improve the textbooks and teaching methods. This resurgence of interest in ELT has been labelled a renaissance by Adamson (2004a), but was relatively short, quickly stifled by the momentous changes of the Cultural Revolution.

1.3.3 The Cultural Revolution

The Great Leap Forward, the People's Communes and the Sino-Soviet split increased tension and divisiveness within the Chinese Communist Party (CCP). The more pragmatic leaders started to doubt the practice of agricultural collectivization, industrial expansion and the emphasis on ideology (i.e. so-called 'redness'). They grew increasingly critical of Maoist policies, viewing them as out of tune with the changing times. Boldly, they proposed an alternative course, even at the risk of offending Mao Zedong (1893–1976). Mao sensed this danger and initiated the Cultural Revolution (1966–76) to eliminate his opponents in order to maintain his supremacy (Hsu, 2000). The Cultural Revolution caused great turmoil both politically and socially in China. With the fall of Liu Shaoqi (1898–1969), the late Chairman of the PRC, and Deng Xiaoping (1904–97), the late senior party leader, political, social, cultural and academic life, even daily routines, throughout the country was disrupted (Dzau, 1990). Mao instructed that every class in every school across China should be temporarily suspended for the purpose of 'making revolution'. Schools throughout the country were all closed. Cultural Revolution policies not only discredited elite secondary schooling in China, but also destroyed any interaction with the world beyond China's borders. Ross (1993) points out that the historical connection in China between foreign interests and privilege linked foreign language proficiency to exploitation. The Cultural Revolution aimed to eradicate the 'four olds' – old ideas, old culture, old customs and old habits of exploitation. English language teaching and learning was seen as the hothouse for cultivating bourgeois and revisionist ideas and intellectuals and therefore was banned. Learning anything foreign was impossible (Lam, 2002), hence many teachers of English were persecuted, and treated as foreign secret agents or spies. During this period of time, textbooks developed locally were crowded with political slogans in order to meet the need of proletarian propaganda. Many schools even stopped offering English due to the lack of teachers. Standards fell, policies often changed, and English reached its nadir in terms of popularity.

1.3.4 Opening up to the outside world

The Cultural Revolution ended in 1976 with the death of Mao Zedong and the arrest of the Gang of Four.[2] The Central Committee of the Communist Party of China held the Eleventh Party Congress in August 1977, in which the Open Door Policy was confirmed to realize the four modernizations (agriculture, industry, national defence and science and technology) in China. In 1978 the Ministry of Education held an important conference on foreign language teaching. English was given prominence again in schools, on a par with Chinese and mathematics. By the early 1980s the Ministry of Education had restored English as a compulsory subject in the national college entrance examination. The fervour for learning English was fanned by teach yourself English programmes on television, watched by hundreds of millions of people (Boyle, 2000). This stimulated enthusiasm for learning foreign languages throughout the country (Ng and Tang, 1997). By 1981, out of the total of 263,646 foreign language teachers in secondary schools, 259,054 were teaching English (Fu, 1986). The large number of ELT teachers reflected the strong resurgence of demand for English learning in China. Social, economic and political forces were important factors in the massive expansion of ELT (Cortazzi and Jin, 1996). From 1982 to 1993, as China increasingly opened up to the West and Chinese scholars were allowed to go abroad, the need for both social and academic English became apparent. As markets also opened up and more foreigners were allowed into the country to do business, the appetite for Business English among all levels of Chinese people became insatiable (Boyle, 2000). A good command of English was seen as giving individuals opportunities for higher education, for career advancement, for better jobs with better pay in foreign-funded joint ventures, for study and travel abroad (Dzau, 1990). English was also seen as the key to an enormous store of readily available knowledge essential to speed up the modernization process, since English was the international language of science and technology. By 1993, 85 per cent of all information in world-wide informational storage and retrieval networks was in English (Anderson, 1993). Great efforts to improve ELT involved many of the best qualified and most experienced teachers, both foreign and Chinese, including scholars and teachers who had come back from studies in Britain, the USA, Canada, Australia and other countries. A new and improved syllabus for ELT in China's universities, colleges and foreign language institutes was promulgated, new teaching materials were prepared, new methods were tried out, albeit on a small scale, and obvious progress in teaching and learning was made (Dzau, 1990).

During this period, two new English textbook series were published for secondary school teaching. The 1978 version consisted of six textbooks in the form of sentence and dialogue drills, reading passages, and grammar exercises. This version followed the principle of the syllabus, that is, listening and speaking first; then reading and writing, integrated training, emphasizing reading (Tang, 1983). In other words, this version stressed balance between knowledge and usage of language. The 1982 version consisted of nine textbooks, cassette tapes of reading passages and practice drills, teacher's books and wallcharts. The main organization of this version was in the form of sentence and dialogue drills, reading passages, vocabulary, and grammar exercises.

From 1993 onwards, as a result of the huge increase in demand for ELT in the PRC, many scholars in China and abroad (e.g. Adamson, 1998; Liu, 1995; 1996; 2001; 2002; Wang, 1999; 2007) became interested in researching ELT curriculum policies and development in the PRC. Adamson (1998), in particular, undertook an elaborate analysis of the process of curriculum development and the nature of the English Language curriculum, as constructed by the People's Education Press (PEP), the curriculum development agency in the Ministry of Education. However, although Adamson (1998; 2002; 2004a), Gong (1999), Mei (2004), Shu (2004), Zhang (2001), and other scholars have contributed some articles on classroom pedagogy and a number of secondary school teachers of English have also written up many self-reflective articles about their teaching strategies, complemented by surveys (e.g. Ng and Tang, 1997), there has not yet been any significant classroom-based studies of the implemented English language pedagogy in Chinese secondary schools.

1.4 Methodology vs. pedagogy

In educational research, the terms 'methodology' and 'pedagogy' are often used interchangeably. For the purpose of this research study, we wish to draw a distinction between them. The study of methodology includes the study of the nature of language skills and procedures for teaching them, the study of preparation of lesson plans, materials and textbooks for teaching language skills, the evaluation and comparison of language teaching methods (e.g. the direct method and the audiolingual method), and such practices, procedures and principles themselves (Adamson, 2004b; Larsen-Freeman, 2000; Richards and Rodgers, 2001). We view pedagogy as closely associated with classroom teaching and it is defined as the teacher's personal construct of teaching beliefs, attitudes and practices that encompasses all aspects of a teacher's identity. Thus, the essential distinctions between methodology and pedagogy can be summarized in terms of three key factors – scope of goals, influences and applicability. Methodology is more narrowly focused and tends to be more prescriptive and theoretically coherent in its application, as it targets language learning as its main goal, it is largely based on individual theoretical insights, and it is by definition assumed to be applicable in different contexts; pedagogy has broader educational goals, is influenced by a wider range of theories and curricular influences and tensions, and is more rooted in and responsive to the practical realities of a particular classroom. Table 1.2 shows the differences between methodology and pedagogy. More detailed analysis of methodology and pedagogy are discussed in Chapter 2 and Chapter 3 respectively.

Table 1.2 Differences between methodology and pedagogy (Zheng, 2005)

	Methodology	Pedagogy
	• 'Top-down'	• 'Bottom-up'
	• Generalized	• Particularized
	• External construct	• Personal construct
Scope and goals	• Biased and relatively narrow	• Broader
	• Tends to be prescriptive	• Descriptive
Influences	• Narrow and theoretical base, usually coherent and clearly articulated	• Wide range of theories and influences, often conflicting
Applicability	• Assumed to be applicable to a wide range of classrooms, irrespective contexts	• Rooted in and responsive to the practical realities of a particular classroom

1.5 Overview of this book

This book is written for teachers, teacher-educators, and researchers who are interested in teachers' cognition and practice, teachers' professional development and teacher knowledge in general. This opening chapter has briefly described the aims and genesis of the book and has provided a brief historical review of ELT in the PRC, locating the study firmly within the context of wider sociocultural, educational and political change. The theoretical framework for the book has also been briefly described and its origins explained.

Chapter 2 sets out to define methodology as an external construct. By tracing innovation and change in ELT internationally, this chapter provides a brief historical review of methods in ELT (Larsen-Freeman, 2000; Richards and Rodgers, 2001; Willis, 1996) and of the post-methods era (Bell, 2003; Kumaravadivelu, 2003), concluding that methods are not universal, context-free nor teacher-free, nor even necessarily desirable or needed. Chapter 2 also argues that social and political factors can have a strong impact upon what happens inside the classroom (Lantolf, 2000; Pennycook, 2000). It concludes with a brief review of the history of ELT curriculum innovation and change in the PRC since 1949 (Adamson, 2004a), in which there is a clear and noticeable trend towards China adapting ELT methods to China's circumstances – the transformation of methods.

In Chapter 3, we argue that to understand English language methodological change and its effects, it is not sufficient to analyse the intended curriculum and the promoted methods; the teachers' own interpretations of and relationships with these factors are equally important, if not more important. We argue for an alternative construct to the notion of methodology explored in Chapter 2, proposing a distinction between pedagogy and methodology. We point out that pedagogy, like methodology, can be conceptualized as having three interlinked levels: teachers' beliefs, teachers' designs and teachers' practices. However, unlike methodology it is a highly individualized, contextualized and specific construct. Elaborating on this notion, we define the nature of teachers' beliefs, and then discuss the relationship between teachers' beliefs and practices so as to provide a clear understanding of why teachers do what they do or don't do, as the case may be, in their classroom teaching (Borg, 2003; Davison, 2001; Freeman, 2002; Tsui, 2003; Woods, 1996). Chapter 3 also argues that teachers' thinking and action, whether tacit or explicit, are influenced and constructed by the situated contexts that surround teachers and teaching (e.g. Fullan, 2001; Hall and Hord, 2000; Hargreaves, 1994). This chapter also clarifies the nature and process of change, and the role of situational factors and individual experiences in change, and at the same time, it also explores how teachers deal with change, especially in their own pedagogic settings (Markee, 1997; Riley, 1998; Stoll and Fink, 1996). The purpose of this is to examine what it is that impels or inspires teachers to change or what it is that hinders or impels teachers not to change.

Chapters 4, 5 and 6 then introduce the three teachers of English – Mr Yang, Miss Wu and Ms Ma – drawing on a range of very rich detailed material to explore their everyday classroom interactions in the rapidly emerging and changing PRC from a range of different perspectives. Together the teachers represent three generations of ELT teacher in the PRC: the young teacher just trained and eager to try out new ideas, the mid-career teacher struggling to reconcile familiar and new routines, and the 'senior' teacher who has lived through the Cultural Revolution but still sees possibilities in change. Each chapter introduces us to the teacher by means of a biographical profile, which helps us to understand their beliefs and practices and the factors which have helped shape their implemented pedagogy, such as ELT curricular renewal, the rigid national college entrance examination and the promoted communicative methods. Each chapter gives a vivid account of how each teacher mediates diverse conflicting situational factors in their specific context, including the diverse needs of students, parents, colleagues and principal.

Chapter 7 provides an authoritative discussion of issues arising from a comparison of the implemented pedagogy of these three teachers, arguing the case for a refined model of the impact of external, internal and situated forces on teachers and the resulting pedagogical innovation and change. From the discussion, this chapter argues that English language teachers in the PRC are open to new teaching methods; however, the process of their pedagogical change is not radical, but incremental and pragmatic, constrained by internal, external and situated forces (Zheng, 2005). This chapter also calls for more teacher support, and a reform of the national assessment system to complement the promoted curriculum in a more coherent and harmonious way. The final chapter concludes with a summary of the major findings of the study and suggestions for more effective practice and much-needed research.

Notes

1. Adamson adopted this framework from Johnson (1989).
2. The Gang of Four, Wang Hongwen (1936–1992), Zhang Chunqiao (1917–2005), Jiang Qing (1914–1991) and Yao Wenyuan (1931–2005), were a group of CPC leaders in the PRC who were arrested and removed from their positions in 1976, following the death of Mao Zedong, and were primarily blamed for the events of the Cultural Revolution.

Chapter 2

ELT as methodology

2.1 Introduction

This chapter focuses on defining and describing methodology in ELT, as well as analysing the underlying construct of methods, and its critique, and drawing out the implications for the nature of the implemented pedagogy of secondary school teachers of English in the PRC. The purpose of this is to show how there are many changes that teachers need to cope with, that is, changes in the ELT discipline as well as in the educational and sociopolitical context both inside and outside China. This will also help to establish the distinction between methodology and pedagogy, to be proposed in Chapter 3.

2.2 The definition of methodology

According to Richards (1985: 8–9), methodology in language teaching refers to the practices and procedures used in teaching, and the principles and beliefs that underlie them. Methodology includes the study of the nature of language skills and procedures for teaching them, the study of preparation of lesson plans, materials and textbooks for teaching language skills, the evaluation and comparison of language teaching methods (e.g. the direct method and the audiolingual method), and the practices, procedures, principles and beliefs themselves (Richards *et al.*, 1985). Rodgers (2001) provides a more succinct definition of methodology by asserting that methodology links to theory and practice. He points out that theory statements include theories of what language is and how language is learned or, more specifically, theories of ELT. Such theories are linked to various design features of language instruction. These design features might include stated objectives, syllabus specifications, types of activities, roles of teachers and learners, materials and so forth. Design features in turn are linked to actual teaching and learning practices as observed in the environments where language teaching and learning take place. This whole complex of elements defines ELT methodology (see Figure 2.1).

Again, Rodgers (2001) points out that within ELT methodology a

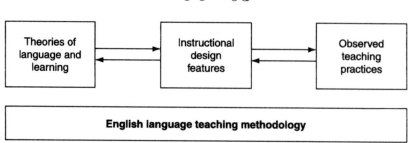

Figure 2.1 Language teaching methodology (adapted from Rodgers, 2001)

distinction is often made between methods and approaches, in which methods are held to be fixed teaching systems with prescribed techniques and practices, whereas approaches represent language teaching philosophies that can be interpreted and applied in a variety of different ways in the classroom. This distinction is probably most usefully seen as defining a continuum of entities ranging from highly prescribed methods to loosely described approaches. Based on the above notion, we redefine *methodology* as an external and generalized theory for practice in this book, which will be contrasted with the other key term *pedagogy*, to be discussed in detail in Chapter 3.

Sutton (2000) believes that methods are the kinds of structured activities for students and the various kinds of methods used by teachers/trainers in the teaching–learning process. In other words, methods refer to the teaching skills that teachers use to impart the specialized knowledge/content of their subject area(s). Effective teachers display a wide range of skills and abilities that lead to creating a learning environment where all students feel comfortable and are sure that they can succeed both academically and personally. In contrast, Larsen-Freeman (1986: xi) sees methods as superordinate, comprising both 'principles' and 'techniques'. The principles involve five aspects: the teacher, the learner, the teaching process, the learning process and the target language culture. Taken together, the principles represent the theoretical framework of the method. The techniques are the behavioural manifestation of the principles, in other words, the classroom activities and procedures derived from an application of the principles.

Richards and Rodgers (1986; 2001), adopting a similar three-part analysis focus proposed by Anthony (1963), see methods as an umbrella term comprising approach, design and procedure. According to Richards and Rodgers (2001: 20), 'a method is theoretically related to an approach, is organizationally determined by a design, and is practically realized in procedure'. By approach, they mean the underlying theory of language and of language learning. By design, they mean how those theories determine the objectives, syllabus, teaching–learning activities, teacher–learner roles, and the role of the instructional materials. By procedure, they mean how techniques derived from a particular approach and design are performed in practice. Bell (2003: 327) observes that Richards and Rodgers' perspective has become increasingly influential.

The three dimensions of Richards and Rodgers' model, namely, a theoretical dimension (approach/theory), a design dimension (design/design features), and a practice dimension (procedure/teaching and learning practice), are shown in Figure 2.2. Richards and Rodgers' model helps to establish a useful framework for the systematic description and comparison of methods at the levels of theory, design and practice. Very few methods are explicit with respect to all of these dimensions.

According to Richards and Rodgers (1986; 2001) the theoretical dimension of a method refers to explicit theoretical statements and/or curricular manifestations that reflect theories of language and language learning, which focus on curriculum objectives, syllabus specifications, design of activities, examination specifications, nature and roles of teachers, learners and resources and so forth. The design dimension of a method refers to the general and specific objectives of the method, criteria for the selection and organization of linguistic and/or subject-matter content, roles of learners and teachers, types of learning and teaching activities, the role of instructional materials and so forth. With regard to the practice dimension, it depends on classroom tactics and strategies, practices and behaviours that different teachers and learners use when the method is used. Table 2.1 summarizes the nature of methods at three levels in terms of theory, design and procedure. This framework for discussing methods will be used to demonstrate methods in ELT about the major changes in the last fifty years, which is critical for the context of this book.

The following section will briefly discuss the key methods in ELT which have been most influential in the People's Republic of China: the grammar-translation method, the audiolingual method, communicative language teaching, and task-based learning.

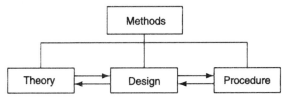

Figure 2.2 Three levels of methods: theory, design and procedure (adapted from Richards and Rodgers, 2001: 33)

Table 2.1 Method, design and procedure (adapted from Richards and Rodgers, 2001: 33)

		Methods
Theory	Scope	Explicit theoretical statements and/or curricular manifestations that reflect theories of language and language learning
	Focus	• Teachers' guides • Curriculum objectives • Syllabus specifications • Examination specifications • Design of activities • Nature and roles of teachers, learners and resources
	Approach	Interviews with curriculum designers; analysis of syllabus, examinations, resources and Teacher's Books
Design	Scope	Design of content for teaching and learning
	Focus	• Choice and organization of content • Objects of learning • Nature and role of resources • Types of activities • Roles of teachers and learners
	Approach	Analysis of syllabus, resources and Teacher's Books
Procedure	Scope	
	Focus	
	Approach	

2.3 Brief history of ELT methods

2.3.1 The grammar-translation method

The historical development of the grammar-translation method can be traced back to more than three centuries ago when the classical languages, such as Latin and Greek, were taught. This mode of language teaching was initially employed for the acquisition of the skills necessary to read and understand these classical languages (Chastain, 1988). The principal characteristics of the grammar-translation method are summarized as follows:

- The theory of learning could be best summarized as 'what is taught is learned'. Language learning is viewed as an intellectual activity involving rule learning and the memorization of rules and facts related to first language meanings by means of a lot of translation practice (Stern, 1983).
- It is characterized by its emphasis on reading and writing; little or no systematic attention is paid to speaking or listening. Knowledge of the grammar is taught deductively, that is, from rules to examples (Richards and Rodgers, 2001).
- Vocabulary selection is based solely on the reading texts used; vocabulary is introduced in long word lists with their translation equivalents, which are memorized by rote learning (Celce-Murcia, 2001).
- These lists of structures and vocabulary form the basis of any syllabus. Textbooks using the grammar-translation method have lessons which include: a reading passage in the target language, a list of vocabulary items and their translation, and an explanation in the native language of important points of grammar contained in the text. The methodology is restricted to grammar exercises, translation and dictation (Celce-Murcia, 2001).
- The teacher is at the centre of the classroom teaching–learning process. The teacher is 'he who knows': he directs the classroom activities, asking questions and setting tasks, and is considered as an authority. The learner would learn vocabulary and conjugations off by heart. The learner is no more than a passive receptor (Omaggio, 1986).
- The learning process is conceived of as a process of memorizing rules and examples; accuracy is much emphasized (Larsen-Freeman, 1986).

The main drawbacks of this method from the perspective of modern educators and linguists such as Rivers (1968) and Richards and Rodgers (1986; 2001) are that little emphasis is laid on speaking practice and thus communication skills are neglected. Too much emphasis is laid on learning rules and exceptions, some of which may be rare, old fashioned or have little or no pragmatic value. The role of the students in the classroom is mostly a passive one, with overloaded written exercises, which most students consider tedious and laborious.

It is noteworthy that none of the basic orientations of the grammar-translation method can be justified by research findings. The concept of language underpinning grammar-translation is not upheld by linguistics; the conception of the learner and learning is not based upon any formal psychology. However, in spite of the method's indifference to speech and oral communication, and despite its being disparaged by leading language educators for decades, grammar-translation is still widely employed today (Rao,

1999; Stern, 1983; Wyss, 2002). The unique aspect of this method is that it can be applied to masses of students by teachers who lack verbal fluency in the target language in terms of both understanding and producing speech (Steinberg, 1993). Steinberg further maintains another strong point of the grammar-translation method is its extraordinary capacity to adapt to ever-changing psychological and linguistic theories. The distinguishing features of the method, its explication of grammar and the use of translation can be adapted to any psychological or linguistic theory.

2.3.2 The audiolingual method

From 1850 to 1900, the language teaching reformers, particularly in Europe, attempted to make language teaching more effective by a radical change from the grammar-translation method. Since the grammar-translation method was not very effective in preparing students to use the target language communicatively, the direct method gained in popularity. The direct method had one very basic rule: no translation was allowed. Diller (1978) stated that the direct method received its name from the fact that meaning was to be conveyed directly in the target language through the use of demonstration and visual aid, with no recourse to the students' native language. The direct method enjoyed considerable popularity at the end of the nineteenth century and the beginning of the twentieth century, but it was difficult to use, mainly because of the constraints of high cost, time and classroom size. In addition, the direct method also set too high a demand on teachers' language competence. However, such was the demand for 'real' communication that a few decades later, interest in the direct method was revived in the form of the audiolingual method (Brown, 2000).

The emergence of the audiolingual method was linked directly to military operations in World War II (Richards and Rodgers, 2001). In order to provide personnel who could speak fluent German, French, Italian, Chinese, Japanese and other languages, the US government developed the Army Specialized Training Program (ASTP). ASTP adopted the techniques of the informant method, which used a native speaker of the language – the informant – to serve as a source of phrases and vocabulary and who provided sentences for imitation, and a linguist, who supervised the learning experience. ASTP turned out to be most successful in small classes of mature and highly motivated students, enabling them to achieve conversational proficiency in as short time as possible. After World War II, when thousands of overseas students poured into the USA for study, there was a great demand for English language learning. Language teaching specialists began to develop a method that was suitable for US colleges and classrooms. They drew on the Army

Method, structural linguistic theory and behavioural psychology to develop what was termed 'the audiolingual method' (e.g. Richards and Rodgers, 2001; Steinberg, 1993; Stern, 1983). According to Chastain (1988), structural linguistics focused on the phonemic, morphological and syntactic systems underlying the grammar of a given language, rather than the traditional categories of Latin grammar. As such, it is held that learning a language involved mastering the building blocks of the language and learning the rules by which these basic elements are combined from the level of sound to the level of sentence. The audiolingual method was also based on the behaviourist theory of learning (Steinberg, 1993), in which language is elicited by a stimulus and that stimulus then triggers a response. The response in turn then produces some kind of reinforcement, which, if positive, encourages the repetition of the response in the future or, if negative, its suppression. When transposed to the classroom, this gives us the classic pattern drill – Model: Mary went to the cinema yesterday. Stimulus: library. Response: Mary went to the library yesterday. Reinforcement: Good! (Brown, 1980; Skinner, 1957).

The audiolingual method aimed to promote mechanical habit-formation through repetition of basic patterns. Accurate manipulation of structure was meant to lead to eventual fluency. Spoken language came before written language. Dialogues and drill were central to the approach. Accurate pronunciation and control of structure were paramount. This method was one of the first to have its roots firmly grounded in linguistic and psychological theory (Brown, 1994; 2000), which added to its credibility and probably had some influence on the popularity it enjoyed over a long period of time.

The principal features of the audiolingual method were the use of dialogue as the chief means of presenting the language, and the emphasis on certain practice techniques including imitation, repetition, memorization and pattern drills. Another feature was that learners were not encouraged to speak before listening, to read before speaking, or to write before reading (Chastain, 1988). The objective of the audiolingual method was to focus on the fundamental skills, i.e. listening and speaking. In other words, listening and speaking were given priority or, to be more exact, in the teaching sequence, listening and speaking preceded reading and writing (Brooks, 1964). The teacher's role was central and active. The teacher was encouraged to correct every false utterance immediately; in other words, errors had to be avoided at all costs. However, the learner played a reactive role by responding to stimuli, and thus had very little control over the content, pace or style of learning (Rivers, 1968).

Stern (1983) indicates that in the early 1960s the audiolingual method raised hopes of ushering in a golden age of language teaching; however, by the end of the decade it became the scapegoat for all that was wrong with language teaching. There are two major reasons for this pendulum swing. On the one hand, the practical results of the method did not meet its expectations, and on the other hand, changes in linguistic theory in the 1960s challenged the structural view of language as well as the behaviourist view of language learning. Chomsky's theory (1959) of transformational grammar argued that language was not a process of habit formation. According to Chomsky (1965), innovation and the formation of new sentences and patterns allow for the generation or creation of new utterances from the learner's underlying knowledge of abstract rules. Chomsky's references to 'innate aspects of the mind' contrasted and conflicted with Skinner's emphasis on observable behaviours. With respect to practical classroom teaching, Rivers (1968: 46) notes that 'the techniques of memorization and drilling that this method implies can become intensely tedious and boring, causing fatigue and distaste on the part of the students'. Moreover, the method was also very demanding on the part of classroom language teachers. As Rivers (1968: 49–50) elaborates:

> The audiolingual method makes considerable demands upon the teacher. It demands of him a near-native articulation and intonation if he is to model utterances for the students (if he is lacking in this area he must learn to use a tape model and work along with the class at making up his deficiencies). The method calls for considerable energy if the teacher is to keep oral practice moving smartly and imagination and enterprise in using persons and situations in the classroom if foreign language-learning material is to acquire reality and relevance. It also demands of the teacher careful preparation and organization of material. For those reasons, it is difficult for a teacher to teach a number of parallel classes during the day by this method without becoming weary of material and physically and emotionally exhausted.

The dissatisfaction with the audiolingual method was one of a number of factors that set the stage for another shift in methods, that is, to communicative language teaching, with its fundamental idea that a language can only be learned if it is used in a meaningful way. Such a focus centred on speaking and listening skills, on writing for specific communicative purposes, and on 'authentic reading texts' (Brown, 2000; Richards and Rodgers, 2001; Steinberg, 1993).

2.3.3 Communicative language teaching

Communicative language teaching (CLT) began in Britain in the 1960s as a replacement to the earlier structural method, called situational language teaching. This was partly in response to Chomsky's (1957) criticisms of structural theories of language and partly based on the theories of British functional linguists, such as Firth (1957) and Halliday (1973), as well as American sociolinguists, such as Hymes (1968), Gumperz and Hymes (1972) and Labov (1972), and the writings of Austin (1962) and Searle (1969) on speech acts. Since it first came into being, CLT has undergone a number of phases. Leading scholars, such as Bachman (1991), Bachman and Palmer (1996), Brumfit and Johnson (1979), Canale and Swain (1980), Celce-Murcia *et al.* (1997), Chomsky (1965), Hymes (1972), Munby (1978), Prabhu (1987), Savignon (1983), Widdowson (1978; 1979; 1990; 1998) and Wilkins (1976), have been working hard to explore its rationale and have done much to develop its rich and eclectic theoretical base. Larsen-Freeman (2000) defines the aims of CLT broadly as making communicative competence the goal of language teaching and acknowledging the interdependence of language and communication.

The development of sociolinguistics and psycholinguistics played an important role in the emergence of the theoretical basis of CLT. Socio-linguistics maintains that the social function of a language is to serve, as a tool, various communicative activities in the community, which involves what to say (notion), how to say (use) and why to say (function) (see Coupland and Jaworski, 1997; Gumperz and Hymes, 1972; Holmes, 1992; Hudson, 1996; Labov, 1972; Romaine, 1994; Ronald, 2002; Whorf, 1956). Hence, the emphasis of language teaching should be placed on equipping the learners with communicative competence so as to enable them to use the language to communicate effectively and efficiently. Psycholinguistics (cognitive psychology) holds that every child possesses an inborn capacity for acquiring language, which enables him or her to master a language (e.g. Cairns, 1999; Herdina, 2002; Steinberg, 2001). Therefore the communicative approach pays heed to developing this inborn capacity.

Finocchiaro and Brumfit (1983: 91–3) list 22 pedagogical features of CLT. In essence, the key implications for teaching are as follows:

- Teaching is learner centred and responsive to students' needs and interests.
- The target language is acquired through interactive communicative use that encourages the negotiation of meaning.
- Genuinely meaningful language use is emphasized, along with unpredictability, risk-taking and choice-making.
- There is exposure to examples of authentic language from the target language community.
- The formal properties of language are never treated in isolation from use; language forms are always addressed within a communicative context.

- Students are encouraged to discover the forms and structures of language for themselves.
- There is a whole-language approach in which the four traditional language skills (speaking, listening, reading and writing) are integrated.

Richards and Rodgers (2001: 172) have also summarized the main principles of CLT as follows:

- Learners learn a language through using it.
- Authentic and meaningful communication should be the goal of classroom activities.
- Fluency is an important dimension of communication.
- Communication involves the integration of different language skills.
- Learning is a process of creative construction and involves trial and error.

These principles are all related in some way to the theories of language learning that were discussed above. To summarize these: language acquisition is an unpredictable developmental process requiring a communicatively interactive and cooperative negotiation of meaning on the part of students; the subsequent integration of comprehensible input and output influences the learner's developing language system.

Howatt (1984: 279) argues that there are two forms of communicative language teaching: the 'weak' form and the 'strong' form. Howatt defines the weak form as learning to use English while the strong form as using English to learn it. In the strong form of CLT the teacher is required to take a 'less dominant role' and the students are encouraged to be 'more responsible managers of their own learning' (Larsen-Freeman, 1986: 131). Celce-Murcia *et al.* (1997: 141) suggest that there has been a move away from strong CLT to a weaker version 'whereby new linguistic information is passed on and practiced explicitly'. Thornbury (1998) observes that strong CLT has been and remains a chimera and that in fact, from a communicative perspective, CLT is not only weak but very weak. To illustrate, the weak form regarded knowledge of grammar as an integral part of communicative competence and it held that grammar rules should be learned so as to facilitate and assist correct and better use of target language in communication.

In communicative language teaching, learners participate in different activities, expressing their own ideas, giving information, sharing and exchanging ideas. There may not be only one correct answer to different questions. Conversational interaction is the main means of developing communicative competence, which has been called an indirect approach (Celce-Murcia *et al.*, 1997: 141). It relies heavily on the students' own abilities to interactively negotiate meaning with each other. In the process, unfamiliar language forms and rules are made comprehensible to the students, and presumably integrated into their developing language systems. The importance of comprehensible input which challenges learners to stretch their understanding was expressed by Krashen and Terrell as the 'input hypothesis' (Richards and Rodgers, 1986: 130). More recently, emphasis has also been placed on the importance of language production in this acquisition process (Kumaravadivelu, 1994: 34). Breen and Candlin (1980: 110) have described the learners' role within CLT in the following terms:

> The role of learner as negotiator – between the self, the learning process, and the object of learning – emerges from and interacts with the role of joint negotiator within the group and within the classroom procedures and activities which the group undertakes. The implication for the learner is that he should contribute as much as he gains, and thereby learn in an interdependent way.

Several roles are assumed for teachers in CLT, such as controllers, monitors, facilitators, participant analysts, advisers and process managers (Richards and Rodgers, 2001). Teachers are constantly adapting their roles in accordance to the requirement of different activities. They are expected to give appropriate help to students without discouraging their motivation and interrupting their communication. They are not supposed always to correct students' errors and leave more space for self-correction. Breen and Candlin (1980: 99) describe teacher's roles as follows:

> The teacher has two main roles: the first role is to facilitate the communication process between all participants in the classroom, and between these participants and the various activities and texts. The second role is to act as an independent participant within the learning–teaching group. The latter role is closely related to the objectives of the first role and arises from it. These roles imply a set of secondary roles for the teacher; first, as an organizer of resources and as a resource himself, second as a guide within the classroom procedures and activities ... A third role for the teacher is that of researcher and learner, with much to contribute in terms of appropriate knowledge and abilities, actual and observed experience of the nature of learning and organizational capacities.

In relation to materials, the primary role in communicative language teaching is to promote the learners' communicative language use. Materials are typically described as 'text-based', 'task-based' and 'realia', including bridging information gap, information transfer and problem-solving (Richards and

Rodgers, 2001: 168). The materials are claimed to be 'authentic' or at least 'semi-authentic', which means learners can use authentic language to solve 'real' problems in their classroom. The materials are also generally integrated, which demands listening, speaking, reading and writing (Nunan, 1999: 78–81).

Though CLT has been implemented internationally for two to three decades, many problems still remain. If we look at mainstream course books such as *Headway* (Soars and Soars, 2000), *Language in Use* (Doff and Jones, 2000) or *Matters* (J. Bell and Gower, 1997), we find each unit organized according to grammar and vocabulary, as well as functional language skills. It would be wrong to see textbooks as a reflection of actual practice, but it would seem to indicate that a strictly communicative syllabus has not been widely embraced. It is not only in the area of classroom activities and overall syllabus that the application of a communicative approach has been problematic; for teaching to be accountable it requires the monitoring and assessment of learning. In this area communicative approaches have encouraged us to see language development as an ongoing process rather than a static product (Prabhu, 1990). A qualitative assessment of communicative competence would seem to provide a more realistic view of a student's progress than a quantitative measurement of errors or mistakes. But unfortunately, as Savignon (1991: 266) has pointed out, 'qualitative evaluation of written and oral expression is time-consuming and not so straightforward'.

Although the various difficulties in applying a communicative approach, as discussed above, do not require us to question its methodological principles as such, the changing models of syllabus design in the communicative era, from the early experimentation with notional-functional syllabuses to the more recent attempts to design syllabuses with a number of organizing categories, lead into the discussion of syllabuses based upon communicative tasks, and therefore task-based learning (TBL).

2.3.4 Task-based learning

Since Prabhu's (1987) experiment, groundbreaking in its organization of courses around tasks, much has been written about the use of tasks as the unit of analysis of language learning, including Breen (1987), Candlin (1987), Ellis (1994; 2003), Long (1985), Long and Crookes (1992), Skehan (1995; 1996; 2003) and Willis (1996).

Prabhu (1987) points out that the term 'task-based learning' (TBL) is derived from the literature on language education. It refers to 'an approach to the design of language courses in which the point of departure is not an ordered list of linguistic items, but a collection of tasks' (Nunan, 1999: 24).

It has evolved in response to a better understanding of the way languages are learned. Long (1985: 389) describes task-based learning as:

> A piece of work undertaken for oneself or for others, freely or for some reward. Thus, examples of tasks include painting a fence, dressing a child, filling out a form, buying a pair of shoes, making an airline reservation – in other words, by 'task' is meant the hundred and one things people do in everyday life.

Prabhu (1987: 24) further defines what he sees as a task as follows:

> An activity which requires learners to arrive at an outcome from given information through some process of thought, and which allowed learners to control and regulate that process.

However, this definition is not clear enough to help us to see what would count as a task and what would not. In the latter part of his same article Prabhu makes a clearer point by defining four types of classroom activities: 1. rule focused; 2. form-focused; 3. meaningful; and 4. meaning focused. Prabhu's procedural syllabus received attention as well as criticism (see Long and Crookes, 1992; Nunan, 1989). Then Candlin (1987: 10) provided a much more detailed but rather confusing definition of task in his paper:

> One of a set of differentiated, sequencable, problem-posing activities involving learners and teachers in some joint selection from a range of varied cognitive and communicative procedures applied to existing and new knowledge in the collective exploration and pursuance of foreseen or emergent goals within a social milieu.

However, Long and Crookes (1992) commented that Candlin's task-oriented 'process' syllabus still failed to present explicit provision for a focus on language. In contrast, Skehan (1994) has argued that the key to task-based learning is how to preserve a controlled approach to language development and ensure a balance between the competing pressures of restructuring complexity, accuracy and fluency. The tasks must be challenging for the language learner – not too difficult, so that achieving meaning predominates, and not too simple, as in this case nothing is being learned or developed. Skehan (1996: 20) offered his definition of task-based learning as follows:

> [Tasks are] . . . activities which have meaning as their primary focus. Success in tasks is evaluated in terms of achievement of an outcome, and tasks generally bear some resemblance to real-life language use. So task-based instruction takes a fairly strong view of communicative language teaching.

Skehan (2003: 1) observes that like CLT there are also 'weak' and 'strong' versions of TBL:

> In general, proponents of the weak position tend to assume that tasks are not the driving force for syllabus design; that the use of tasks is an adjunct to structure-based teaching; and that it may be possible to 'clothe' structures through tasks without compromise. This approach tends to assume an automatisation or practice view of learning. In contrast, those who take the stronger view of tasks have generally seen the engagement of acquisitional processes as central, although views on the conditions which engage such processing have changed.

Willis (1996) set out to make the transition to task-based learning as easy as possible, and in her book provides a very comprehensive description of how to teach a task-based lesson. Willis (1996: 53) defines a task-based learning approach as:

> A goal-oriented activity in which learners use language to achieve a real outcome . . . learners use whatever target language resources they have in order to solve a problem, do a puzzle, play a game, or share and compare experiences.

Experienced teachers may resent the rather dictatorial style used in her book, but for new teachers it seems that her approach is quite helpful. Following from Long and Crookes (1992) and Skehan (1995), Willis (1996) includes a focus on form in her approach to task-based learning. Regarding focus on form, Long and Robinson (1998) made the distinction between focus on form, focus on formS, and focus on meaning (see Table 2.2).

Despite these shifts and differences of opinions in task-based learning, there

Table 2.2 Differences between focus on form, focus on formS, and focus on meaning (adapted from Long and Robinson, 1998: 16)

Option 2	*Option 3*	*Option 1*
analytic	analytic	synthetic
focus on **meaning**	focus on **form**	focus on **formS**
←		→
Natural Approach	TBLT	GT, ALM, Silent Way, TPR
Immersion	Content-Based LT (?)	
Procedural Syllabus	Process Syllabus (?)	Structural/N-F Syllabuses
etc.	etc.	etc.

are common and language learning assumptions about the nature of language, underlying current approaches to TBL (Richards and Rodgers, 2001: 226–9):

- Language is primarily a means of making meaning.
- Multiple models of language inform task-based instruction.
- Lexical units are central in language use and language learning.
- Conversation is the central focus of language and the keystone of language acquisition.
- Tasks provide both input and output processing necessary for language acquisition.
- Task activity and achievement are motivational.
- Learning difficulty can be negotiated and fine-tuned for particular pedagogical purposes.

Task-based learning procedures are typically based on three stages, a tripartite division into which Willis (1996: 53) refers to as the pre-task, the during-task and the post-task stage elements, which is shown in Table 2.3.

Similarly, Richards (2002) points out there are potentially three points at which a focus on form can be provided in task work – prior to the task, during the task and after the task, which is summarized in Table 2.4.

The primary roles of learners in the task-based learning approach are group participants, monitors, risk-takers and innovators. These roles not only require the learners to be active in pair work, and group work, but also facilitate learning and reflection. Moreover, the learners are also required to create and interpret messages for which they lack full linguistic resources and prior experience (Richards and Rodgers, 2001).

Regarding the roles of teachers in the task-based learning approach, in addition to the roles that teachers play in CLT, teachers are expected to be the selectors, and sequencers of the tasks, which means teachers should be able to choose, modify and create tasks to suit the learners' needs, and demands in an instructional sequence. At the same time, teachers should be well prepared to provide partial demonstration of task procedures, to help students to learn or recall words and expressions in order to succeed in achieving their task performance. Besides, teachers must also be aware of one aspect in terms of

Table 2.3 Procedures for task-based learning (adapted from Willis, 1996: 53)

Pre-task	Introduction to the task, brainstorming, pre-teaching vocabulary where necessary
During-task	Task-planning and report
Post-task	Analysis, feedback and practice

Table 2.4 Task work – prior to the task, during the task and after the task (adapted from Richards, 2002)

Accuracy prior to the task	• By repeating certain linguistic forms that can be used while completing a task. • By reducing the cognitive complexity of the task. • By giving time to plan the task.
Accuracy during the task	• Participation: whether the task is completed individually or with other learners. • Procedures: the number of procedures involved in completing the task. • Resources: the materials and other resources provided for the learners to use while completing the task. • Order: the sequencing of a task in relation to previous tasks. • Product: the outcome or outcomes students produce, such as a written product or an oral one.
Accuracy after the task	• Public performance: after completing a task in small groups, students now carry out the task in front of the class or another group. This can have the effect of promoting them to perform the task at a more complex linguistic level. Aspects of their performance that were not initially in focus during in-group performance can become conscious, as there is an increased capacity for self-monitoring during a public performance of a task. • Repeat performance: the same activity might be repeated with some elements modified, such as the amount of time available. • Other performance: students might hear more advantaged learners completing the same task, and focus on some of the linguistic and communicative resources employed in the process.

'focus on form', which suggests a variety of form-focusing techniques be used, in other words, attention-focusing pre-task activities, text exploration, guided exposure to parallel tasks, use of highlighted materials, and so on and so forth (Richards and Rodgers, 2001: 236).

To conclude, from the above discussion, each underlying method contains three interlinked components in terms of theory, design and procedure, as summarized in Table 2.5.

As can be seen from Table 2.5, ELT has undergone enormous changes in terms of its underlying concepts of language and language learning in the past few decades, from analytical structure, behaviourism, cognitive code and task-based learning. Although theories change and evolutions go on, methods are based on idealized concepts geared towards idealized contexts. Since language learning and teaching needs, wants and situations are unpredictable and numerous, no idealized method can visualize all the variables in advance

Table 2.5 Key features of some major ELT methods (adapted from Adamson, 2004a; Larsen-Freeman, 2000; Richards and Rodgers, 2001)

Method	Features
Grammar-translation method	• Primary skills are reading and writing • Constant reference to mother tongue • Focus on language forms • Memorization of grammatical paradigms • Teacher-centred
Audiolingual method	• Listening and speaking, then reading and writing • Absence of mother tongue • Communication through habit-formation • Drilling of sentence patterns • Teacher orchestrates students
Communicative language teaching	• Integration of the four skills • Mother tongue available as resource • Focus on communication in context • Systemic teaching and creative production • Teacher as manager and helper
Task-based learning	• Emphasis on communicative fluency • Mother tongue available as resource • Learning through performing a series of activities • Focus on process rather than product • Learner-centred

in order to provide situation-specific suggestions that practising teachers sorely need to tackle the challenges they confront every day of their professional lives. As a predominantly top-down exercise, the conception and construction of methods have been largely guided by a one-size-fits-all, cookie-cutter approach, which by necessity assumes a common clientele with common goals. The following section takes up recent criticisms of Richards and Rodgers' model, and the limitations of the notion of approaches such as the idealized model that can be applied universally.

2.4 Critique of methods as universal and context-free

Although the theoretical model proposed by Richards and Rodgers (see Section 2.2) assumes that methods proposed by developers will normally be implemented in practice, and although ELT professionals know that what is realized as methods in the classroom emerges over time as a result of the interaction between teachers, students, and materials and activities (Richards, 1990), the shift from methods to practice is inevitably influenced by many other different factors, such as socioeconomic, sociocultural and sociopolitical forces (Bell, 2003; Bolton, 2005). This section attempts to challenge the Richards and Rodgers model by arguing that ELT is a complex activity with multiple dimensions: intellectual, cultural, social and political. These challenges come from recent widespread changes in views of language and language learning, as well as views of the relationships between teacher and context.

According to Lantolf (2000), the recent emergence of Vygotskian sociocultural theory (Vygotsky, 1978) in ELT has profoundly changed our understanding of English language teaching and learning. Sociocultural theory maintains that social interaction and cultural institutions, such as schools and classrooms, have important roles to play in an individual's cognitive growth and development (Donato and McCormick, 1994: 453). According to Mitchell and Myles (1998), later theoreticians, such as Bruner (1985), Rogoff (1990) and Wertsch (1985; 1991; 1998), have taken up the germinal ideas of Vygotsky and promoted them. Some recent approaches have tended to focus on semiotic means of mediation (Wertsch, 1991) whereas others have tended to focus more on the activity system in which actions take place (Engestrom, 1993). Many other educational researchers (e.g. Edwards and Mercer, 1987; Mercer, 1995) have applied them in classroom studies. So far researchers and scholars in this field have appealed to a number of theoretical constructs, such as private speech, activity theory, zone of proximal development (ZPD) and scaffolding, and efforts have been made to address a variety of aspects of language learning. Although the studies to date are relatively small in scale, they help to broaden the base of theories for ELT, which is valuable in facilitating and explaining effective language teaching and learning in several ways. When he illustrates the usefulness of sociocultural theory for examining important and relevant psychological, affective, linguistic, social, and individual conditions of foreign and second language classrooms, Donato (2000: 44–7) summarizes three themes that directly address the questions of the contribution of sociocultural theory to advancing both practical and technical knowledge in the field of foreign and second language instruction. First, sociocultural theory underscores the importance of conceptualizing language learning as a developmental process mediated by semiotic resources appropriated from the classroom (Wertsch, 1991; 1998). These semiotic resources include print materials, the physical environment, gestures and, most notably, classroom discourse. This theme contrasts sharply with cognitive approaches based solely on the acquisition metaphor of development, which rigidly ascribes language learning to various internal mental processes such as the construction of interlanguage representation, encodings and decodings between individuals, input processing and attentional operations by the learners, or the biological unfolding of linguistic universals. Second, sociocultural theory emphasizes that during instruction awareness of the structure and function of language is developed by using it socially. Therefore, the theory adds greater clarity to the issue of modified interaction and negotiation of meaning in classroom setting. Third, sociocultural theory is about language classrooms where agency matters. That is, learners bring to interactions their own personal histories replete with values, assumptions, beliefs, rights, duties and obligations. In other words, a central concern in sociocultural theory is that learners actively transform their world and not merely conform to it (Lantolf, 2000). Therefore, the important implication of sociocultural theory, we argue, is that teaching and learning in ELT is socially situated, which is a dimension not emphasized in previous approaches to methods.

The social nature of ELT learning is seen even more clearly in what goes on outside the classroom, in the wider community. The concept of inseparable linkages between language, society and culture helps our understanding of the social and cultural nature of English language teaching (Nunan, 2003). English has often been the outside language imposed on native languages, resulting in their subjugation to a secondary status along with the cultures they represent (see Canagarajah, 1999; Phillipson, 1992). At other times, the teaching of English is seen as a tool to propagate the economic, cultural or religious values of dominant world powers (see Crystal, 1997; 2003). Counter to this have been other studies, research and theories which propose either that such imperialism was or is not at the heart of ELT (e.g. Tollefson, 2000), or that the relationship between language, politics and economics has evolved into something different from what it once was (e.g. Gabrielator, 1998). Yet others have held that the English language classroom serves as the ideal arena in which such possibilities can be examined by students and teachers alike (Pennycook, 2000).

No matter how people debate or argue, one thing is clear, namely, ELT is not just simply an issue of psycholinguistics and methods; it is also an issue of politics, society and culture. McKay and Wong (1988) argue that sociopolitics profoundly affects teaching activities through many channels, such as the funding of language programmes, teacher education, curriculum requirements and community support (see also Nunan, 2003). Benson (1997) states that sociopolitical concepts in education embrace issues such as the societal context in which learning takes place, roles and relationships in the classroom and outside, kinds of learning tasks, and the content of the language that is learned. Auerbach (1995) indicates that methodological choices about curriculum development, content, materials, classroom processes and language use are inherently ideological in nature, with significant implications for learners' socioeconomic roles, even when methods appear to be informed by apolitical professional considerations. She further points out that the classroom functions as a kind of microcosm of the broader social order, in other words, the political relationships in the world outside the classroom are reproduced within the classroom. Similarly, Pennycook (2000) points out that we can perceive everything we do in the classroom as social and political. He asserts that the classroom is not only a place where social relations are reproduced, but also a place where social relations are linked to ideologies (see also Holliday, 1994; Phillipson, 1992). Another important point for us to bear in mind is that, as Pennycook puts it, if we want to understand the macro–micro relationship clearly, we need to consider the relationships between classrooms and schools or community centres, between these and local communities, between communities and larger social institutions, and between classrooms and global relations.

The two important notions proposed by Pennycook are of great importance for us to understand the far-reaching implications of viewing the classroom as a social and cultural space. First, if we take the classroom as an intersection of different ideologies and cultures, language learning becomes not a mere abstract cognitive process where bits of language are absorbed in the brain. Rather, it becomes a highly complex social and cultural process. Second, if we understand students and teachers are not living in a vacuum but in real society, the cultural politics that happen inside and outside the classroom will inevitably influence what is learned and taught. In fact, many critical applied linguists see classrooms as sites where identities are multiple and shifting, continually reproduced and changed, and inextricably tied to language and language learning. Hall and Eggington (2000: 1) maintain:

> [. . .] if we look closely enough, it becomes clear that rather than being peripheral to our tasks as teachers, the political, cultural, and social dimensions of English language teaching are embedded in each and every decision we make. Language policies, both officially and unofficially sanctioned, cultural expectations about the roles of teacher and student, and our identities in terms of, for example, gender, race, ethnicity, and nationality at the same time inform and constrain what we do in the classroom. Our actions, in turn, both shape and constrain the social, academic, and linguistic consequences for our learners. Thus, as important to the development of English language teacher expertise as knowledge of effective classroom practices may be is our understanding of the more macro dimensions of pedagogy and how they shape both our roles as teachers and our students' roles as learners.

Thus, from a sociopolitical and sociocultural perspective, the language classroom becomes a site of contestation, where different codes, different visions of the world and different methods are in continual competition and conflict (Pennycook, 2000).

Such critical theorists argue that the spread of English throughout the world is closely connected with many cultural, economic and political forces: the rise of the USA as a global superpower, the role of international corporations, the spread of particular forms of culture and knowledge and the conformity of the new world order (Pennycook, 1994; Phillipson, 1992). Living in this world, teachers of English cannot escape the implications of these global connections; obviously, such connections are reflected in classroom teaching and learning. Pennycook (2000) proposes that although the ELT classroom is not determined by the outside world, it is part of the world, both affected by what happens outside its walls and affecting what happens within. Drawing on two research studies (see Canagarajah, 1993; Morgan, 1997), Pennycook (2000) illustrates how everything from student annotations in textbooks to preferred learning style and resistance to the teacher's preferred teaching pedagogies are connected in complex ways to the social and cultural worlds both inside and outside the classroom, and how classrooms and students in terms of social class (mixed and homogeneous types), age, ethnicity, gender and location are shaped by the broader social, cultural and political context.

Such ideas have given rise to a recent concern in ELT with 'postmethods', a term signifying a search for an alternative to method rather than an alternative method (Kumaravadivelu, 1994). For Kumaravadivelu (2001: 557), method 'has had a magical hold on us'. In order to break away from method, Kumaravadivelu (2003) proposes that an alternative to method has to be found in order to transcend its marginalizing effect and he believes that postmethods with its ideals of particularity, practicality and possibility offers one such option. Kumaravadivelu (2003: 544–5) defines what he calls postmethod pedagogy as follows:

> Postmethod consists of the parameters of particularity, practicality and possibility. The parameter of particularity is based on the belief that any language teaching programme 'must be sensitive to a particular group of teachers teaching a particular group of learners pursuing a particular set of goals within a particular institutional context embedded in a particular sociocultural milieu' (Kumaravadivelu, 2001: 538). Such a pedagogy is responsive to and responsible for local individual, institutional, social and cultural contexts in which learning and teaching take place. While making themselves aware of the principles and practices of the colonial construct of method, teachers rely mostly on context-sensitive local knowledge to identify problems, find solutions and try them out to see what works and what doesn't in their specific context. The parameter of practicality refers

to the relationship between theory and practice. One long-standing colonial representation is the Weberian idea that theory construction is the hallmark of the West and that the East preoccupies itself with discrete facts and figures, unable to derive any unifying theory. In a sense, it is this kind of (mis)representation that has led the West to marginalize local knowledge. The unfortunate and unproductive division of labour we find in applied linguistics between the theorist and teacher – that is, the theorist produces knowledge, and the teacher consumes knowledge – can also be traced to this colonial construct of marginality. The parameter of practicality goes beyond this marginalizing dichotomy and aims for a personal theory of practice generated by the practising teacher. The parameter of possibility is derived mainly from Freirean critical pedagogy that seeks to empower classroom participants so that they can critically reflect on the social and historical conditions contributing to create the cultural forms and interested knowledge they encounter in their lives. Their lived experiences, motivated by their own sociocultural and historical backgrounds, should help them appropriate the English language and use it in their own terms according to their own values and visions. Such an appropriation assumes greater importance in these days of economic and cultural globalization because classroom participants cannot afford to ignore the global sociocultural reality that challenges identity formation inside and outside the classroom. The three parameters of a postmethod pedagogy interweave and interact with each other in a synergic relationship where the whole is greater than the sum of its parts. Together, they constitute a conceptual rationale necessary to construct a postmethod pedagogy as a postcolonial project.

However, Bell (2003: 330) criticizes Kumaravadivelu's view by arguing that it is one-sided and exaggerated for postmethods to deny the functions and influences of methods in practice:

Postmethod pedagogy is derived on the local level from CLT and on the larger level from the ideas of postmodernist thinking. Postmodernism is characterized by 1. the failure of the enlightenment period – the unconditional belief in the value of scientific progress for the common good – and the downgrading of absolute conceptions of truth as well as the growth of pragmatism; 2. the growth of intracommunal ethnic diversity; and 3. the ever-growing pace of social, economic and technological change (Best and Kellner, 2001). The implication for education has been a strengthening of progressive approaches, especially the influence of John Dewey and the emphases on learner centredness; vocationalism; student autonomy; problem solving, experimentation, and critical thinking in the framework of group and project work; and subject integration within an overall multicultural context (Winch and Gingell, 1999), notions shared by postmethod pedagogy.

Bell (2003: 331) suggests that it is positive to understand postmethods as a synthesis of various methods and that it has a potentially dialectical relationship with methods. He maintains:

> Roughly speaking, methods impose practices top-down; postmethod constructs practices bottom-up. Taken together, they may mediate the negative features of each viewpoint taken in isolation. For its part, postmethod has quite rightly warned of the dangers of notions of one-size-fits-all in methods. Yet in the rush to bury methods, postmethod pedagogy has obscured the positive aspects of method ... Methods can be seen as vehicles for innovation and challenge to the status quo.

To conclude, although methods such as communicative language teaching have wide-scale application in practice, they are not universal, context-free nor teacher-free, nor even necessarily desirable or needed. Methods including their views of competences, strategies, grammar, pronunciation, syntax, tasks, exercises, drills, and activities in classrooms only form a small part of what we need to understand in terms of ELT pedagogy. The above discussion demonstrates that external forces, such as social, political and economic changes, and internal forces, such as theoretical developments in disciplines including philosophy, sociology and psychology, can also have a strong impact upon what happens inside the classroom (see Figure 2.3).

To be more specific, how teachers of English prepare their lessons, how they teach, what they select to teach and select not to teach, what kinds of role they play and how they organize the types of activities, what materials they use, and how they assess the students, all these things are connected to the social, political and cultural environment outside the classroom. With this in mind, the next section aims to examine how so-called universal trends in ELT methodology have been adopted and promoted in the *Chinese* context by *Chinese* educators in the PRC.

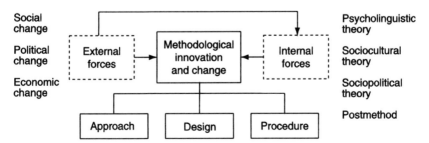

Figure 2.3 Factors that influence methodological innovation and change in ELT (Zheng, 2005)

2.5 The transformation of ELT methods in the PRC

This section aims to illustrate how different methods have been promoted and transformed in different periods in the PRC since 1949. As illustrated in Section 1.3, curriculum innovation and change in the PRC has undergone five major historical periods: the Soviet influence (1949–60), the First Renaissance (1960–66), the Cultural Revolution (1966–76), opening to the outside world (1978–93) and globalization (1993 onwards). One of the most important factors that has affected curriculum innovation and change in the PRC has been the changing political situation. In addition, the concept of *zhong xue wei ti, xi xue wei yong* (study China to extract the cultural essence, study the West for practical techniques), outlined in Chapter 1, seems to have played an important role in the process of innovation and change.

Influenced by these factors and others, in fact, when leading Chinese educationalists have over the years made changes to the ELT curriculum for the secondary school, they have not slavishly adopted Western methods. Instead, they have attempted to research different methodological approaches, rejecting the dross and assimilating the essence, to make them serve China in accordance with China's national conditions. The purpose of this section is to provide an overview of these methodological changes in ELT in the PRC, primarily as demonstrated in the textbooks produced by the government to support promoted methods.

2.5.1 The grammar-translation method

In the literature, researchers such as Dzau (1990), Ford (1988) and Liu and Adamson (1998) point out that the grammar-translation method was promoted for many years in ELT in China, partly because it resembled strategies for mother-tongue learning, partly because of the influence of missionary teachers and Soviet educationalists, and partly because China's previous political and geographical isolation had largely limited interaction with the English language to journals and books. This section attempts to briefly review the grammar-translation method in the PRC, as it is one of the most popular methods and has been long promoted.

As indicated earlier, in the period of Soviet influence, the People's Education Press (PEP) published two series of secondary school textbooks: the 1957 version and the 1960 version; the 1957 version consisted of two text-books. The organization of this series was integrated topic based with a linear sequence. The linguistic components focused on pronunciation, grammar and vocabulary. In this period of time, Soviet educational theories influenced China enormously, Kairov's methods in particular (Tang, 1983). Penner

(1991b) identifies Kairov's methods as having five steps, that is, reviewing old material, siting new material, explaining the new material, consolidating newly learned material and giving assignment. A study of those textbooks showed that some lessons designed in the 1957 version echoed Kairov's methods by having the teacher explain the new material in a reading passage, and a class reviewing newly learned material by reading the passage aloud. The grammar items to be taught were sited in a short passage or dialogue first. The next section of the lesson presented the new vocabulary in a box, followed by the grammatical structure in tabulated form, to facilitate explanation of the material. This structure was then practised for consolidation through various exercises, such as transformation, translation (from/into both Chinese and English), blank-filling (with or without a cue word in Chinese) or substitution exercises (e.g. replacing italicized phrases with a pronoun). The approach to grammar exemplified by such exercises (and which runs throughout the series) – a graded, linear syllabus starting with the present simple tense, presented in reading passages, explained in Chinese and practised through translation or transformation exercises – was consistent with the structural approach blending with the grammar-translation method. Emphasizing reading and writing skills; making constant references to, and explanations in, the learners' mother tongue; focusing on grammatical forms; requiring memorization of grammatical paradigms; and being highly teacher centred were the typical features of the 1957 version (Tang, 1983). The focus on language form rather than on communication can be seen through pupil activities that involved reading aloud, reciting and writing, but which produced language that was neither spontaneous nor freely generated by the students (Adamson, 1998). From the description above, it is clear that the promoted method reflected a strong Soviet influence on the views of teaching and learning underpinning the 1957 version, and that the structural approach and the grammar-translation method were promoted in this version.

The 1960 version consisted of three textbooks. The linguistic components remained much the same as those of the 1957 version, that is, they were organized in a linear syllabus, which accorded with the structural approach. Like the 1957 version, the 1960 version adopted a thematic approach, in that the central focus was the reading passages, to which the presentation of new vocabulary, grammar and phonetics was related. This implied a high status being accorded to reading, although this version did contain some dialogues and classroom expressions for oral use. It is obvious that the 1960 version still recommended the grammar-translation method as the key method because it focused on reading and writing, discrete grammatical forms and memorization. Reading was supported by grammar practice in which the teacher was still the centre while students only followed the teacher, doing mechanical translation and structural manipulation exercises, including phonetic transcriptions, dictation, grammar practice and recitation of the reading passage. There was thus no change in the promoted method – a blend of the structural approach and the grammar-translation method which merged Soviet principles and traditional Chinese ELT practices (Adamson, 1998; 2004a).

2.5.2 The audiolingual method

A study of teaching materials showed that the audiolingual method did not become widely promoted in secondary schools in the PRC until the mid-1970s although its influences started to emerge in the teaching materials of the 1960s. As illustrated in Section 1.3, in the early 1960s, the relationship between China and USSR started to deteriorate due to ideological conflict. English became popular again as it was treated as a useful vehicle to approach modernization and an important medium for communication with the outside world. In this period of time, three series of textbooks called the 1960 new version, the 1961 version and 1963 version were compiled for teaching. The 1960 new version had 18 textbooks which focused on reading and vocabulary. The main purpose of this series was to develop the students' four language skills (reading, writing, listening and speaking). Pronunciation and grammar were also emphasized. The design of this series was for intensive reading, which meant that the passages should be taught and learned thoroughly both syntactically and grammatically in order to understand the precise meaning and structure of each sentence, and students were encouraged to recite some of the typical sentence patterns so that they could memorize those sentences for future communication. The teacher felt free to choose suitable materials for extensive study, for writing in different genres (letters, diaries, compositions) and revision work. At this stage, the main promoted method was still grammar-translation, as the new words were presented with Chinese translations and the exercises were predominantly concerned with translation and reciting parts of the passages. Few chances for reading comprehension exercises or real oral communication were presented in this version.

The 1961 version was made up of three textbooks with a teacher's handbook. Unlike the previous three versions, it added another methodological approach, the strategies of recitation and memorization, to the two identified approaches in the previous versions. Paine (1997) argues that recitation and memorization is part of the tradition of mimetic teaching and learning practices in China and was introduced to meet the requirement in the curriculum guidelines to develop students' oral skills (see also Adamson, 1998). In the 1961 version three distinct promoted methods were included, namely, the grammar-translation method, structural approach and the strategies of recitation and memorization that were similar to the audiolingual method, which was emerging internationally as the preferred second language method at that time. Some passages in this version suggested that students wanted to speak English correctly but they did not know how to do it. The teacher advised them that they should practise speaking English as much as possible, that they should not be afraid of making mistakes and that they should try their best to memorize expressions and whole sentences. From this we can see speaking was treated as an important skill in this version. According to Adamson (1998), this approach was characterized as emphasizing oral skills before written skills and encouraging students to use English as much as possible, and learning through habit formation. However, the evidence did not show this approach as strongly enhanced because there were no further sentence pattern drills for oral practice in the exercises, which were a central feature of the audiolingual method (Larsen-Freeman, 1986).

The 1963 version comprised six textbooks, tape recordings and Teacher's Books. The promoted methods in this version, as spelt out in the syllabus, stressed practice by the students to develop all four language skills. Adamson (1998) indicates that teachers felt free to offer the students clear explanations, but they were strongly recommended to encourage the students to read aloud, recite passages from memory, have questions and answers according to the contents of a passage, give dictation, and have the students write sentences, and translate and compose passages. Some extra work was proposed in the syllabus to create more chances for the students to practise, such as reading simplified novels; singing English songs; making wall posters; having a handwriting exhibition, spelling contests, speech competitions and dialogue performances; and using gramophone records, tape recorders, slides and microphones. Adamson (1998) points out that using gramophone records and tape recorders may indicate the audiolingual method had started to influence the ELT in the PRC at the time. Price (1979) has commented on this phenomenon by saying that gramophone records and tape reels produced by companies such as Linguaphone were a popular means of promoting self-study in foreign languages, most notably through the use of pattern drills, and that there were also methodological experiments using Linguaphone and similar materials for secondary school English teaching. Liu (1996) points out that David Crook, Isabel Crook and Margaret Turner, three of the consultants for the 1963 version, were instrumental in introducing this method to the PRC. Thus, we can conclude that the 1963 version echoed the methods promoted in the syllabus to give particular attention, with Chinese characteristics, to spoken skills, plus the familiar combination of the structural approach and the grammar-translation method.

As described in Chapter 1, with the advent of the Cultural Revolution, English was ousted from the school curriculum for the second time. All the textbooks were heavily criticized, then banned. Standards fell, policies often changed. When English finally reappeared in the curriculum around 1969, it was distorted. The textbooks were locally produced and the English in the textbooks was not the English of any English-speaking country, but political slogans for the purpose of meeting the need of proletarian propaganda. The grammar-translation method, based on the studies of the textbooks compiled by Beijing, Shanghai, Guangzhou and Fujian during this period of time, was still the main promoted method.

As discussed in Chapter 1, the death of Chairman Mao Zedong brought an end to the Cultural Revolution. Deng Xiaoping's open door policy aimed to realize the four modernizations (agriculture, industry, national defence and science and technology) in China. In this period of time, two series of textbooks (the 1978 version and the 1982 version) were published for teaching. The 1978 version consisted of six textbooks in the form of sentence and dialogue drills, reading passages and grammar exercises. This version followed the principle of the syllabus, that is, listening and speaking first; then reading and writing (*ting shuo ling xian, du xie gen shang*), integrated training, emphasizing reading (*zhong he xun lian, ce zhong yue du*) (Tang, 1983). In other words, this version stressed balance between knowledge and use of language. On the whole, the promoted method of this version was a combination of the structural approach and the audiolingual method, together with the grammar-translation method. Since the 1963 version, the trend towards paying more attention to oracy steadily increased. The 1978 version advocated the improvement of students' ability in speaking through practice-theory-practice steps. The influence of the grammar-translation method was still evident but less dominant.

The 1982 version consisted of nine textbooks, cassette tapes of reading passages and practice drills, Teacher's Books and wallcharts. This series was arranged in the form of sentence and dialogue drills, reading passages, vocabulary, and grammar exercises. The methods promoted in this version were the structural approach with the audiolingual method, the grammar-translation method and functional/notional approach. The components were presented, explained and practised. Apparently, the dominant promoted method in this version was a structural approach, although there was a greater degree of communicative contextualization than in previous versions (Adamson, 1998). In the early stages of the course, the focus was on short dialogues and sentence patterns for oral drilling – features consistent with the audiolingual method. In other words, before their reading and writing skills were developed, students' oral skills were highly emphasized. Suggestions were made to provide a variety of extra-curricular activities focusing mainly on oral skills. As the course progressed, reading passages showed greater prominence, and some exercises focused on the grammar of the passage and English–Chinese and Chinese–English translation, in accordance with the grammar-translation method. Features of the functional/notional approach, as noted above, were also evident. This approach presented and practised realistic English within its appropriate sociolinguistic setting. In the 1982 version, there were fragments or complete dialogues that were directly transferable to everyday situations, and thus provided scope for communicative activities such as role-plays. However, the functional/notional aspects were limited, because other features of the approach were lacking.

2.5.3 Communicative language teaching

As described in Section 1.3.4, from 1993 onwards, as China opened more to the outside world, it sought to reform its secondary school curriculum with the help of foreign education institutions. In 1993, for the first time in the PRC's history, PEP/Longman collaborated to produce a series of textbooks called Junior English for China (JEFC) and Senior English for China (SEFC), which were labelled by their promoters as a 'structural/functional/notional' series. Linguistically, the JEFC/SEFC resembled previous versions in many ways; for example, they prescribed the teaching of grammatical and lexical items. The main change was the addition of real-life contexts in which certain functions of English were prevalent. Methodologically, although the communicative approach was promoted, existing traditional Chinese ELT teaching experiences were also preserved and followed (Liu and Adamson, 1999). In fact, this echoed Chairman Mao's idea to make foreign things serve China. In other words, when methodological methods are adopted in ELT practices in China, dross should be eliminated and essence absorbed in order to make them serve China best according to China's conditions (Liu, 2002). On the whole, JEFC/SEFC encouraged language learning to be an interactive activity and the teacher's role shifted from the teacher-centred position to a multifaceted position, i.e. a demonstrator, an actor, an organizer, a conductor, a monitor and a guide (Harmer, 2001; Liu, 2002; Liu and Adamson, 1999; Wang, 1999). Nevertheless, the form of CLT promoted by the 1993 English Curriculum in the Chinese context belonged to the very weak form.

2.5.4 Task-based learning

In 2000, PEP revised the 1993 English Curriculum. The revised 2001 English Curriculum, also called the English Curriculum Standard (PEP, 2001), claimed that special attention in ELT should be paid to quality education so as to arouse students' interests, help them build up their confidence and help to develop their efficient learning strategies in the learning process so that students can primarily establish comprehensive abilities in using the target language. The objective of the revised 2001 English Curriculum focused on the formation of students' abilities in comprehensive language application, based on the holistic development of their language competence, linguistic knowledge, emotional attitude, learning strategy, and cultural awareness. This objective orientation was intended to enhance the holistic development of students in terms of knowledge, competence, self-learning ability and good personality so as to lay a good foundation for their lifelong study and long-term development (Liu, 2002; Wang, 1999).

One of the most prominent features of the revised 2001 English Curriculum was to include learning strategies. Students were encouraged to use the English they learned to improve their performance, through the strategies to develop their language competence, and thinking, communicative and collaborative abilities. It was the first time that psychological and socio-cultural theories (e.g. perception, memory, imagery, comparison, analysing, deducing, monitoring, self-evaluation and adjustment) had been so explicitly promoted in classroom teaching.

The key promoted method of the latest curriculum was task-based learning, together with the functional/notional approach and the grammar-translation method. The revised 2001 English Curriculum proposed that teachers should focus clearly on language use in both in form and meaning by using the concept of 'tasks' so that students could learn more actively with clearer goals, which conveyed the message that teachers should help students to complete their tasks in the process of practising, thinking, investigating, discussing, communicating and cooperating. The aim of this was to develop students' language ability, to enhance their study motivation, to increase their study interest, to form their learning strategies, to nurture their spirit in cooperation and to help them to have better understanding of multicultures. Teachers were advised to adopt effective teaching methods in accordance with their own situation and students' needs in order to suit the needs in the transitional period, that is, from examination-oriented education to a more student-centred learning. Task-based learning promoted by the revised 2001 English Curriculum resembles the weak version defined by Skehan (2003).

The 2001 revised English Curriculum was first tried out and implemented in the 38 national experimental districts throughout the country. The new curriculum was then implemented in the provincial experimental districts in autumn 2002, which reached 10–15 per cent of the entire student population.

In 2004, its implementation expanded to 2,576 cities and counties and 65–70 per cent of students (Li, 2003). The curriculum innovation is expected to be implemented throughout the country by 2007 (Liu, 2004).

To sum up, as suggested in Chapter 1, a number of factors have influenced Chinese curriculum innovation and change in ELT. External forces, such as the ideological conflict between the Soviet Union and China, the Cultural Revolution, social and economic changes, such as the Open Door Policy and China's entry to the WTO, as well as internal forces, such as educational policies including quality education, Confucian philosophy, and Chinese traditional teaching methods with deep memorization[1] as their key characteristic, have permeated the process of methodological innovation and change in ELT in terms of curriculum design, methodological adoption and textbook compilation. Although the audiolingual method and communicative language methods are increasingly promoted and enhanced in the PRC, it seems that the grammar-translation method has never lost its prominence in ELT. On the other hand, discussion of postmethods and the ideological debates around ELT have not yet penetrated mainstream discourses on English language education in China, and certainly have not been incorporated into any public policy documents or teaching materials. Table 2.6 summarizes the document promoted methods in ELT in the PRC from 1957 to 2001.

2.5.5 Implications for this book

Several implications for this book can be drawn from the above discussion. First, the roles and status of English in the PRC have been and continue to be determined by the political situation; second, the adoption of certain methods by Chinese educators and curriculum planners is strongly influenced by the need for the English language in the particular social context and always based on the accumulated experience of teaching the language and the principle of *zhong xue wei ti, xi xue wei yong* (study China to extract the cultural essence, study the West for practical techniques); and third, the 1993 English Curriculum, the revised 2001 English Curriculum and methodological change were not a sudden breakthrough but an incremental change from the previous ones. In summary, methodological innovation and change in the PRC has been influenced by a number of factors that are shown in Figure 2.4.

Table 2.6 Promoted ELT methods in the PRC (adapted from Adamson, 2004a)

PEP publication of ELT textbooks (1957–2001)	*The methodology promoted in each version*
The 1957 version	Structural and grammar-translation: teacher-centred, focus on accuracy and written language, memorization, Kairov's five steps
The 1960 version	Structural and grammar-translation: teacher-centred, focus on written language, pronunciation and grammatical structures, memorization
The 1960 new version	Grammar-translation: teacher-centred, focus on written language, memorization
The 1961 version	Reading aloud, memorization, structural approach, grammar-translation
The 1963 version	Reading aloud, memorization, oral practice, sentence writing, students' independent learning, structural approach, grammar-translation
The Cultural Revolution versions	Structural approach, grammar-translation and audiolingualism
The 1978 version	Mainly audiolingualism and structural approach; some grammar-translation
The 1982 version	Predominantly structural approach with audiolingualism, grammar-translation and functional/notional approach
The 1993/2001 versions: JEFC/SEFC	Structural approach (with a linear grammatical progression and a focus on sentence patterns) and audiolingualism (with behaviourist drills to aid memorization); emphasis on reading for meaning; paying attention to the cultivation of communicative competence and performance in English

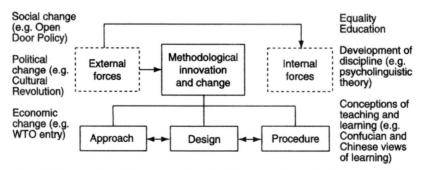

Figure 2.4 Factors that influence methodological innovation and change in ELT in China (Zheng, 2005)

2.6 Conclusion

Methods in ELT generally have undergone a tremendous transition over the past hundred years, that is, from the grammar-translation method, to the audiolingual method, then to communicative language teaching and task-based learning. This has been the result of the influence of both external and internal forces, including social, political and economic changes, as well as development of the foundation disciplines of ELT. What is less apparent in the histories of methods in ELT is the human factor. This book argues that methodological innovation and change is a fundamentally social activity that is affected by ethical and systemic constraints, the personal characteristics of potential adopters, the attributes of innovations, and the strategies that are used to manage change in a particular context (Markee, 1997). The next chapter explores the differences between the promoted methodology in ELT and the implemented pedagogy, and then examines the deeper meaning of pedagogy, pedagogy and change, influences on pedagogy in ELT in the PRC, and pedagogy and change in the PRC.

Note

1. Deep memorization is a new way of regarding memorization and under-standing as intertwined and enhancing each other. The process of repetition contributes to understanding and can be distinguished from the mechanical memorization that characterizes rote learning. Some studies (Marton and Wenestam, 1987) demonstrate that when a text is memorized, it can be repeated in a way that deepens understanding and that different aspects of the text are focused on with each repetition.

Chapter 3

Pedagogy in ELT

3.1 Introduction

In the previous chapter it was argued that to understand English language methodological change and its effects in the PRC, it is not sufficient to analyse the intended curriculum and the promoted methods. The teacher's own interpretations of and relationships with these factors are equally important, if not more important. This point may be captured by a distinction between *methodology* and *pedagogy*. Pedagogy, like methodology, can be conceptualized as having three interlinked levels: teachers' beliefs (orientation), teachers' designs (intended) and teachers' practices (implemented). This chapter first describes the concept of pedagogy as used in this book, then examines the nature of teachers' beliefs, and the relationship between teachers' beliefs and practices so as to provide a clear understanding of why teachers do what they do or don't do, as the case may be, in their classroom teaching. Then, the chapter focuses on exploring pedagogy and change, and the influences on pedagogy in general, and pedagogy and change in the PRC in particular. The last section of the chapter presents a conceptual framework which theorizes how individual English language teachers in the PRC cope with change and reconcile potential and actual conflicts in internal, external and situational forces in their individual teaching contexts.

3.2 Pedagogy: an alternative to methodology

3.2.1 The definition of pedagogy

Pedagogy is seen by many both inside and outside the teaching profession as a somewhat vague concept. In the Anglo-American tradition of educational research, pedagogy is subsidiary to curriculum, sometimes implying little more than 'teaching method'. The concept of curriculum itself has both a broad and a narrow meaning, what is formally required to be taught which comes closer to continental European 'didactics' without capturing the sense in *la didactique* or *die Didaktik* of a quasi-science comprising subject knowledge and the principles by which it is imparted. The concept of curriculum is more prominent in educational discourse where it is contested, less prominent where it is imposed or accepted as a given. In contrast, in the central European tradition, it is the other way round: pedagogy moves centre stage and frames everything else, including curriculum – in so far as the word is used – and didactics (Alexander *et al.*, 2000: 540–56; Moon, 1998). In this sense, pedagogy offers those involved with teaching a useful conceptual framework with which to examine their own professional practice and offers those outside of this group a way to understand the often complex approaches that are needed (Ireson *et al.*, 1999).

Because the range of meanings attaching to pedagogy varies tremendously in English – quite apart from differences between English and other languages – the use of the term needs to be carefully defined. For the purpose of this research study, *pedagogy* is seen as closely associated with classroom teaching and is defined as the teacher's personal construct of teaching beliefs, attitudes and practices that encompasses all aspects of a teacher's identity. It is used in contrast to the term *methodology*, which denotes the study of the explicit system or range of methods that are used in teaching. As discussed in Section 2.2 the study of methodology includes the study of the nature of language skills and procedures for teaching them, the study of preparation of lesson plans, materials and textbooks for teaching language skills, the evaluation and comparison of language teaching methods (e.g. the audiolingual method), and the practices, procedures, and principles themselves. The essential distinctions between methodology and pedagogy can be summarized in terms of three key factors – scope, key influences and applications. Methodology is more narrowly focused and tends to be more dogmatic and theoretically coherent in its application, as it targets language learning as its main goal. Methodology is explicitly based on theoretical constructs, and by definition it is assumed to be applicable in different contexts (see Section 2.5); whereas pedagogy has broader educational goals, is influenced by a wider range of implicit as well as explicit theories and curricular influences and tensions, and is more rooted in and responsive to the practical realities of a particular classroom (Adamson, 2004b: 605). Table 3.1 shows these key differences between *methodology* and *pedagogy*.

In Chapter 2 the chief elements of English language teaching methodology, the interlinked levels of theories of language and learning, instructional design and teaching practice were identified (see Figure 2.1). Based on the discussion above, we propose that pedagogy in the ELT context can be defined as beliefs and practices of individual teachers in preparing, delivering and evaluating English language lessons. Thus, pedagogy is the bridge between the intended and the implemented curriculum (see Figure 1.1), making teachers crucial

Table 3.1 Differences between methodology and pedagogy (Zheng, 2005)

	Methodology	*Pedagogy*
	• 'Top-down' • Generalized • External construct	• 'Bottom-up' • Particularized • Personal construct
Scope	• Biased and relatively narrow • Tends to be prescriptive	• Broader • Descriptive
Key influences	• Narrow and theoretical base, usually coherent and clearly articulated	• Wide range of theories and influences, often conflicting
Application	• Assumed to be applicable to a wide range of classrooms, irrespective of contexts	• Rooted in and responsive to the practical realities of a particular classroom

agents in the curriculum process. Therefore, a parallel conceptualization of levels of pedagogy can be defined in the same way as was done for methodology. This conceptualization includes teachers' explicit and implicit theories, their designs and their practices (see Figure 3.1).

The following section discusses teachers' theories and the relationship between teachers' theories and their designs and practices.

3.2.2 The nature of teachers' theories

The terms ' theory', 'principle' and ' belief' are often used interchangeably in educational research about teacher development (Cumming, 1989; Davison, 2001; Pennington, 1989). Davison (2001: 82) uses the term 'theory' to refer to formal and explicit explanations, the term 'principle' to refer to fundamental generalizations and the term 'belief' to refer to implicit or explicit assumptions (see Figure 3.2), with each term reflecting increasing levels of abstract low.

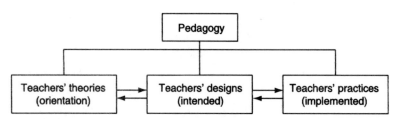

Figure 3.1 Three interlinked levels of pedagogy: teachers' theory, teachers' design and teachers' practice (Zheng, 2005)

As illustrated in Figure 3.2, she argues that theories, principles and practices can be in open contestation; values and beliefs may also be in conflict. Each factor relates to the other, and impacts on the other with ways of thinking being open to change and rarely entirely consistent with one another. For the purpose of this research study, however, we do not need five such levels of analysis. Hence, we will use the terms 'theory' and 'beliefs' interchangeably to mean teachers' articulated beliefs and also teachers' explicit personal theories and principles.

Teachers' beliefs, representing an amalgam of personally constructed explicit and implicit views of language and language learning, serve as a mediator for experiencing, negotiating and responding to the environment. In turn, teachers' beliefs are shaped by complex external factors in the situated context. Therefore, teachers' beliefs are a product of a dynamic and evolving socioculture, hence also value-laden and inherently political.

As shown in Figure 3.2, teachers' beliefs or theories, implicit or explicit, form a part of a teacher's pedagogy. In order to understand how teachers approach their work, it is necessary to understand the beliefs and principles they operate from. Much discussion about teachers' beliefs has been con-ducted in the literature from different perspectives. Those discussions include a range of psychological and cognitive science perspectives such as Abelson (1979), Clark and Peterson (1986), Kagan (1992), Nespor (1987), Pajares (1992) and Richardson (1996). According to Pintrich (1990), beliefs are the most valuable psychological construct in teacher education. Hodge (1953)

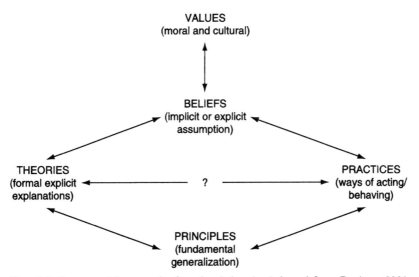

Figure 3.2 Conceptual framework of teachers' theories (adapted from Davison, 2001: 82)

defines belief as a moral act for which the believer is to be held responsible. In his review of teacher beliefs, Borg (2001; 2003) conceptualizes belief as a proposition which may be consciously or unconsciously held, is evaluative in that it is accepted as true by individuals, and therefore imbued with emotive commitment; furthermore, it serves as a guide to thought and behaviour. Kagan (1992) describes belief as a particularly provocative form of personal knowledge and argues that most of a teacher's professional knowledge can be regarded more accurately as belief. According to Kagan, this knowledge grows richer and more coherent, as a teacher's experience in classrooms grows, and thus forms a highly personalized pedagogy or belief system that actually constrains the teacher's perception, judgement, and behaviour. In terms of belief as personal knowledge, Kagan (1992: 74) explains:

> A teacher's knowledge of his or her profession is situated in three important ways: in context (it is related to specific groups of students), in content (it is related to particular academic material to be taught), and in person (it is embedded within the teacher's unique belief system).

Like Clark (1988) who equates 'implicit theories' with beliefs, Nespor (1987: 324) explained how beliefs become personal pedagogies or theories to guide teachers' practices:

> teachers' beliefs play a major role in defining teaching tasks and organizing the knowledge and information relevant to those tasks. But why should this be so? Why wouldn't research-based knowledge or academic theory serve this purpose just as well? The answer suggested here is that the contexts and environments within which teachers work, and many of the problems they encounter, are ill-defined and deeply entangled, and that beliefs are peculiarly suited for making sense of such contexts.

Accordingly Brayan and Atwater (2002) conclude that there is a consensus in the literature that beliefs are part of a group of constructs that describe the structure and content of a person's thinking and that are presumed to drive his or her actions. Rust (1994), in describing beliefs as socially constructed representational systems, also argues that these systems are used to interpret and act upon the world. Since beliefs are generally contextualized and associated with a particular situation or circumstance (Kagan, 1992), systems of beliefs may contradict each other (Ennis, 1994). Wide variance can be found among the systems of beliefs of different teachers from within a similar group (Bussis *et al.*, 1976). Wehling and Charters (1969) discuss beliefs in terms of complex organizations consisting of discrete sets of interrelated concepts. They include beliefs in the category of representations, or cognitive maps of the external world that serve as mediators for experiencing and responding to reality. This conception of beliefs fits with the notion of beliefs as personal knowledge, personal pedagogies and implicit theories.

Davison (2001: 80–3) points out that all the research literature on teacher knowledge and teacher change suggests that teachers develop their professional knowledge from practice up, rather than education down. She states that teacher practice, inside and outside the classroom, is shaped both by the external context, that is, the institutional, sociocultural and political practices of the society in which the teacher operates, and by the complex interactions between learners and between teachers and learners. Thus, in any construct of professional knowledge, theoretical and pedagogic knowledge interact with and are influenced by other sorts of implicit and explicit contextual knowledge, including institutional, sociocultural and political knowledge. Together these 'epistemologies' or 'knowledges' can be perceived to form teachers' professional knowledge and are both reflected in and shaped by practice (Davison, 2001: 81).

To sum up, teachers' beliefs are shaped by many factors, which may include the influence of discipline subculture, learning experiences as a student, teaching experiences, professional education, pedagogical content knowledge, life history and opportunity for collegial interaction which leads to self-reflection (Bean and Zulich, 1992; Brousseau *et al.*, 1988; Carter, 1990; Cherland, 1989; Freeman, 2002; Richards *et al.*, 1987). These factors affect teachers' planning and their interactive thoughts and decisions as well as their classroom behaviours (Carter, 1990; Nisbett and Ross, 1980). In other words, teachers' beliefs play a crucial role in terms of how teachers interpret information about learning and teaching and how they translate it into classroom practices (Clark and Peterson, 1986; Johnson, 1994; Kagan, 1992; Richards, 1996). The next section examines this relationship between teachers' beliefs and practices.

3.2.3 The relationship between teachers' beliefs and practices

This section first briefly reviews the history of mainstream educational research on the relationship between teachers' beliefs and practices. Next it examines how teachers' beliefs influence classroom practices in general. Then it focuses on exploring English teachers' beliefs and how these beliefs affect classroom practices. The purpose of this is to attempt to establish a conceptual framework to examine the relationship between teachers' beliefs, designs and practices for this research study.

Research on teachers' beliefs and practices has undergone three stages, from the period leading up to the mid-1970s to the decade of change

(1980–90) and more recently to the decade of consolidation (Freeman, 2002). In research through the mid-1970s classrooms were seen primarily as sites of educational delivery in a sense that teachers' practices were essentially defined as behaviour. During the 1980s, practices were perceived as more complex as they were situated in personal and institutional histories and seen as inter-active or dialogical with others – students, parents and community members and colleagues – in the settings in which they unfolded. In comparison to the 1980s, the ten-year period from 1990–2000 has consolidated and deepened that understanding. The notion that teachers possess access to unique knowledge about teaching has become increasingly widespread (Freeman, 2002).

Numerous studies on teacher beliefs and how they influence classroom practices have been conducted during the past two decades. Shavelson and Stern (1981) are two of many researchers who have suggested that such behaviour is directly influenced by teacher thoughts, judgements and prior decisions. Clark and Peterson (1986), however, have argued that teachers' beliefs influence both their thinking and their teaching performance. Some describe how beliefs appear to be resistant to change (Brousseau *et al.*, 1988; Golombek, 1998; Roberts, 1998), whereas other researchers (e.g. Bailey, 1992) affirm the notion that changes in teachers' beliefs precede changes in their teaching practices. Although some studies have indicated that teachers' beliefs and practices are consistent (Richardson *et al.*, 1991), a number of studies have highlighted that there are inconsistencies between teachers' beliefs and their observed practices in the sense that teachers do less than they claim (Desforges and Cockburn, 1987; Galton *et al.*, 1980), particularly in terms of alternatives to didacticism. The inconsistent relationship suggests, on the one hand, that there are other factors determining teachers' behaviour; and on the other hand, the inconsistency is attributed to the discrepancy between their theoretical beliefs and the complexities of the teaching reality (Fang, 1996). Poulson *et al.* (2001) point out that the relationship between teachers' beliefs and practices is complex, and explain that it is 'dialectical' rather than 'uni-lateral' and therefore practice does not always come after beliefs, but may sometimes precede them.

Some studies (e.g. Cimbricz, 2002) show that one of the major factors that influence teachers' beliefs and practices are high stakes tests; other studies (e.g. Freeman, 2002) suggest that context also plays a very important role in the relationship between teachers' beliefs and practices. Key questions in regard to the complex relationship between beliefs and practices and other influencing issues include: To what extent do high stakes tests influence teachers' beliefs and practices? How do contextual factors influence the definition of the teaching task – of what needs to be accomplished? What cultural capital do teachers bring into teaching as they accomplish the tasks they set? How do cultural backgrounds influence definitions of success and failure in teaching? Why do teachers do what they do (or not, as the case may be)? These are the very issues that we would like to investigate in this research study.

While mainstream educational research was fully engaged in exploring how teachers' beliefs influenced practice in the 1980s, classroom-based research into English language teaching still focused on effective teaching behaviours, positive learner outcomes and teacher–student interactions which were believed to enhance ELT (Chaudron, 1988). Johnson (1994) has argued that the field of ELT has lagged behind mainstream educational research in that learning to teach had been largely viewed as a matter of mastering content at the linguistic and meta-linguistic levels, practising classroom methods and techniques, and learning theoretical rationales for them, and that such a view has failed to give adequate attention to the affective dimensions of ELT. Only since the late 1980s and early 1990s have researchers begun to shift to consideration of the influence of teachers' thoughts, decisions and judgements on ELT (Freeman, 1989; Johnson, 1992; Richards and Nunan, 1990; Tsui, 2003).

Johnson's (1994) study of the beliefs of pre-service English teachers found that teachers' beliefs were largely based on images from their formal language learning experiences and that these beliefs may have been responsible for ineffectual teaching practices. Johnson's findings concur with Freeman's (1991) study of the evolution of perceptions and understandings of four foreign language teachers, in which issues of classroom management led to tensions in teachers' thinking which helped to clarify the need for genuine and spontaneous interaction in order to promote language development. Williams and Burden (1997) affirm that beliefs play an important role in the language learning process and that, for this reason, teachers must understand their own beliefs, theories or philosophy. They argue that teachers must maintain a continual process of personal reflection and that it is by becoming aware of their beliefs that they come to understand their own implicit educational theories and the ways in which such theories influence their professional practice (see also Tsui, 2003). Williams and Burden (1997: 56) further point out that, although a syllabus or curriculum may be set down precisely for teachers, it is personally shaped by the teachers' own belief systems:

Teachers' beliefs about what learning is will affect everything they do in the classroom, whether these beliefs are implicit or explicit. Even if a teacher acts spontaneously, or from habit without thinking about the action, such actions are nevertheless prompted by a deep-rooted belief that may never have been articulated or made explicit. If the teacher-as-educator is one who is constantly re-evaluating in the light of new knowledge his or her beliefs about language, or about how language is learned, or about education as a whole, then it is crucial that teachers first understand and articulate their own theoretical perspectives.

Woods (1996) considers how teachers' beliefs, assumptions and knowledge shape their understanding of teaching and their decisions. Woods contributes to the knowledge of second language teaching by clarifying how teachers' beliefs, attitudes and experiences influence classroom practices. He argues strongly in favour of recognition and acceptance of their personal pedagogies and multiple interpretations of theory and top-down curriculum. He further argues that there is insufficient research on what the second language teacher brings to the process of second language learning. Woods found that, given a new curriculum and two different teachers, two very different interpretations result in the course to be taught. Teachers' underlying beliefs, assumptions and knowledge (BAK) about 'what language is, how it is learned, and how it should be taught' resulted in differing classroom experiences for the learners. Given a new curriculum, two teachers in his study experienced conflict between interpreting the curriculum in a way that would be consistent with their BAK as opposed to interpreting it in a way that would be more consistent with the 'institutional system'. Woods found that teachers not only interpret curriculum innovations in accordance with their BAK, but also interpret theoretical and pedagogical concepts related to second language learning.

Freeman (2002) asserts that concern for subject-matter representation, or redefining how content and teaching processes fit together in the language classroom, has been a central concern for English and foreign language teaching this decade. For teachers, thought processes depend on point of view, or position. Thinking reflects social identity – who you are, your background and experience, your purposes, and your social contexts. Thus, what has been called teacher decision-making in the 1980s becomes a complex, contingent and amorphous set of relationships among meaning, context of the mind and public activity.

As discussed above, teachers' beliefs or theories, teachers' designs and teachers' practices together form their dynamic and often very complicated pedagogy. In pedagogy, teachers' beliefs or theories, that is, their orientation to teaching, are demonstrated by both the teachers' explicit and implicit statements and/or curricular manifestations which reflect personal beliefs regarding language and language learning. For this book, interview, analysis of lesson plans, lessons observations and journals are used to examine and interpret teachers' beliefs which are relevant to learning objectives, priorities in teaching and learning, preference of activity selection, consideration of nature, and roles of teacher, learner and resources. Two other layers of analysis are also included, design and practice. In pedagogy, design refers to teachers' intentions, that is, their choice and organization of content, object in learning, nature and roles of resources, types of activities, and roles of teachers and learners. Interviews, analysis of resources, teachers' lesson plans and journals are used to examine and interpret teachers' design. Teachers' practices refer to their actual classroom implementation of proposed lessons, which is examined and interpreted through analysing the teacher's process of teaching and learning, content and focus, teacher's roles, learners' roles, organization, types of activities and resources. Table 3.1 summarized the distinction between methodology and pedagogy in terms of these three components or layers: theory, design and practice. The parameters in the right-hand column of Table 3.2 are used to examine the internal forces of teachers' pedagogy; the left is the model of methodology based on Richards and Rodgers (2001).

To summarize, this section has argued for the need for an alternative construct to the notion of methodology explored in Chapter 2, that is, pedagogy. The definition of teachers' theories for the purpose of this study has also been established. The nature of teachers' beliefs and the relationship between their beliefs and practices has been explored and a conceptual framework that will be used to examine the internal factors relating to a teacher's pedagogy has been described. The following section moves to an examination of pedagogy and change, which is very important in understanding the situated nature of teachers' pedagogy and the ways in which pedagogy is influenced by external and contextual forces.

3.3 Pedagogy and change

3.3.1 The nature of change

Pedagogy, which includes the way in which teachers think and act, differs across the world (Alexander, 2000). Variations exist in the way teachers relate to their students, in the goals that teachers have for student learning, in the way teachers approach the curriculum and the textbook, in the way knowledge is communicated to students and in the way teachers interact verbally with their students. In addition to a variety of factors related to the economic, political and demographic contexts that fuel this difference, teacher thinking and action, whether tacit or explicit, are influenced and constructed by the situated

Table 3.2 A comparison of methodology and pedagogy

Components		Methodology	Implemented pedagogy
Theory	Scope	Explicit theoretical statements and/or curricular manifestations that reflect theories of language and language learning	Explicit and implicit statements and/or curricular manifestations that reflect personal beliefs regarding language and language learning
	Focus	• Teachers' guides • Curriculum objectives • Syllabus specifications • Examination specifications • Design of activities • Nature and roles of teachers, learners and resources	• Brief statements • Learning objectives • Priorities in teaching and learning • Design of activities • Nature and roles of teacher, learners and resources
	Approach to analysis	Interviews with curriculum designers; analysis of syllabus, examinations, resources and teachers' books	Interview; analysis of lesson plans, journal, etc.; lesson observation
Design	Scope	Design of content for teaching and learning • Choice and organization of content • Objects of learning • Nature and role of resources • Types of activities • Roles of teachers and learners	Design of content for teaching and learning • Choice and organization of content • Objects of learning • Nature and role of resources • Types of activities • Roles of teachers and learners
	Approach to analysis	Analysis of syllabus, resource and Teacher's Books	Interviews; analysis of resources, lesson plans and journal
Practice	Scope		Procedures for bringing about learning
	Focus		Process of teaching and learning Types of activities Roles of teachers and learners use of resources
	Approach to analysis		Lesson observation, analysis of resources, lesson plans and journal

contexts that surround teachers and teaching. In other words, cultural, economic, political and other factors always mediate the possibility of change (Markee, 1997). This section clarifies the nature and process of change, and the role of situational factors and individual experience in change. It also explores how teachers deal with change, especially in their own pedagogic settings. The purpose of this is to examine what it is that impels or inspires teachers to change or what it is that hinders or impedes teachers not to change.

In general, educational change can be initiated in two distinct ways. One form of change refers to that initiated by policy-makers, with research attempting to find ways of assisting schools to implement a particular innovation. This strategy is labelled as 'top-down', 'from above' or 'imposed change' (Fullan, 1991: 31). The other form of change is initiated by teachers and often undertaken with outside support. This form is regarded as 'bottom-up', 'grassroots' or 'voluntary change' (Fullan, 1991: 31; Wideen, 1994). Regardless of the direction of change, all real changes involve loss, anxiety and struggle (Fullan, 1991).

Wideen (1994: 9–27) examines the areas of educational change and proposes five major domains: curriculum development, school improvement, school effectiveness, teacher research and teacher development. According to Wideen, each area or perspective has its own approach to change. First, the curriculum development domain proposes to improve education by the implementation of better curriculum materials. The school improvement approach focuses on the school as the unit for change and primarily gives attention to the problems and internal conditions in one or more schools. The school effectiveness approach has an outcome focus in terms of student achievement and those characteristics that are correlated to achievement. In the teacher research approach the teacher is involved as a researcher in the change process. This is a kind of teacher emancipation directed towards addressing classroom problems. Finally, teacher development is a recent line of research that has grown out of the previous mentioned developments. Teacher development focuses upon the teacher as a learner and an active change agent. This approach places the teacher more centrally within school reform and educational change rather than simply seeing the teacher as a means to implement innovations. Although these domains do not have clearly defined boundaries, from a specific point of view, Wideen argues that each area provides a rich source of knowledge about education in general and educational change in particular. In a very general sense, curriculum reform, school improvement and school effectiveness represent a paradigm within which the stimulus for change comes from those who either direct or support change. In contrast, the fields of teacher research and teacher development represent a paradigm in which the teacher initiates or is central in educational change

(Fullan, 2001). This book incorporates these concepts from the different areas that are identified as affecting teachers' pedagogy.

According to Fullan (1991), the essence of educational change is putting something new into practice. Fullan (2001: 39) points out that in most situations educational change occurs along several dimensions. These dimensions include the possible use of new or revised materials (instructional resources such as curriculum materials or technologies), the possible use of new teaching approaches (teaching strategies or learning activities) and/or the possible alteration of beliefs (e.g. pedagogical assumptions and theories underlying particular new policies or programmes). Fullan argues that educational change restricted to one of these dimensions, for instance the use of a new textbook or materials without any alteration of teaching strategies, is a minor change. If an innovation covers all three dimensions of potential change, it is seen as a more complex innovation.

It is important to notice that it is difficult to define an innovation objectively as more or less complex. The degree of complexity is not primarily a characteristic of the innovation itself but also depends on the teachers' current materials, strategies and beliefs. Therefore, complexity of an innovation is a characteristic of the individual teacher and refers to the discrepancy between the state of existing practice and beliefs of the individual teacher, and the future state when a change has taken place. From this perspective the complexity of an innovation is associated with the subjective meaning of educational change. As will be seen in Chapter 8, this point emerges as a critical factor in this book.

The theory of educational change is described by Fullan (1991: 110) as a 'theory of probing and understanding the meaning of multiple dilemmas'. He characterizes the current knowledge base as a situation in which 'no one knows for sure what is the best'. The problem is not only the number, but also the instability of the factors which interact and affect the process of educational change. The next section discusses the phases in the process of educational change and the key factors affecting this process in more detail.

3.3.2 The role of external and situational factors in change

This section identifies the key elements of external and situational factors that affect change so as to demonstrate that teachers' pedagogy is not an isolated entity. Teachers' practices are inevitably influenced by external and situational factors; thus, it is important to identify the significant features of these factors.

Fullan (2001) identifies a number of external and situational factors that influence implementation, which he lists into two main categories relating

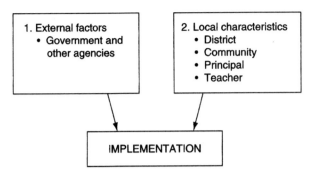

Figure 3.3 Interactive factors affecting the implementation of change (adapted from Fullan, 2001: 72)

to external factors and local characteristics (see Figure 3.3). According to Fullan, external forces include the department or ministry of education of each province or state, faculties of education, regional institutions, and other external partners who attempt to support educational implementation across the country. In times of competitiveness and perceived economic crisis, there are waves of moral panic about how to prepare future generations for the new world order. At moments like these, education in general and schools in particular become what Halsey *et al.* (1980) called 'the wastebasket of society'. Few people want to do much about the economy, but everyone – politicians, the media and the public alike – wants to do something about education (Hargreaves, 1994). Following public concerns that the educational system is not doing an adequate job in developing career-relevant skills for the economic system, producing effective citizens and/or meeting the needs of at-risk children – children of poverty, recent immigrants and special needs children – the external agents identified by Fullan (2001) have been preoccupied with new policies and programmes, initiatives such as the introduction of a subject-by-subject, stage-by-stage national curriculum; the establishment of detailed, age-related attainment targets; the creation of a new public examination system; a threatened reversion to traditional teaching methods; the extent and type of system implementation support; and the inauguration of a nationwide system of standardized testing (see Calderhead, 1984; Doll, 1996; Goodson, 2003; Hargreaves, 1994; McLaughlin, 1998; Morris, 1996; White, 1988). However, according to Fullan (2001), whether or not implementation occurs or succeeds depends on the congruence between the reformers and local needs, and how the changes are introduced and followed through. If policy-maker and practitioners are ignorant of each other's subjective worlds, the innovation and implementation will fail. In other words, the quality of relationships across this gulf is crucial to supporting change efforts when there is agreement, and to reconciling problems when there is conflict among these groups: between state ministries, and local school boards, administrators and teachers; between state departments and local districts; and between state project officers and local authorities.

The difficulties in the relationship between external and internal groups are central to the problem and process of change. Not only is the meaning of change difficult to grasp when two different worlds have limited interactions, but misinterpretation, attribution of motives, feelings of being misunderstood and disillusionment on both sides are almost certain. Nevertheless, to some extent, with the increased focus on larger-scale reform, government agencies are becoming more adept at combining 'pressure and support' forces in order to stimulate and follow through in achieving greater implementation (Fullan 2001: 87).

In Fullan's (1982; 1993) framework, situated forces can be described as two different levels, one at school district, school board and community level, and the other at school level including principals, teachers, school culture, and peer relationships. According to Fullan (2001), studies show that the local implementation process at the district level is essential if substantial improvement is the goal. The chief executive officer and other key central administrators set the conditions for implementation to the extent that they show specific forms of support and active knowledge and understanding of the realities of attempting to put a change into practice. To illustrate this most forcefully, district administrators affect the quality of implementation to the extent that they understand and help to manage the set of factors and the processes. In regard to the roles of communities and school boards, they can indirectly and directly affect implementation by hiring reform-oriented superintendents. Demographic changes often put increasing pressure on schools to adopt, if not implement, new policies. To sum up, the role of communities and school boards is quite variable ranging from apathy to active involvement – with the latter varying from conflicting to cooperative modes depending on the conditions.

In relation to the school level, Fullan (2001) points out that the main agents of change are the principals and teachers. To some extent, school culture and peer relationships also affect change. However, a neglected factor in most current conceptualizations of change is the role of students and their parents. These factors will be briefly elaborated.

In relation to the role of the principal, Fullan (2001) argues that research on innovation and school effectiveness shows that the principal strongly influences the likelihood of change. However, Fullan points out that most principals do not take instructional or change leadership roles, but mainly the roles of planners, organizers and evaluators, who are supposed to interpret the general national intentions into more specific curriculum meaning and integrate it into the ongoing curriculum system. The decision-making of school principals is especially crucial to 'bringing successful school improvement into sharp focus' (Fullan, 1995: 96).

Principals' actions also serve to legitimate whether a change is to be taken seriously and to support teachers both psychologically and with resources (see also Wideen, 1994: 100–2). Berman *et al.* (1979: 128) note that one of the best indicators of active involvement is whether the principal attends workshop training sessions. If the principal does not gain some understanding of dimensions of change, that is, beliefs, teaching behaviour and curriculum materials, he or she will not be able to understand teachers' concerns – that is, will not be able to provide support for implementation. The principal is the person most likely to be in a position to shape the organizational conditions necessary for success, such as the development of shared goals, collaborative work structures and climates, and procedures for monitoring results. When illustrating the problems that the principal might confront, Fullan (2001: 83) states:

> The subjective world of principals is such that many of them suffer from the same problem in 'implementing a new role as facilitator of change' as do teachers in implementing new teaching roles: What the principal should do specifically to manage change at the school level is a complex affair for which the principal has little preparation. The psychological and sociological problems of change that confront the principal are at least as great as those that confront teachers. Without this sociological sympathy, many principals feel exactly as teachers do: Other people simply do not seem to understand the problems they face.

In brief, the issue surrounding the role of the principal in school innovation remains complex and context-specific. He or she may develop a culture or environment which might be favourable or unfavourable to introducing changes (Morris, 1996). A supportive and collaborative school environment is a powerful force to facilitate teachers' acceptance of an innovation (Fullan and Hargreaves, 1992) and is conductive to sustainable changes (Fullan, 1995).

Teachers obviously play critically important roles in the implementation of educational change (Fullan, 1991; Kelly, 2004; Stenhouse, 1975). According to Hargreaves and Evans (1997: 3), 'teachers are the indispensable agents of educational change. Where educational change is concerned, if a teacher can't or won't do it, it simply can't be done'. It is teachers' understanding and interpretation of the change that shapes what happens in the classroom, as will be elaborated below.

However, teachers themselves are not autonomous agents; they are part of an interacting network or community of teachers. They spend a great deal of time both socializing and working together and such relationships contribute significantly not only to their core work of teachers, but also to the development of distinctive teacher cultures. Hargreaves (1994: 166) proposes that such cultures can be viewed from two different aspects: content and form. He proposes that the content of teacher cultures can be seen in what teachers say, do and think, based on shared values, beliefs and assumptions of the teaching group, whereas the form of teacher cultures is to be found in how relations between teachers and their colleagues are articulated. Relationships may change over time, affecting beliefs, values and attitudes. This suggests that the form of culture is a very powerful and significant element in the life and work of teachers in schools.

Learners are a somewhat neglected factor in the analysis of innovation (Johnson, 1989; Tsui and Cheng, 2000), which is rather ironic, given that the primary aim of any educational innovation is generally to promote students' learning. However, students are themselves powerful forces in the implementation, and ultimate sustainability, of any innovation (Adamson and Davison, 2003). They vary considerably in terms of their needs and concerns, learning experiences, language proficiencies, family backgrounds, learning strategies and personalities, all of which shapes their learning experience and perceptions of teachers' practices. Yet what students are willing or able to do in the classroom determines to a large extent the success or failure of any pedagogic innovation. They may view the innovation quite differently from their teachers, and will react to teachers' initiatives in a range of ways determined by their own experiences, needs, purposes, learning styles, and relations with their peers, teachers and parents (Erickson and Shultz, 1992; Tsui and Cheng, 2000). Even more significantly, teachers' attitudes towards a specific innovation may be strongly influenced by their predictions and concerns about students' responses, although there is surprisingly little research in ELT investigating students as a factor in innovation.

This section has briefly examined the major forces, both external and situational factors, which might influence and affect teachers' pedagogy. The following section examines the role of individual experience, which determines implementation.

3.3.3 The role of the individual experience

Moreover, Hargreaves (1994) points out that teachers are not just technical learners, but also social learners. They must have not only the capacity, but also the desire for change. Teachers have always struggled with the current needs and expectations of society, with the state of learning in their particular discipline, and with their own personality and skills to find the best mode of teaching, which has created the pragmatic attitude that demonstrates teachers' approach to the process of change (Fullan, 2001).

The reason teachers have an important role to play in implementing change lies in the nature of classroom practice. First, classroom processes are complex and often unpredictable. Due to the varied contexts in which teachers work, situations may present themselves differently, and demand quite different responses. Second, teachers themselves bring their own values and beliefs to teaching which inevitably predispose them to the selection of particular strategies and the seeking of particular outcomes (Calderhead, 1984). According to Pehkonen and Törner (1999), surface changes cannot influence teachers because they can adapt to a new curriculum, for example by interpreting their teaching in a new way, and absorbing some of the ideas of the new teaching materials into their old style of teaching. At the heart of change for most teachers is the issue of whether it is practical (Hargreaves, 1994). Judging changes by their practicality seems, on the surface, to amount to measuring abstract theories against the tough test of harsh reality. There is more to it than this, though. The ethic of practicality among teachers is a powerful sense of what works and what does not; of which changes will go and which will not – not in the abstract, or even as a general rule, but for the particular teacher in the particular context in which they work (Hargreaves, 1994: 12).

Shaw *et al.* (1991) propose a useful framework for understanding the teacher's roles in change, i.e. cultural environment, vision, perturbance and commitment (see Figure 3.4). According to Shaw *et al.*, the cultural environment is different for each teacher. Some central cultural elements, such as the support given by others, time, money, other resources, taboos, customs, common beliefs and so on, have their impact on the process of change. Perturbance denotes uncertainty or confusion. Change cannot occur without perturbance in teachers' thinking and action; that is, the crucial point at which teachers change is when they begin to realize that their current practice might be problematic (Cobb *et al.*, 1990). For instance, students, colleagues, parents, administrators, teacher-educators, textbooks, self-reflection may act as a result of perturbance. Commitment is a personal decision to realize the change as a result of one or more perturbances. Teachers in the process of change need to form a personal vision of what teaching and learning can look like in their classes. Although more factors need to be taken into account, such as the role of the teacher's projected self in the vision, the decision to make changes within a given context, the level of cultural awareness and reflexivity and so on (Edwards, 1994), the model given by Shaw *et al.* (1991) can serve as a valuable indicator to help examine how teachers cope with change and reconcile these different factors in their situated contexts.

Figure 3.4 A framework for teacher change (adapted from Shaw *et al.*, 1991)

There is a rich store of literature, research and practical understanding on teacher change. Some research shows that teacher change is a long process (see Becker *et al.*, 1995), some demonstrating that teachers show little change in beliefs about their roles (see Martens, 1992). In contrast, other research shows that the teacher learned and consequently changed beliefs and practice through actual practice (see Feikes, 1995), some demonstrating that teachers can make significant changes in their teaching behaviours after only ten hours' training (see Sparks, 1984). However, a common theme in the literature is both a resistance to and a compliance with change in their practices. The next section aims to examine different models of change which help to show the experience of change from the teachers' perspective.

3.3.4 The nature of adaptation to change

This section aims to explore the level of adaptation to change, first introducing the Concerns-Based Adoption Model (the CBAM), a model for change in individuals that applies to anyone experiencing change, that is, policy-makers, teachers, parents and students (Hall and Hord, 1987; 2000). Then the nature of the concerns model of change is explored to help to identify different ways in which teachers adapt innovation to their unique situation.

Hall and Hord (1987; 2000) propose the CBAM – a conceptual framework which describes, explains, and predicts probable teacher behaviours in the change process. The three principal diagnostic dimensions of the CBAM are stages of concern, levels of use and innovation configurations (see Table 3.3). Stages of concern, the first principal diagnostic dimension of the CBAM, identifies and provides ways to assess seven stages of concern including those ideas of scales such as awareness, informational, personal, management, consequence, collaboration and refocusing (see Table 3.4).

According to Hall and Hord (1987; 2000), these seven stages have several

Table 3.3 The three principal diagnostic dimensions of the Concerns-Based Adoption Model (adapted from Hall and Hord, 2000)

Stages of concern	Seven different reactions that educators experience when they are implementing a new programme
Levels of use	Behaviours educators develop as they become more familiar with and more skilled in using an innovation
Innovation configurations	Different ways in which teachers adapt innovations to their unique situations

Table 3.4 Innovation stages of concerns (adapted from Hall and Hord, 2000: 60)

Stage of concern		*Expressions of concern*
Impact	6. Refocusing	I have some ideas about something that would work even better.
	5. Collaboration	How can I relate what I am doing to what others are doing?
	4. Consequence	How is my use affecting learners? How can I refine it to have more impact?
Task	3. Management	I seem to be spending all my time getting materials ready.
Self	2. Personal	How will using it affect me?
	1. Informational	I would like to know more about it.
	0. Awareness	I am not concerned about it.

implications for professional development. First, they highlight the importance of attending to where people are and addressing the questions they are asking at the time that they are asking them. Second, this model emphasizes the importance of paying attention to implementation for a certain period of time, because it takes at least three years for early concerns to be resolved and later ones to emerge. Teachers need to have their self-concerns addressed before they are ready to attend hands-on workshops. Management concerns can last at least a year, especially when teachers are implementing a school year's worth of new curricula and also when new approaches to teaching require practice and each topic brings new surprises. Last, but not least, with all the demands on teachers, it is often the case that once their practice becomes routine, they have little time and space to focus on whether and in what ways students are learning. This often requires some organizational priority setting, as well as stimulating interest and concern about specific student learning outcomes. In fact, administrators, parents, policy-makers and professional developers also have their own concerns. It is critical to acknowledge their concerns and address them in the process of change.

The second principal diagnostic dimension of the CBAM is called levels of use of the innovation. When defining the levels, Hall and Hord (1987; 2000: 83) state that heavy emphasis was placed on developing definitions of what can be seen and observed and that each level represents a different behavioural approach. Table 3.5 summarizes the different levels of use of the innovation.

As shown in Table 3.5, we can see that at Level 0, the individual has no interest in innovation and therefore takes no action; at Level I the individual takes action to learn more detailed information about the innovation; at Level II the individual makes a decision to use the innovation by establishing a time to begin; at Level III, the individual begins first use of innovation; at Level IV(A) routine pattern of use is established; at Level IV(B) the individual changes use of the innovation on formal or informal evaluation to improve expected benefits; at Level V the individual initiates changes in the use of the

Table 3.5 Innovation levels of use (adapted from Hall and Hord, 2000: 84)

Levels of use	Behavioral indicators of level
VI. Renewal	The individual is seeking more effective alternatives to the established use of the innovation.
V. Integration	The individual is making deliberate efforts to coordinate with others in using the innovation.
IV(B). Refinement	The individual is making changes to increase outcomes.
IV(A). Routine	The individual is making few or no changes and has an established pattern of use.
III. Mechanical	The individual is making changes to better organize use of the innovation.
II. Preparation	The individual has definite plans to begin using the innovation.
I. Orientation	The individual is taking the initiative to learn more about the innovation.
0. Non-use	The individual has little or no knowledge of innovation, no involvement with it, and is doing nothing towards becoming involved.

innovation based on input from and in coordination with colleagues to improve expected benefits; and at Level VI the individual begins exploring alternatives or major modifications to the innovation presently in use. When addressing the significance of the levels of use concept, Hall and Hord (2000: 87) maintain:

> The categories cut across the Levels of Use and have unique sets of behavioural indicators within each level. Interestingly, this work expanded our understanding of what use means. The categories reflect behaviour occurring both inside and outside the classroom. What is typically thought of as direct use of the innovation, that is, what happens in classrooms, is grouped under the Performing category. All other categories and behavioural indicators represent innovation-related behaviour occurring outside the actual classroom. This significant characteristic of the Levels of Use concept should help facilitators appreciate the significance of the range of activities teachers become involved with when an innovation is introduced. The activity that occurs within the classroom plus the innovation-related behaviours exhibited before and after classroom performance combines to form the totality of innovation use. This perspective broadens the change facilitator's field of vision and range of intervention opportunities. In both innovation non-use and use categories significant amounts of activity occur before and after classroom time.

Innovation configurations is the third principal diagnostic dimension of CBAM. It deals directly with characteristics of the innovation and what use means when the innovation is the frame of reference. The differences in how innovations are used led researchers to propose the concept of innovation configurations (Hall and Loucks, 1978). An innovation configuration is an established and well-researched format developed by experts in a national/ state research centre studying educational change (Hall and Hord, 2001; Hord *et al.*, 1987). It identifies and describes, in operation, the major components of new practice. Studies of how policies, programmes and processes have been implemented show that innovations typically are implemented in various ways and with varying levels of quality (Roy and Hord, 2004). Somewhat parallel to the definition of the complexity of an innovation is the dilemma of two different ways in which an innovation can be implemented, namely, the fidelity approach and the mutual adaptation approach (Snyder *et al.*, 1992). The fidelity approach is based on the assumption that an already developed innovation exists and the task for the teacher is to implement it faithfully in practice in the way the developer intended, while the mutual adaptation approach stresses that change is often a result of adaptations and decisions made by teachers as they work with new materials (Berman and McLaughlin,

1975). Having authorities mandate, experts request or colleagues agree to adopt an innovation does not guarantee the change will be implemented with fidelity. The teacher's situation and the new materials are mutually determining the outcome as teachers are the decision-makers in their classroom (Clandinin and Connelly, 1992). Some studies demonstrate that successful implementation required mutual adaptation – that change succeeds when there is some adaptation of the innovation at the particular school site and some adaptation of the local school's practices as the innovation is implemented (see, for example, Hall and Hord, 2000). The concept of the innovation configuration was born from this recognition that individual teachers adapt or modify the components of new practices as they implement them (Roy and Hord, 2004). The innovation configuration maps identify the innovation's major components and describe various uses ranging from ideal implementation to non-use along a continuum. The innovation configuration answers two questions: What does the innovation look like in practice? and Has quality implementation occurred? This description helps create an image of the innovation that we can carry in our minds. With innovation configurations, decision-makers, evaluators, teachers, principals and others can learn a great deal about the characteristics and expectations of an innovation.

However, there is also often resistance to innovation and slippage in its implementation (Adamson *et al.*, 2000; Tong *et al.*, 2000). Most researchers find that if methods and practices are incompatible with teachers' classroom realities or threaten existing routines, teachers tend to reject the innovation (Chan, 2002; Prabhu, 1987), although responses can range from compliance and appropriation to retreatism and outright resistance (see Table 3.6), reminding us that accommodating to change is not a smooth, linear nor necessarily predictable process.

To sum up, this section first explored the nature of change. Then it examined the roles of external, situational and internal factors that can influence and affect pedagogy and change. Finally this section reviewed the levels of adaptation to change. As discussed, we can see that pedagogy and curriculum change is a very complex issue, which contains multidimensional factors that interact and affect one another. Each factor has its own role to play in the process of change. It is important to realize that teachers are strongly influenced by their own reasons and desire for change, or not as the case may be, and by their own capacity for change. Teacher change is very much a product of not only top-down or bottom-up forces, but also situated and individual forces. The next section attempts to examine the relationship, as such, between those external, situated and individual forces in ELT pedagogy in the PRC.

Table 3.6 Teachers' responses to innovation (cited in Zhang, 2005: 64)

Response	Explanation
Compliance/ appropriation	Acceptance of the imposed changes and adjustment of teachers' professional ideology accordingly, so that greater central control was perceived as acceptable or even desirable.
Incorporation/ assimilation/ accommodation	Appearing to accept the imposed changes but incorporating them into existing models of working, so that existing methods were adapted rather than changed and the effect of change was considerably different from that intended.
Creative mediation/ convergence	Taking active control of the changes and responding to them in a creative, but possibly selective, way; the most significant elements of the innovation are integrated into existing practice to create something fundamentally new.
Pseudo-compliance	The teacher pays lip-service to the innovation, but does not actually implement it.
Retreatism	Submission to the imposed changes without any change in professional ideology, leading to deep-seated feelings of resentment, demoralization and alienation.
Resistance	Resistance to the imposed changes in the hope that the sanctions available to enforce them would not be sufficiently powerful to make this impossible.

3.4 Influences on ELT pedagogy in China

As discussed above, pedagogy and change are affected by a number of factors. This section intends to examine which factors are most likely to have impacted on teachers' pedagogy in ELT in the PRC. The purpose of this is to set up a tentative theoretical framework for this research study to look at the dynamic entities of the teacher's pedagogy.

As indicated in Chapter 1, the introduction of the new curriculum, the creation of new public examinations, and the promotion of new teaching methods have been increasing the demands upon teachers in the PRC to change. However, teachers of English – the real decision-makers in practice – with different views of language, and conceptions of teaching and learning from different backgrounds or motives, are not necessarily willing to adopt new curricula without any adaptation, implement promoted methods without any change or neglect their own classes to help their students attain good academic results in public examination. Hence, their pedagogy is likely to be more pragmatic than purist, influenced by both external and situated forces, as well as their own lived experiences and perceptions of change.

As demonstrated in Chapter 2, in addition to the social, political, and economic changes in the PRC in the past few decades, ELT policy and curriculum have also undergone tremendous change, with a clear trend from political-oriented to expertise-oriented change (Adamson, 2001). The State Education Development Commission (SEDC), as a representative of the central government, is in a position to make educational policies and determine the goals, curriculum, course books and even teaching methods throughout the country (Liao, 2000). As indicated earlier, in response to these changes, new textbooks, for instance the Junior English for China and Senior English for China series (JEFC/SEFC) have been co-compiled with Longman International. This joint venture has been used for the technical transfer (Adamson, 2001) and promotion of new teaching methods, such as communicative language teaching and task-based learning in the PRC (Anderson, 1993; Cortazzi and Jin, 1996; Liao, 2000; Liu and Adamson, 1999).

Communicative language teaching (CLT) has been judged by many as more effective than the traditional grammar-translation method in terms of improving students' sociolinguistic and strategic competence in using English (Liao, 2000), incorporating more authentic materials, and stimulating more lively classroom activities (Chen *et al.*, 1988). However, CLT has also been seen as one of many 'Western-thought packages' (Marton, 2000), which are openly promoted as a replacement for traditional methods of learning and teaching in China (Anderson, 1993; Burnaby and Sun, 1989; Rao, 1996; 1999). Traditional sociocultural attitudes and values are considered by some researchers as the main reason CLT has failed to be implemented more widely (Cortazzi and Jin, 1996; Ng and Tang, 1997; Tang and Absalom, 1998); that is, CLT is constructed in opposition to so-called Confucian culture and values.

However, it is more likely that CLT has been compromised by more practical considerations such as large class sizes[1] (Anderson, 1993; Hu, 2002; Wu, 2001), limited instruction time,[2] a shortage of materials, the poor training and low pay of teachers (Hui, 1997), the lack of practical support (Ng and Tang, 1997), a rigid top-down school culture, unrealistic demands from educational authorities and rising parental expectations[3] (Anderson, 1993; Hu, 2002; Wu, 2001). A significant problem is the popularity of national and local grammar-based examinations (Rao, 1996; Zheng and Adamson, 2003), and the backwash effect of the Matriculation English Test (MET) – a national college entrance examination developed by the SEDC (Gao and Watkins, 2001; Zheng and Adamson, 2003). Given such external and situated factors, exacerbated by perceived inadequacies in teachers' English language proficiency and pedagogical ability (Rao, 1996), it is no wonder that teachers confronted with pedagogic innovation are likely to feel uncertainty, even confusion – what Shaw *et al.* (1991) term a perturbance.

However, there has been little or no research into secondary English language teachers' perceptions and responses to the new English language curriculum, and the effects on their implemented pedagogy in the PRC (but see Zhang, 2005, for a recent study of the impact of curriculum implementation on primary teachers in Shenzhen). If we are to examine the dynamic entity of teachers' pedagogy, it is necessary to take all these influential factors into consideration. Only by so doing can we see which factors have been of most influence on teachers' pedagogy and explore it from a dialectical and interactive point of view to understand the real nature of teachers' pedagogy in the PRC. Figure 3.5 summarizes the factors listed above that are likely to critically influence ELT pedagogy in the PRC. This model of influences will serve as a tentative theoretical framework for this research study.

3.5 Conclusion

As demonstrated above, implemented pedagogy is affected and shaped by a great number of complex factors, i.e. external, situated and internal factors. Although both Chinese and Western scholars, such as Adamson (1998), Anderson (1993), Cowan *et al.* (1979), Dzau (1990), Liu (1988; 1995), Paine (1990; 1997) and Penner (1991a) have contributed to the embryonic literature on Chinese ELT policy and curriculum studies, there has been little empirical research and study in relation to how teachers' beliefs, designs and practices are negotiated and implemented in the rapidly evolving and changing world of ELT in the PRC. Thus, this book is even more important.

The tentative research framework established above was used as a starting point to explore this dynamic and complex phenomenon in the analysis of the beliefs and practices of the three case study teachers: Mr Yang, Miss Wu and Ms Ma (all pseudonyms), who were working at three very different secondary schools in Fuzhou, Fujian, the PRC. The focus of the next three chapters is on the teachers' stories and demonstrations of mutual adaptation, as they negotiated and modified the promoted methods in the new ELT curriculum in the process of their teaching to suit their local context.

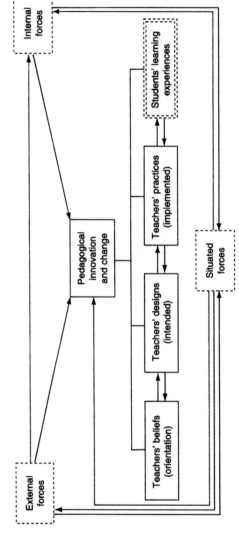

Figure 3.5 A tentative theoretical framework for this research study (Zheng, 2005)

Notes

1. According to Lam (2005) in some secondary schools, particularly in the less economically advantaged interior, the number of students in a class is often 50-plus and may even be as high as 70, which makes it difficult for students to have much opportunity for interactive practice in English.

2. In secondary schools in China, there are usually 2 semesters with 18 to 22 weeks each semester. Lessons are generally 45 minutes long. Hence, the total number of class hours spent on studying English in the 6 years of secondary school ranges from 1,080 to 1,210 lessons or 810 to 908 hours.

3. In China, as in many Asian countries, parents are demanding that schools begin English lessons earlier and earlier. However, the shortage of teachers of English at this level means that many schools have only one teacher of English who has to teach all five grades from Primary 2 onwards (Lam, 2005). Schools do not usually offer English in Primary 1 because in their first year of school students have to learn *hanyu pinyin*, the alphabetical script for representing Putonghua (Mandarin), and there is widespread concern that they may get confused if they have to attach different sounds to the same letters.

Chapter 4

Mr Yang's pedagogy[1]

4.1 Introduction

This chapter explores how Mr Yang handled the demands of the curriculum: in particular how he mediated his own beliefs and practices (i.e. his personal pedagogy) with the promoted methods to soothe the tension between his beliefs and practice. Section 4.2 provides a brief biographical profile of Mr Yang, exploring his personal and family background, his own experience of learning English, his teaching experience and professional development. Following the analytical framework constructed in Chapter 3.2, Section 4.3 describes the teaching and learning processes, content and focus, teacher's roles, students' roles, organization, types of activities and resources in Mr Yang's classroom teaching. Section 4.4 focuses on identifying the relationship between Mr Yang's beliefs and his classroom practices by using content analysis to identify and describe Mr Yang's beliefs – both articulated and implicit. Section 4.5 discusses how Mr Yang's epistemic beliefs influenced his design and shaped his practices and how issues arising from his practice impacted on his beliefs and refined or transformed them.

4.2 Mr Yang's biographical profile[2]

Mr Yang is a senior teacher with a BA degree from an average university in Fujian province. He was 55 years old with over thirty years of teaching experience at the time of the study. He had been teaching the 1993 English Curriculum for more than seven years. We approached Mr Yang to participate in this study following a seminar in Fuzhou in which Mr Yang had made articulate and forthright contributions to a discussion of the challenges of English language teaching in secondary schools in the PRC, and he readily agreed to be interviewed and observed in the classroom.

Mr Yang's school was located in the inner-city area of Fuzhou, and was an average school in terms of school resources, teacher qualifications, student admission requirements and student achievement. The school was still using the JEFC and SEFC textbook series, which was based on the earlier version of the curriculum, but Mr Yang was aware of the contents of the revised curriculum published in 2001, and had some knowledge of task-based learning. Besides his academic title as a senior teacher, Mr Yang was also head of the Teaching and Research Group of English in his school. His position as a leader, to some extent, represented the subgroup members in his school in terms of social values, teaching views, political acts, school culture and so on. We felt that Mr Yang had the potential to help reveal the changing nature of an English language teacher's pedagogy over the past two decades.

However, it was difficult at first to involve Mr Yang in the study. His principal was worried about the damage to the school's image and reputation if Mr Yang did not perform well. Although Mr Yang was a senior teacher, he had never done any videotaping before. We explained to Mr Zhang, principal of the school, that when we reported the findings, we would not use Mr Yang's real name or the name of the school. Meanwhile we called Mr Yang to persuade him to support us. He said it would be a big extra load for him; he had never been videotaped before and he was not sure if he could do a good job:

> School leaders usually have great concerns about videotaping. They think they will choose the best teacher to do the videotaping in order to represent the highest teaching level of the school. So I think you should ask him to choose someone else for you.

We realized the school principal may not want Mr Yang to do the video and Mr Yang had felt hurt by the principal's words. We revisited Mr Zhang, the school principal, to persuade him to support us. Luckily, Mr Zhang finally agreed to let Mr Yang do it on condition that no materials should be given to outsiders. We made a call to Mr Yang, telling him that the principal had agreed to support the videotaping and asked him to participate. Mr Yang was moved by our perseverance and finally agreed to help.

In terms of his family background, Mr Yang came from working-class origins. His parents did not have any knowledge of English. When he was a middle school student in the early 1960s, he learned Russian for two years. Due to the deterioration of the Sino-Soviet relationship in 1960s, China turned to the West, so Mr Yang then learned English for two years. However, the Cultural Revolution in China broke out in 1966. As a result, the schools were closed, and like thousands of educated youth, Mr Yang went to settle in a remote village in the northern part of Fujian, where he worked as a farmer in the field during the daytime and in the evening he taught himself some English by listening to broadcast English programmes because he felt that he could not idle away his youth. In 1977, China resumed its national college entrance examination after being suspended for more than ten years due to the political chaos. After taking part in the national college entrance examination, Mr Yang went to an average university in Fujian. He recalled that when he studied at university most of his teachers paid special attention to grammar, translation and linguistic accuracy. Grammar, in particular, was systematically taught; Mr Yang said that he did not have much chance to practise speaking and listening. Upon his graduation, he went into teaching immediately in a rural secondary school. Unlike most urban students in China, who start to learn English in primary school, Mr Yang's students did not start to learn English until they went to secondary school. Mr Yang found it difficult to handle the large number of students. For him, being strict with his students was effective in terms of classroom management. He felt comfortable keeping his students quiet and making them listen to him carefully and attentively. He recalled that he used to stand at the front of the class transmitting knowledge by reading aloud new words and expressions for his students to imitate, reading out texts sentence by sentence, and explaining grammar and language points in detail.

The turning point of Mr Yang's professional life started in 1993 when he transferred to teach in a key secondary school in the city of Fuzhou. When he came to this school, facing a new teaching task, Mr Yang felt that his pedagogical content knowledge should be updated. At the same time, Fuzhou Institute of Education organized a training programme to help teachers of English understand the 1993 new curriculum and the intended communicative methods. The training programme introduced Mr Yang to the new rationale of communicative methods, instructional practices both inside and outside China, and a series of wider educational issues. Mr Yang also had a chance to take a course on the psychology of learning. He said that the course helped him not only to reflect on his past teaching, but also to see things from his students' perspective. According to Mr Yang, the 1993 English Curriculum, the promoted communicative methods together with the training programme served as activators to stimulate him to change. He also mentioned that his collegial network also considerably affected him to change. However, there were a lot of obstacles in the way of change: the traditional rigid national college entrance examination, his school authorities' expectations, parental expectations, tight timetable and so on created a dilemma for Mr Yang. On the one hand, he did not want to chain himself to beliefs about the primacy of grammar, nor did he want to make a big change in his teaching by completely rejecting his beliefs. On the other hand, Mr Yang realized his students would eventually be faced with the multiple uses of English in the real world which would require comprehensive skills in speaking, listening, reading and writing. As a compromise, he followed the requirements of the examination oriented system by spending approximately half of his teaching time going over the language points, grammar and doing translations, which was congruent with his beliefs. The other half of his time he would help his students to develop their skills in speaking, listening, reading and writing. To achieve the latter, Mr Yang tried out innovative teaching methods. The above description helps to give a general idea of Mr Yang's life story, learning experience, professional development, in-service education and so on. The following section will discuss how Mr Yang's beliefs were implemented and reflected in his practice.

4.3 Mr Yang's practice[3]

4.3.1 Processes of teaching and learning

According to Richards and Rodgers (2001), processes of teaching and learning refer to the way a teacher handles the presentation, practice and feedback phases of teaching and learning in the classroom. The analysis of Mr Yang's teaching plans showed that when he made his plans, Mr Yang primarily followed the sequencing recommended by the textbook, the teacher's book, which included asking questions about the pictures, reading the dialogue, listening to the tape, explaining the grammar and language points, doing practice, checking homework. The following tables (Table 4.1, Table 4.2 and Table 4.3) illustrate what Mr Yang intended to do in class when he planned to teach Lesson 37 (a dialogue lesson), Lessons 38–39 (two longer text lessons) and Lesson 40 (listening comprehension, word study and composition).

However, in his actual lesson Mr Yang made some changes to his plans in order to meet his students' demands.[4] One prominent change was that Mr Yang gave priority to speaking and listening, followed by reading and writing. As will be seen, this was quite different from the belief that Mr Yang held

Table 4.1 Sequencing of Lesson 37

---

1. Teaching words and expressions
2. Listening to the tapes
3. Practising speaking by asking questions and answers
4. Reading and understanding the dialogue
5. Doing exercises
6. Explaining language points and grammatical items
7. Doing exercises to consolidate what has been taught
8. Student oral performance

Table 4.2 Sequencing of Lesson 38 and Lesson 39

---

1. Revision of what has been taught in previous lessons
2. Listening to the tapes and doing questions and answers
3. Doing the exercises provided by the textbook in order to get comprehensive understanding of the text
4. Focusing on explaining the language points and grammar
5. Doing plenty of translation from Chinese into English; occasionally from English to Chinese
6. Checking the homework and helping the students with the problems that emerged in class

---

Table 4.3 Sequencing of Lesson 40

---

1. Revision of what has been taught in previous lessons
2. Listening to the tapes and filling in the blanks
3. Explaining the word study (teacher's talk)
4. Doing translation from Chinese into English; making sentences by using the words

---

about the order of the four skills. The Teacher's Book did not provide clear instructions regarding how to teach new words and expressions. Mr Yang taught all the new words and expressions in the first teaching period. He believed this would help his students to become familiar with all the new words so as to remove any obstacles to the students' understanding of the dialogue and the texts. It is interesting to see that in the vocabulary teaching Mr Yang handled listening and speaking before reading and writing. When he taught dialogue and longer texts, Mr Yang had his students listen to the tapes before they were asked to answer questions. After the listening and speaking practice, he started to explain some language points and grammar, which he thought was a very important component in his whole teaching process. When he finished his talk, Mr Yang had his students do oral practice and some written practice and checked the exercises on the workbook.

4.3.2 Content and focus

Content and focus refers to the textbook materials in each unit, such as dialogue, reading, listening, writing, grammar, exercises on the students' workbooks, word study, language points and so on. In his lesson plan, Mr Yang intended to cover all the content from Lesson 37 to Lesson 40 by focusing on the dialogue, texts, grammar, exercises, listening, word study and writing. However, due to the change in the demands and problems occurring in the real classroom teaching as well as time pressure, Mr Yang was unable to cover all the content planned, so what he did do was to cut down some of the exercises, including the composition writing. The classroom observation showed that Mr Yang spent 75 minutes out of the total 280 minutes in explaining grammar, the language points and having his students engaged in doing different kinds of activities relating grammatical items. Grammar talk was one of Mr Yang's major foci. The classroom observation also showed that he spent altogether 74 minutes in helping his students with listening and speaking to understand the dialogue, the texts and the exercises on listening comprehension. Presumably, listening and speaking was another major focus in his practice. Judging from his time allocation, we could see that Mr Yang paid attention not only to transmitting knowledge, but also to cultivating the students' comprehension abilities. A third focus of his practice was translation; classroom observation showed that Mr Yang spent almost 47 minutes organizing activities to get his students involved in doing translation from Chinese into English or vice versa. Table 4.4 summarizes Mr Yang's major foci, content and time allocation in practice.

4.3.3 Teacher's roles

Teacher's roles refers to the types of functions teachers are expected to fulfil, the degree of control the teacher has over how learning takes place, the degree to which the teacher is responsible for determining the content of what is taught and the interactional patterns that develop between teachers and learners (Richards and Rodgers, 2001). In his practice, Mr Yang played multiple roles. Most of the time during the lessons, he talked, explained, provided the information and encouraged his students to speak. English was the chief medium in the lessons, but sometimes when special grammatical

Table 4.4 Mr Yang's major foci and content in practice

Time (minutes)	Content and focus
75	Grammar, language points and exercises
74	Listening and speaking to understand the dialogue and the texts
47	Doing translation to consolidate sentence patterns, key words, collocations, etc.
84	Revision, checking homework, explaining the background, culture, student's recitation, performance and other activities
Total time 280	

terms and difficult words occurred, Chinese was used to help the students understand the meanings. Mr Yang checked the exercises, arranged the word competition, organized the students to act out the dialogue, and explained the reading lessons in detail by asking a number of questions. Later, he provided a diagram to demonstrate how Bill Banks, the protagonist in the text, escaped from the spies. The students were divided into small groups to discuss and then one of the students was asked to report their discussion. The student had some difficulties in reporting the principal content of their discussion and Mr Yang tried to scaffold the student's language use. The following text is an example to show how Mr Yang scaffolded the student's language:

	Student	*Mr Yang*
2.	. . . Bill hurried into the bathroom . . . he went up to Room 511 . . . er . . . er . . .	
3.		Did you mean Bill went up to Room 511 directly from the bathroom?
4.	No, there was a staircase in the bathroom . . . mmm . . . Bill climbed up the staircase and went into another room, where there were twelve more steps leading to Room 511. As soon as he was in Room 511, he opened the front door and let Mick in . . . er . . . er . . .	
5.		Why did he let Mick in? What could Mick do for Bill?
6.	Oh, yes, Mr Yang. Bill gave the important computer program to Mick and asked him to go to airport immediately . . .	

Mr Yang commented that an overemphasis on grammar would lead to underemphasis on the holistic understanding of the text; the teacher's emphasis on grammar might mislead the students. Therefore, in actual teaching, Mr Yang tried to help students understand not only the language points, but also the holistic meanings of the texts. For example, before he explained the grammar, he required his students to read the whole lesson carefully and then he asked them to answer some general questions in order to make sure they had had a good understanding of the text. Then he encouraged his students to speak English as much as possible. From the observation data, we can see Mr Yang explained grammatical points in great detail. For instance, when teaching the attributive clause, Mr Yang repeatedly explained in English what an antecedent and a relative pronoun meant, and how to join the main clause and the subordinate clause together. After he finished explaining, Mr Yang used the following three pairs of sentences to show how they could be joined as complex sentences:

1. *The person* is Mr Ball. You need to speak to <u>him</u>. → *The person* <u>whom</u> you need to speak to is Mr Ball.
2. *The hospital* was a very old building. I was born in <u>it</u>. → *The hospital* in <u>which</u> I was born was a very old building.
3. *The noodles* were delicious. I cooked <u>them</u> yesterday. → *The noodles* <u>which</u> I cooked yesterday were delicious.

After that, Mr Yang gave out more than ten sentences for his students to practise. In this process, we can see from the observation data that there were interactions between him and the students. Mr Yang walked around the classroom and gave help where necessary; five minutes later, he had his students report what they had done. He tried to lead them to the conclusion, and gave them immediate feedback in both oral and written forms. Mr Yang's role in actual practice can be summarized in Table 4.5.

Table 4.5 The teacher's role in Mr Yang's class

1. Organizer   2. Helper   3. Resource provider   4. Controller   5. Consultant
6. Memory activator   7. Prompter   8. Marker/assessor   9. Demonstrator/presenter

4.3.4 Students' roles

According to Richards and Rodgers (2001), students' roles refers to their contribution to the learning process, which is seen in the types of activities they carry out, the degree of control they have over the content of learning, the patterns of student groupings adopted, the degree to which they influence the learning of others, and the view of the student as processor, performer, initiator and problem-solver. According to the observed lessons, for most of the time during the lessons, Mr Yang's students listened to him carefully, made notes and did exercises in accordance with Mr Yang's instruction. They had no way to control the content of the focus or the teaching methods. When asked to do the discussion, it seemed that they could follow Mr Yang's directions clearly; however, they felt rather shy, apparently timid to express themselves in English. At the beginning, most appeared very quiet. Later, with Mr Yang's encouragement, a few bolder students tried to utter a few words or a sentence. From such collaboration, the students developed their points of view bit by bit, and wrote them down in their exercise books for later reference. Although Mr Yang encouraged his students to ask questions when he was conducting his

Table 4.6 The students' roles in Mr Yang's class

---

1. Performers   2. Problem-solvers   3. Participants   4. Listeners   5. Knowledge receptors

---

teaching, few actively raised any questions. The students' roles in Mr Yang's class are summarized in Table 4.6.

4.3.5 Organization

Organization refers to the way a method handles the presentation, practice and feedback phases of teaching. Revision, presentation, drill, practice and consolidation are highly recommended as the five-step approach in the teacher's reference book, very important teaching material for Mr Yang. From the observed lessons, we can see that Mr Yang mainly followed these steps, for each using different ways to organize teaching for interaction and activities. Teacher talk was one of his main methods; he spoke to the whole class to transmit knowledge and information. Mr Yang used this mode as a primary means of controlling his students' behaviour. Requesting his students to ask and answer questions, he arranged them in pairs or small groups. Individual study was also used when he needed his students to do reading. The interactions between teacher and individual student were also observed. Table 4.7 summarizes the organization of Mr Yang in his practice.

Table 4.7 Mr Yang's teaching organization in practice

---

1. Revision   2. Presentation–practice   3. Practice–presentation   4. Consolidation

---

4.3.6 Activities

Activities refers to kinds of tasks and practice activities employed in the classroom through the organized and directed interactions of teachers, students and materials. According to the observation data, Mr Yang had the students read out the words, and corrected their pronunciation when necessary. Furthermore, he gave definitions of most of the words in English. Mr Yang commented that the purpose of doing so was to provide his students with some opportunities to practise their listening and speaking and it also helped them to think in English. Some examples of word definitions Mr Yang gave to his students in actual teaching include:

Pause = temporary stop in speech or action
Turn up = arrive unexpectedly

Adventure = strange or unusual happening, especially an exciting or dangerous journey or activity

Fear = be afraid of

The moment = as soon as

According to the observation data, sometimes Mr Yang read out the word and his students gave the definition, and sometimes he gave the definition and they read out the word. The whole class was active in participating in this activity. By doing so, many here-and-now discourses emerged. Mr Yang made active use of the chance to talk with the students and correct their mistakes.

When the lesson moved to the dialogue, Mr Yang first separated his students into small groups to read and discuss the text. While they were discussing the text, Mr Yang was walking around to help. After that, each group or pair chose one student to present their opinions about the text to the whole class. The students got some chances to share their ideas with their classmates. At this stage, Mr Yang listened to them carefully rather than making any comments. One example is given here to show how the students shared their ideas in class. According to the observation data, one student from Group 4 stood up to make the following comment:

After the discussion, most of us agreed that something must have happened to Linda Bell. According to Linda's classmates, she was a very responsible student and she had never missed any classes before. But this time without asking for leave beforehand, she did not turn up for two days. It was very strange. What is more, when her classmates went to her dorm to check, they found there were only a few loose coins at the back of the drawer. Her purse was missing. We really feel worried about her.

(A student's report in Mr Yang's class)

With these activities done, Mr Yang had the students listen to the tapes three times so that they would have the chance to listen to native speakers, in particular to become familiar with pronunciation and intonation. After that, Mr Yang organized question and answer practice. He asked his students not only to practise listening and speaking in the dialogue lesson, but also to spend some time explaining the key sentences of the dialogue and some grammatical points. He showed some examples by using transparencies and gave some exercises for the students to practise. These exercises were designed to build up the students' ability in applying the knowledge of those key sentences and grammar to their real-life situation and examination. The exercises included oral translation and making up sentences. Interactions between Mr Yang and his students were obviously frequent and positive. In addition to this, Mr Yang also had some of his students act out the dialogue in front of the class.

It was obvious that he encouraged them to memorize the dialogue. Here are some examples to show how Mr Yang interacted with his students on the dialogue:

Mr Yang:	What do you do if people disappear?
Student A:	Well, if I am at school, I will first report to my teacher.
Mr Yang:	If you are not at school, whom do you first choose to call?
Student B:	Well, I will call 110.
Mr Yang:	110? What does it mean?
Student B:	Everybody knows this number. It is a special number to call police in emergencies.
Mr Yang:	Very good! What did Linda's friends do when they found out that she was missing?
Student C:	I guess they called the police.
Mr Yang:	What did the policemen ask Linda's friends to report when they arrived?
Student D:	Er . . . the policemen asked when they last saw Linda, if she missed classes very often . . .

Lesson 38 and Lesson 39 of this unit are about a story entitled 'The Trick'. First, Mr Yang played the tapes several times in order to give his students sufficient chances to understand the lessons. After that, he asked 14 why or how questions to see if the students could understand the general meaning of the lessons. This required the students not only to think hard after they listened to the tapes, but also to give specific answers. During the discussion and inter-action processes, Mr Yang gave consistent encouragement, dropping hints when he saw some of the students fail to answer the questions correctly, so that they could feel confident to respond:

Mr Yang:	Why did Bill pretend to admire something in the shop window?
Student A:	Well, er . . . er . . .
Mr Yang:	OK, what did Bill want to know for certain before he entered the hotel?
Student A:	Oh, yeah, Mr Yang, I understand now. Bill stopped and wanted to see if the two men were following him.
Mr Yang:	That's right! Very good!

From this description, we can see that Mr Yang did not teach the texts by reading them or explaining them sentence by sentence, which might break up the whole complete lessons into incomprehensible pieces. Instead, he tried to help his students to obtain a clear general idea of the lessons in their mind through collective discussion. Once he achieved this goal, Mr Yang moved to the second step of his teaching, a retelling exercise.

After completing the retelling, Mr Yang assumed that most of his students understood the general idea of the lessons and then he asked his students to rearrange the order of the events that happened in the story. It appeared that the students could do this without much difficulty. Mr Yang used this method in order to achieve two things. First, he wanted to make sure his students could understand the content from the discussion, and second, he wanted to consolidate this understanding and comprehension in written form, which he believed could give useful help to some 'slower' students to understand the texts better.

The third step saw Mr Yang engaging in explaining the texts. He did not explain the whole texts sentence by sentence. Instead, he focused on some key sentences and some language points and he also had his students do some translation, both from English into Chinese and vice versa. Here are some sentences that Mr Yang wanted his students to translate:

1. _____ (看起来) (It seems) Linda Bell has done something wrong.
2. _____ (显然) (Obviously) she has got something important to do.
3. _____ (我猜想) (I guess) her mother might have fallen ill.
4. _____ (我确信) (I am sure/I believe) she must have had some trouble.

Normally, teachers of English in PRC dominate the talk at this stage, as discussed in Chapter 2. In contrast, Mr Yang had plenty of interaction with his students, giving some examples and exercises on transparencies. After this, he went on to explain grammar (subjunctive mood) in Chinese to the students and gave some more examples to illustrate this grammatical point. According to the observation data, we can see that when grammar paradigms were taught, Mr Yang chose to explain in Chinese and that he did pay attention to the language forms and grammar paradigms. At the same time, he tried to avoid talking too much himself. Instead, he tried to provide as many opportunities as possible to his students to participate in the interaction. From the observation data, we can also see that Mr Yang gave particular attention to some useful idiomatic expressions and phrases and spent adequate time explaining how to use them.

After finishing all the grammatical items and the language points, Mr Yang moved to his fourth step, the consolidation, by working out the exercises in the workbook. As was previously observed, Mr Yang had already integrated parts of the exercises that were most relevant to the dialogue and reading texts into his explanation. At this stage, he dealt with the remaining parts of the exercises: grammar exercise and translation exercise. The major grammar items in this unit were direct speech and indirect speech. Although he had already explicitly explained these two grammar items to his students in the grammar talk, we can see that Mr Yang still wanted to make the best use of this chance to help his students review, deepen and enhance their understanding of the grammar by giving the following presentation:

Direct	*Indirect*
'Rose went to Nanjing,' said he.	He said that Rose had gone to Nanjing.
The waitress told George, 'Don't smoke at the food counter!'	The waitress told George not to smoke at the food counter.

After some explanation and presentation, Mr Yang asked his students to practise the following three sentences together:

> 'Put my purse in the desk drawer and lock it.' (she/her husband)
> 'I've met you somewhere before.' (I told the secretary)
> 'Who have you caught for stealing their purse?' (I asked the police)

Here is the conversation between Mr Yang and his students in the discussion:

Mr Yang: Now, class, please first of all observe the differences among these three sentences. Liu Yun, can you tell me what kind of sentence the first sentence is?

Liu: Sorry . . . I don't know how to say that in English. Er, it is a 祈使句.

Mr Yang: Oh, yes. It is an imperative sentence. Good! How about the second sentence, Li Hong?

Li: Well, I think it is a 陈述句.

Mr Yang: You are right. It is a declarative sentence. Very good! OK, can you tell us about the third sentence, Wu Yan?

Wu: Yes, Mr Yang. I think it is a 特殊疑问句.

Mr Yang: Good, it is an interrogative sentence. Now, let's see how we can put these three sentences from direct sentences into indirect sentences.

After this interaction with his students, Mr Yang used the transparency to show them how to change the three sentences from direct speech into indirect speech. When he was doing the presentation, Mr Yang told his students that usually the pattern *ask sb to do sth* or *tell sb to do sth* was used to transfer the imperative sentence, the conjunction *that* was used to transfer the declarative sentence, and the conjunctions *if* or *what* (note: *when, why, how, where, which, who* and *whom*) were used to transfer the interrogative sentence. Finally, Mr Yang had his students practise with the following exercises on the transparency:

'How many languages are spoken in Australia?' asked the boy.
'What is the title of the book you've translated?' I said to the professor.
'Don't ever be late again!' (doctor/student nurse)
'Change your dirty shoes.' (elder sister/younger brother)
'Everybody seems as busy as a bee in the office.' (manager/visitor)
'I promise I won't say anything until I hear from you.' (he said)

After this procedure, Mr Yang moved to work at the translation exercise. Judging by the time that he spent doing the exercises, we can see Mr Yang paid much attention to developing the students' ability in this respect. He used two copies of a transparency, on which there were ten sentences in Chinese, to get his students to do the translation. Some idiomatic phrases from the texts were chosen for the students' reference when they did the translation. Mr Yang requested the students carry out the oral activity first and then based on the practice he asked them to write the sentences down and finally he showed the translated version to the students to compare. Here is one example to show how Mr Yang and his students did the translation:

Mr Yang:	Now, let's put this sentence from Chinese into English: '他问我能不能在他把这篇报告送交大会之前浏览一下?' First of all, can you tell me in the indirect speech part, what kind of sentence it is? An imperative sentence, or a declarative sentence, or an interrogative sentence? Chen Haibing, please.
Chen:	I think it is an interrogative sentence.
Mr Yang:	Correct. Can you find if there is a phrase that comes from our lesson? Song Meiqing, please.
Song	Yes, '浏览'.
Mr Yang:	How do you say that in English, then?
Song:	To glance at or to glance over.
Mr Yang:	Good! How do you say '浏览一下报告'? Wu Ming, please.
Wu:	'To glance over the report.'
Mr Yang:	Good! OK, now, let us translate part of this sentence from Chinese into English first. '你能不能在我把这篇报告送交大会之前浏览一下?' Yao Jiejun, please.
Yao:	'Can you glance over this report before I send it to the conference?'
Mr Yang:	That is right. Now let's put 他问 together with the sentence 'Can you glance over this report before I send it to the conference?' Would you please do this, Zhang Tianye?
Zhang:	Well, let me try. 'He ask can I glance over his report before he send it to the conference.'

Mr Yang: OK. I am going to write what Zhang Tianye said on the blackboard to see if there is anything that needs improving.

Mr Yang wrote Zhang's sentence on the blackboard: 'He ask can I glance over his report before he send it to the conference.' Then he continued discussion with his students.

Mr Yang: Well, let's see the word 'ask'. What is wrong? Liao Hui, please.
Liao: I think we should add ed to the word 'ask'.
Mr Yang: Great! As I told you before, we need to have a conjunction to connect the main clause and the subordinate clause. What kind of conjunction do we need here? Wang Yongdong, please.
Wang: I think we need a word 'if' to connect.
Mr Yang: Can you tell me why?
Wang: 'Can I glance over his report before he sends it to the conference' is an interrogative sentence. It is not a special question, but a simple question. So we need a word 'if' to connect.
Mr Yang: You are right. Is there anything that we need to correct? Ma Lili, please?
Ma: We must change the clause from 'Can I glance over his report before he sends it to the conference' to 'If I could glance over his report before he sent it to the conference'.
Mr Yang: Well done. So the whole translated sentence should be read like this: 'He asked if I could glance over his report before he sent it to the conference.'

To take a holistic and comprehensive view of these activities, Mr Yang's strategy in dealing with the consolidation was very communicative. Though the content and focus included much information relating to grammar and translation, Mr Yang sought to tackle the consolidation by using a more meaning-oriented interactive approach. He attempted to organize different kinds of activities in order to provide his students with the best opportunities to train their comprehension skills in listening, speaking and writing rather than merely delivering the knowledge to them.

The last step of Mr Yang's lessons dealt with the listening comprehension part. According to the workbook, there were three messages that had been recorded on three different answering machines as the end of the story 'The Trick'. Mr Yang asked his students to listen to the tape and write down the name of the caller, the person for whom the message was intended, and the time and the place of the call if it was given (Table 4.8).

Table 4.8 A listening comprehension form in Mr Yang's lesson

	1	2	3
Message for:			
Time of call:			
Caller's name:			
Place of call:			

Mr Yang played the audiotape of the text three times for his students to listen to. Sometimes he paused here and there to give some explanation. He did not push his students to fill in the missing words in a hurry. Instead, he encouraged his students to catch the key words in the messages. After filling in the columns, Mr Yang required his students to write down the message they had heard from the tape:

Mick is flying to _____.
He'll go back to Cairo _____.
Mick _____.
Something _____.
He'll be back in Cairo _____.
He asks Joan to _____.
Mick is well and _____.
He asks Bill to ring his boss David Lightfoot and _____.
He'll _____.

First, Mr Yang made sure that his students had understood the passage well by asking some questions. Mr Yang commented that he did not rigidly follow the proposed steps in the teacher's reference book, that is, to have the students listen to the tape, fill in the missing words and check the answer; instead, he acted in a more flexible way to expose his students to the atmosphere of the target language as much as possible, and encouraged them to deduce the missing words from the context. In fact, this process greatly enhanced the interaction between the teacher and the students and also helped the less developed students in listening comprehension to gain more confidence. Mr Yang used the following questions to remind his students:

Remember, Mick has a special mission at the moment. Which country is he flying to?
You should listen very carefully for the time when Mick will go back to Cairo. At the beginning of the week, or at the weekend?
What made him rush off? Something important has happened?

What help does he need from Joan? To pick her up or to see him off?

What telephone number does he ask Bill to ring his boss? What does he ask Bill to explain to his boss?

Table 4.9 summarizes the different kinds of activities that Mr Yang employed in his practice:

Table 4.9 Different types of activities Mr Yang used in practice

---

1. Listening to the tapes
2. Speaking in class, group, and pair
3. Translation (basically oral activity)
4. Reading aloud
5. Retelling and reporting
6. Word competition
7. Acting out the dialogue
8. Completing sentences
9. Making up sentences
10. Reporting homework
11. Questions and answers
12. Grammar practice

4.3.7 Materials

Materials refers to the primary goal of materials (e.g. to present content, to practise content, to facilitate communication between learners or to enable learners to practise content without the teacher's help), the form of materials (e.g. textbooks, audiovisuals, computer software) and the relation of materials to other sources of input (i.e. whether they serve as the major source of input or only as a minor component of it). The materials that Mr Yang used in his practice included the textbook (Senior English for China, Students' Book 3A), the teacher's reference book (Senior English for China, Teacher's Book 3A), the Listening Cassette, the slides prepared by Mr Yang himself and the cassette player.

The textbook played a major role in the teaching practice. Mr Yang mainly adopted the objectives, contents, learning activities and the teacher's role suggested by the textbook and the teacher's book. However, in the actual class, Mr Yang cut down some of the content. For instance, instead of completing all the exercises, he selected some of the exercises that he believed were important for the students. He did not complete the composition in class for two reasons: first, the time was too limited and second, he thought the students might do the practice outside class themselves. Mr Yang thought the grammar exercises designed by the textbook were not comprehensive enough, so he

Table 4.10 Materials Mr Yang used in practice

---

1. Students' Textbook (SEFC, Book 3A)
2. Teacher's Book 3A (Reference Book)
3. Slides prepared by Mr Yang himself
4. A tape recorder
5. Some listening tapes
6. English Accessorial Exercise Book for Senior Three by local publishing house

---

prepared some slides in addition to help his students to consolidate what they had learned; he believed these additional materials were useful for his students. For example, he designed some Chinese sentences for the translation activity and asked his students to translate them into English. Mr Yang frequently used audio-video aids (mainly the cassette player and slides), which enabled his students to listen to the native speakers' voices and accents and also helped to create more opportunities for practice.

4.3.8 Summary

The above description shows that Mr Yang primarily followed the procedures recommended by the teacher's book to fulfil the content set by the 1993 English Curriculum. It is a top priority to fulfil the curriculum objectives, as the national entrance examination has a very rigid system to test students' knowledge of grammar and language points. Mr Yang tried to use different kinds of methods in the hope of laying a solid foundation in grammar and language points for his students. At the same time, it is clear that he believed it was insufficient for his students only to have a good command of grammar and language points as China badly needs more and more workers who are able to communicate with native speakers orally. Facing this demand and challenge, Mr Yang overcame difficulties in his class, such as unrealistic content expectations and time limits, to assist his students in speaking and listening. His major goal was to involve his students in the teaching and learning process as much as possible. Different kinds of activities were organized in order to provide his students with ample chances to practise listening, speaking, reading and writing. Mr Yang's teaching practice did not come from a vacuum. As discussed in Chapter 3, what a teacher does in practice is greatly influenced or shaped by his or her beliefs and other social, cultural and political factors in the environment. In the following section, we will explore what Mr Yang's beliefs were and how social and political factors influenced his practices.

4.4 Relationship between Mr Yang's beliefs and practices

Interviewing Mr Yang, we can see that his views of language and language learning were greatly influenced by his own experiences learning English at college in the mid-1960s. When he was a student, his teachers emphasized grammar teaching a great deal and paid much attention to the accuracy of the linguistic components. According to Mr Yang, he felt that he had benefited a lot from this kind of teaching in that it laid a solid foundation in grammar, which, in return, helped him to develop his other skills in the language learning process. He admitted that his later teaching perceptions were hugely affected by these learning experiences. He regarded grammar teaching as the primary element in the teaching and learning process and believed that in this process the teacher should play a major role:

> I think grammar is of utter importance for our Chinese students. Personally speaking, I believe vocabulary and grammar are two most important foundations for the students. It is no use talking about learning English well without having a solid command of grammar or building up a considerably good vocabulary.

As discussed in Chapter 2 and Chapter 3, this perception is also influenced by the backwash effect of the high stakes national matriculation examination – in which the implicit view of language and language learning leads to a weak form of communicative language teaching:

> According to our public examination system, our students need to apply their grammar knowledge to solving the problems. Therefore, it is very important for us teachers to transmit the grammatical knowledge to them.

It is obvious from the observation data, with this firm belief in his mind, that Mr Yang regarded his primary role as a knowledge transmitter because he thought learning was a process of acquiring and accumulating knowledge and skills, and he, being a teacher, was responsible to fulfil the objectives assigned by the syllabus and to transmit and deliver the knowledge and skills to his students. From his experience and his deeply embedded Chinese cultural perceptions, Mr Yang believed that rote learning was one of the most effective ways for his students to learn grammar well:

> Normally speaking, I encourage my students to recite the dialogues of each unit because they are usually not very long but contain very good and useful phrases and sentences. If my students can recite them, in fact, they learn grammar underpinning in the dialogues. Regarding the long texts, I only

ask them to memorize some key sentences. I find it very useful for them to do so because they have to read the dialogues several times before they can recite them. This gives them the chance to practise reading English aloud. I believe they will do well in the examinations as their brains are full of those useful things.

In practice, as seen in the previous section, it is clear that Mr Yang followed this orientation very firmly. He spent one third of the total time teaching grammar, explaining language points, transmitting knowledge and information and asking his students to recite the assignments. However, the 1993 English Curriculum, as mentioned in previous chapters, encouraged teachers to pay attention to the cultivation of communicative competence and performance in English rather than merely knowledge of the language. This change had a major impact on classroom teaching. In the school where Mr Yang taught, there were some novice teachers who were between 25 and 35 years old; some were attending postgraduate certificate courses in the local universities and others were working at their master degrees in their spare time. These teachers were active in reflecting on their professional pedagogical knowledge and their teaching methods. It was through this conduit that Mr Yang got a chance both to review what was happening in the classrooms of other teachers, and to access, as far as possible, what the latest developments in ELT research and theory were. Mr Yang commented that frequent interaction and communication with his colleagues helped him to view his teaching from multiple perspectives. He thought it was very useful for him to establish close teaching relationships with his young colleagues by attending each other's lessons, discussing teaching methods, preparing lessons together weekly, giving feedback to each other about the difficulties that they faced in the classroom teaching and so on. Consequently, this led to constant reflection on his pedagogical knowledge and teaching method:

> When I observed the lively, active and vivid teaching demonstrations of my young colleagues, and when I saw the eagerness and enthusiasm from the students to participate in the classroom activities, I started to reflect about my teaching practice. Though I still hold that the teacher should play a leading role [in teaching], yet I now think the classroom teaching without adequate participation and involvement of the students cannot be called as the real teaching and learning. So from the implication of my young colleagues, I had a substantial understanding of the interrelationship of the roles of the teacher, the roles of the students, the content and focus, the interaction, the learning process and the use of materials.

This external force pushed Mr Yang to adopt diverse types of activities to improve his students' speaking and listening abilities, which Mr Yang also considered as primary to communicative competence. He recognized that teachers should not spend too much time delivering grammar knowledge. Instead, teachers, he believed, should teach grammar in context:

> We must change the old conception, that is, we should not teach grammar for the sake of grammar. Instead, while we nurture the students' abilities in using grammar, we should not neglect to nurture their abilities in speaking and listening. When teaching grammar, teachers should not devote all their time explaining the language points and grammatical rules. In fact, it is wise to integrate the form and context closely so that it would be interesting for the students to learn grammar and at the same time to improve their holistic comprehension.

Collegial interaction brought Mr Yang much reflection, which gradually impelled him to change his practices although grammar teaching was still a key part of his classroom teaching. In the past, Mr Yang had verbally dominated the teaching process by spending much time explaining the content and focus to the students. But now, Mr Yang gave adequate explanations to his students and then offered them more opportunities to get involved in as many different types of activities as possible. Based on the content and the focus explained, his students had more opportunities to communicate with him and with peers. The activities observed were duty report, free talk, questions and answers, situational dialogues, oral and written translation, retelling, drilling, group work, pair work, dictation, word competition, recitation and so on. At the same time, Mr Yang changed his role from a single dimensional one of knowledge transmitter to a multidimensional one of organizer, controller and helper, and he regarded his students as performers and problem-solvers. All these aspects of his teaching revealed that Mr Yang was trying to make his teaching more student centred in orientation.

However, this change was not smooth. Mr Yang was often caught in a dilemma as he encountered many complicated problems in his actual teaching environment. He realized that ELT was by no means only a matter of teaching grammar, translation, pattern drill, syntax, linguistic competence or practising method innovation; it was also a social and political issue. In fact, Mr Yang had to cope with many other things, such as negotiating for more resources, more time, and responding to different complaints from his students and their parents. The things that happened both outside and inside his classroom constantly impacted on his unsteady beliefs and, consequently, influenced his choices of teaching methods. One of the biggest problems was the tight time schedule.

Schools allocate different teaching hours for different disciplines in accordance with the national curriculum in China. Mr Yang's school allotted five teaching periods for the teachers of English to conduct lessons. Mr Yang explained that the length of each teaching period in his school was only 40 minutes, five minutes shorter than that of other schools in Fujian province. The reason for this was that his school was undergoing a kind of curriculum innovation, which aimed to offer more subjects to students. In order to make this innovation possible, the school authorities could think of no better way other than to cut five minutes from each teaching period. Mr Yang strongly felt that his personal pedagogy was challenged because of this time adjustment:

> SEFC is a very demanding textbook, which requires our teachers to train the students strictly in speaking, listening, reading and writing respectively. There are too many things to cover. I just feel it impossible to finish everything. What I have to do is cut down something. The choice of cutting down some contents or adding some contents is determined by many factors. First, I think, the influence comes from the national entrance examination. At present, there is no speaking and listening requirement in the national entrance examination. They [the examiners] pay greater attention to the written form, reading, language points and grammar. I would like to fulfil the comprehensive aims of the textbook if I had the time. However, my school leaders, the students' parents and the students themselves are very practical. What they expect to see is to have the good result in the national examination. Personally speaking, I can fully understand it. For students in China now, after twelve years of basic education, going to college is their ultimate goal and expectation. Going to college means the first step up to the social ladder. This is part of our culture. Therefore I must adapt to this situation, in other words, I must cut down some listening and speaking practice so as to squeeze the time for other focus. Second, grammar is not systematically well organized in the textbook; I must add some materials prepared by myself in order to let my students have a good command of it.

From the comments above, it is obvious that Mr Yang was in a quandary. On the one hand, he had to 'feed' his students with the content examined in the national matriculation examination. In doing so, he worried that he might revert too far to the teacher-centred mode as there were lots of grammatical items for him to explain and to cover. On the other hand, Mr Yang fully realized English learning required solid command of the four skills through interactive classroom communication. He mentioned in the interview it was these tensions that made him frustrated and he really wished he had been able to organize as many oral practices as possible for the students to voice their points of views and assist one another.

Under these circumstances, Mr Yang had no other choice but to transmit knowledge first rather than cultivate the students' abilities, although he under-stood clearly that the latter was also very important for his students. Mr Yang held that the teacher should dominate the teaching and learning process, but he said it was not necessary to be teacher centred, implicitly, that it was the teacher who should decide what to teach, how to teach, how to support the students and how to control the pace. In the learning process, Mr Yang insisted that the students' roles should be supportive; in other words, they should mainly follow what they were asked to do, and were not encouraged to challenge the teacher. SEFC and its supplementary materials were regarded as the appropriate teaching materials and their objectives and targets were very clear. However, due to the time limit, Mr Yang realized that when he used the textbook and the materials, he had to cut down some parts of the content. Decisions as to which part of the content in the textbook should be cut down, Mr Yang commented, would depend on the classroom situation. In other words, he was flexible to adjust his teaching design when he perceived it was necessary to do so to meet the emerging problems in practices.

The extremely large class size (usually 55 students) and uneven level of students' academic abilities were further salient problems that bothered Mr Yang in his practice. In his school, classes were separated into 'quick' or 'slow' students in accordance with their grades. The prerequisite for a student to be chosen to study in a 'quick' class was that he or she should be in the top 200 out of the 300 students in the grade. Those who were chosen to study in a 'quick' class hoped to pass the national entrance examination; therefore, they received better attention and care from the school and teachers. For those who were left in a 'slow' class, the school authorities and the teacher believed, their ultimate goals were to graduate and get their secondary school certificates. However, things were not so simple. According to Mr Yang, exceptional situations might occur:

> Nowadays, educational circle is not as clean as before due to the prevailing bad social atmosphere. Some people have power, and others have money. There are very complicated social relationships behind this kind of arrangement. For example, some students whose scores were not good enough also came to these 'quick' classes because their parents manoeuvred their powers or money. This added difficulty for us teachers to teach because those students lagged far behind the majority of the good students. It was very hard for me, indeed. What I could do was to face the reality: my fundamental idea was that I should face the majority of the students. I had to consider their overall abilities, i.e. speaking, listening, reading and writing. At the same time, I really did not want to ignore the existence of those 'poor' students. However, very often, I just felt it very hard to satisfy all

and please all. This is something annoying. If I showed my concern and favour to slow down my teaching pace, good students started to request me to be more communicative because they were not satisfied with the old methods. If I used too much communicative method, poor students obviously got lost. To be honest, I was back and forth and forth and back.

It is clear from the observation data that Mr Yang tried very hard to handle this tension. The salient feature was that he was fully aware that under this kind of circumstance he should not stick to a certain fixed method. He said that he would be flexible enough to use different and appropriate methods to handle outcomes from the real situation as each day he had to face different kinds of contents, and students had different kinds of questions to ask and different kinds of problems to solve. Nevertheless, he thought in teaching there should be a general method to follow. From his design, it was clear that Mr Yang basically adopted the proposed teaching methods and procedures from the SEFC Teacher's Book to prepare his lessons, although he tended towards a structural approach to a greater extent than a functional/notional approach (see Chapter 2). Mr Yang planned his lessons by considering how to adopt these diverse approaches; in the classroom, he adjusted his plan to deal with emergent circumstances. According to his lesson plan, it is obvious that the Five Step Teaching Method, as explained in Chapter 2, was the keynote of Mr Yang's intended method. Mr Yang said he could see nothing improper from this method though he did not completely apply it to the whole teaching process:

> When I wrote my lesson plans, I usually referred to the Teacher's Book. I believe the steps and methods recommended by the Teacher's Book are good. I usually follow the main design of it and also make some necessary changes in order to adapt to the real situations of the teaching and learning in my class. The Five Step Teaching Method covers many procedures that suit Chinese learners. By using this method I think the students will have a lot of comprehensive and overall training opportunities in four skills.

4.5 Discussion

First, judging from his articulated belief, it is quite clear that Mr Yang treats English as an important tool, through which his students could know about the outside world, learn modern science and technology, communicate with foreign friends politically and culturally, find better jobs and higher pay, go abroad for their further and higher education and so on. Second, regarding language learning, we can infer from the data that Mr Yang's belief is that learning has much to do with rote memory, which he strongly believed was deeply embedded in Chinese culture. At the same time, by reflecting on other teachers' innovative teaching in his school, by learning from the promoted methods and by attending some academic presentations and conferences, Mr Yang also believes that language learning is a communicative process as well, in which a teacher should make every possible effort to support students and the students need to be supportive to be fully engaged in the interactions. Third, with regard to language teaching, from the data, it is obvious that he believes that a language teacher should first pay attention to teaching grammar well. According to Mr Yang, only by explaining grammar and language points clearly to the students can they have a solid command of the language; after the students build up a solid foundation of grammar and vocabulary, he thinks it is necessary to train them in the integration of the four skills, namely, listening, speaking, reading and writing. Fourth, in relation to the purpose of teaching, from the data, it is quite apparent that Mr Yang thinks that the main reason for the secondary school students to learn English is to sit for the national entrance examination, which is a common goal for most of society. Hence, the national college matriculation examination has a great influence on classroom teaching. Therefore, he believes that his chief role in teaching is to fulfil the objectives assigned by the syllabus, and transmit and deliver the required knowledge and skills to his students.

Mr Yang feels that he cannot merely train his students to become 'examination machines' because in the future they will use English to attend academic lectures and seminars, to exchange ideas with native speakers, to go abroad for their further studies, to work as clerks in foreign companies in China and so on. Doing this requires them to have comprehensive skills in speaking, listening, reading and writing. Mr Yang's original belief, in which he treated English language teaching as simply a way to deliver and transmit knowledge rather than cultivating the students' language abilities, met with the challenge of real demands and was reshaped. Interestingly, Mr Yang did not want to surrender himself completely to the conventional teaching model, nor did he want to make a big change in his teaching; instead, he adopted a middle course. In practice, he held that he must compromise with the examination oriented system, that is to say, he would spend 'enough' and 'necessary' time going over the language points, grammar and translation, which was considered as an effective way to help students gain good scores in examinations. By doing so, he would feel relaxed as he thought he had taken a very solid step in helping them to succeed. Then he would try to make the best use of remaining time to help his students to lay an essential and fundamental foundation in speaking, listening, reading and writing. From observing young teachers' lessons, and their attempts to adopt new teaching concepts such as collaborative learning and scaffolding, Mr Yang could not help but try to follow this kind of method in order to meet the students' demands and cultivate their learning ability. It is apparent that Mr Yang was trying to resolve his dilemma, the tension between conventional and new teaching trends, in a very pragmatic way.

To resolve the tension, Mr Yang tries out more innovative teaching methods, adopting different kinds of teaching methods under different circumstances. Though he thinks grammar teaching is very important for his students, he also pays great attention to training his students in speaking and listening. This action shows a critical change in his beliefs. From his design, we can see Mr Yang basically adopts the proposed teaching methods and procedures from the Teacher's Book to prepare his lessons. In fact, when compiled, the textbook (SEFC) incorporated different approaches, such as topics and functional/notional approaches, or to be more exact, both the traditional approach and communicative approach (Liu and Adamson, 1998). In his design, Mr Yang takes the content and focus, the organization, the activities, the teacher's role and the students' roles, and the use of materials into full consideration. He is inclined to use different methods to meet different objectives. His choices of different methods appear diverse, which can be clearly seen in the summary of his design.

Mr Yang basically puts what he has planned in his design into real practice though he adjusts his lessons a bit from time to time during his teaching. Table 4.11 details the prominent features identified in Mr Yang's seven classes.

Last, but not least, Mr Yang recognizes that social, cultural and political factors could influence his belief, design and practice:

We live in a society where we are inevitably involved in our socialist system, communist ideology and superstructure. When I was young in the late 1960s and the early 1970s, at that time there was a slogan which stated 'Study English for the revolution'. The curriculum and textbooks were full of political jargons. Language learning became a pure political propaganda . . . More recently, as China is more open to the outside world, the purposes of learning English become more pragmatic. Some want to learn English and sit for TOEFL, IELTS and GRE examinations in order to go abroad; others want to learn English in order to find a better job and get higher pay in the foreign joint ventures. I do think, from the macrocosmic perspective, the social, cultural and political environment does give impetus to the classroom teaching. For example, the Ministry of Education in our country stipulates that in any public matriculation examination at different levels English is mandatory. On the whole, we can say every possible effort has been made to help students score high in the examination by school

Table 4.11 Prominent features of Mr Yang's seven lessons

---

1. Chinese was part of the medium of instruction; it was used to explain new items and to enable comparisons to be made between English and Chinese.
2. About 110 minutes were spent explaining grammar, language points, doing translation into and out of the target language.
3. Language points were explained and taught deductively by presentation and study of some sentence patterns and grammar rules, which were then practised through substitution drilling and translation.
4. Some key structures and sentences from the dialogues and reading were selected and used as the basis for pattern drills of different kinds. Some grammatical explanation was offered to the students, but it was minimized as much as possible.
5. Demands memorization of structure-based dialogues.
6. Linguistic competence was the desired goal.
7. Attempts to communicate were encouraged from the very beginning, during and till the end; 74 minutes were spent on speaking/listening.
8. Students were encouraged to discover the generalization or rules underlying the functional expression or structure.
9. Oral practice – proceeding from guided/controlled to some freer communication activities.
10. Questions and answers based on the dialogues and reading texts; there were some creative activities.
11. Basic communicative expressions and structures were studied that exemplified the function in the dialogues and the texts, and these were applied to students' personal experience but centred around the dialogue and text themes.

---

authorities, teachers and even parents. However, when we talk about the allocation of resources, time and administrative arrangement at the school level, grade level or even at class level, the situation is very tricky.

To conclude, Mr Yang's pedagogy is fundamentally pragmatic, a blended approach. The salient core of his pedagogy is a mix of a communicative orientation and a grammar-translation orientation. Mr Yang's pedagogy is shaped by a number of dynamic factors, including the social and political influences existing outside and inside his classroom; inevitably, they impacted on his intrinsic beliefs. On the one hand, Mr Yang has to implement the prescribed curriculum, which is an important blueprint for the teachers and students to prepare for the national college matriculation examination; on the other, due to the increasingly great changes in teaching methods and more comprehensive demands on the students' abilities from society, he realizes his teaching should shift from a teacher-centred to a more student-centred model. Therefore, from Mr Yang's pedagogy, it is quite clear that communicative skills and grammatical knowledge are viewed as of the same importance, which is a significant difference from the stereotypes in the literature about the pedagogy of secondary school teachers of English in China: teacher centred and grammar translation. However, for Mr Yang, the change is not radical, but incremental; it consists of expanding his repertoire rather than rejecting previous approaches.

Notes

1. In keeping with case study methodology (Yin, 1994) the approach to data collection and analysis described in the next three chapters was descriptive, holistic, heuristic and inductive. However, as Maxwell (1996) points out, we were interested not only in a 'description' of the objective events and behaviour that were taking place, but also in how the participants made sense of those events and actions. As researchers working in such class-rooms and with such teachers over a long period of time, we felt we were in a good position to identify, understand and interpret the genesis, nature and impact of the teachers' modifications and adaptations. However, like other case studies, there are also obvious limitations and caveats relating to the use of the findings, not least our own biases and prejudices.

2. Semi-structured interviews were chosen as one of the primary methods of gaining insight into the teachers' beliefs and practices, as they allowed us to obtain data on predetermined themes (Cohen *et al.*, 2000), yet at the same time allowed us to follow up unexpected issues. Interviews of each teacher were done separately, with each interview normally lasting one hour. It was conducted in Chinese by the first author so that the inform-ants were comfortable about expressing their ideas, then transcribed and translated.

3. As the main purpose of this study was to explore the relationship between teachers' beliefs, designs and practices, we used Richards and Rodgers' (2001) framework as a starting point to develop a short list of tentative codes that related to the processes of teaching and learning, content, types of activities, use of resources, roles of teachers, roles of students and so on. As we continued to review and re-review our database, we expanded the categories. Finally, we related conceptual categories and created themes or concepts, and developed analytic frameworks which we used for further data analysis. This process freed us from entanglement in details of the raw data and encouraged higher level thinking about them, which eventually led us towards theory and generalization.

4. One unit of work undertaken by each teacher was videotaped, giving us a total of 14 45-minute videotaped lessons. The videotaping of the three case

study teachers, which allowed us to revisit the data again and again, was essential to help analyse and interpret the nature of the teachers' practices so that the valid conclusions relating to each teacher's pedagogy could be drawn.

Chapter 5

Miss Wu's pedagogy

5.1 Introduction

This chapter focuses on describing and interpreting Miss Wu's beliefs, design and practices. For the convenience of comparison and analysis, Chapters 5 and 6 follow the same format as Chapter 4 to explore Miss Wu's and Ms Ma's pedagogy. Section 5.2 provides a brief biographical profile of Miss Wu, which introduces Miss Wu's personal life story, language learning experiences, teaching experiences, professional development and so on. Section 5.3 describes Miss Wu's teaching and learning processes, content and focus, teacher's roles, students' roles, organization, types of activities and resources. Section 5.4 identifies the tensions existing between Miss Wu's beliefs and her real practices. Section 5.5 discusses how Miss Wu's beliefs influenced her design and shaped her practices and also how problems that arise from practices affected her beliefs, reshaped her beliefs and influenced her practices.

5.2 Miss Wu's biographical profile

Miss Wu, our second case study teacher, was a relatively inexperienced young teacher, who had only graduated from an average college three years before she joined this study. We met her at a local academic seminar where Miss Wu gave a presentation about how she carried out a demonstration lesson in her school. At that time Miss Wu was trying out a certain teaching model which was designed to teach a long text. We found what she presented at the seminar was full of innovative ideas. After the seminar, we approached Miss Wu and talked for an hour. We invited her to have a formal interview, intending to listen more closely to her beliefs and practices. As a younger teacher who had been trained in CLT methods we thought Miss Wu would add an interesting perspective to the study of implemented pedagogy. Miss Wu was happy to join the study and later readily allowed us to videotape her lessons.

Unlike Mr Yang's school, Miss Wu's school was located in the suburbs, and was much smaller and simply furnished. As it was located in the suburbs and a non-key secondary school, the local government allocated much less funding to the school, and fewer parents were willing to send their children there. Except for some students who were admitted to short-term colleges for their associate degree study, few of the students did well in the national matriculation examination.

Miss Wu came from a well-educated family, both parents being secondary school teachers of science. When she was young, her parents sent her to the local evening school to learn spoken English. When she was at home, her grandfather, who worked in the Customs Office, communicated with her in English. According to Miss Wu, after she left the classroom she still had the chance to practise speaking English. Her grandfather offered her some English storybooks to read. When she was a student in middle school, Miss Wu was very active in speaking English in class. Her English teacher chose her as coordinator to help other students. Fascinated by English fiction, she decided to major in English language and literature after she finished her studies in the middle school. Miss Wu said that her college education gave her good training in listening, speaking, reading, writing and translation.

Besides subject matter knowledge, Miss Wu was also well informed about the latest developments in pedagogical content knowledge both inside and outside China. To Miss Wu's advantage, her department had two teachers of English from Canada and Australia. They often introduced information about the latest trends in teaching methods to students, and they also demonstrated how they applied these teaching strategies in their classroom practices. Miss Wu mentioned that these two teachers' views on learning and teaching and their methods of conducting lessons were a great influence on her later teaching model.

However, her professional life had not always gone smoothly. When she went into teaching after her graduation, Miss Wu was very keen and enthusiastic to teach communicatively. She believed that students should be fully engaged in the teaching and learning process, and that listening and speaking should be heavily emphasized at the initial teaching stage. Therefore, she devoted most of her time to training students in speaking and listening. Her students were very active in acting out different kinds of communicative performances. Her way of teaching, labelled as innovative, was much talked about and commented on by her colleagues. However, to her disappointment, at the end of the school year, the average academic result of her students in the examination was comparatively lower than that of other classes. Immediately, frustrating pressure from school authorities and parents was exerted. Without even asking her about her pedagogy, the school authorities officially informed Miss Wu that for the benefit of the school and students in the national college entrance examination, in the new semester she must remain in the same grade for another year to learn how to teach well, which was considered as a kind of warning and punishment because only when a teacher was considered 'incapable' of teaching was he or she asked to do so. Miss Wu was very disappointed about this unfair treatment, and even considered quitting her job. However, her mentor came to her rescue, and after lengthy discussion, Miss Wu started to reflect on what she had done. She believed that she had done nothing wrong in advocating speaking and listening since many of her students showed positive attitudes towards her teaching. However, she also realized that linguistic competence was a goal required by the syllabus. She figured out that the key point was to achieve a sound balance between the four skills.

This frustration and reflection marked the turning point of Miss Wu's professional development. She started to sit in to observe the lessons conducted by other experienced teachers and held more talks with her colleagues in the common room in order to share their experiences. She strengthened grammar instruction by giving explicit explanations of the structural patterns followed with a lot of language production practice. This description helps to understand, to some extent, Miss Wu's personal life story, learning experience, teaching experience and professional development. The following section will focus on Miss Wu's practice.

5.3 Miss Wu's practice

5.3.1 Processes of teaching and learning

As indicated in Chapter 4, processes of teaching and learning refer to the way a teacher handles the presentation, practice, and feedback phases of teaching and learning in the classroom. Tables 5.1 to 5.4 demonstrate the procedures that Miss Wu adopted when she taught Unit 8, which comprised four lessons.

Table 5.1 Sequencing of Lesson 29 – dialogue

1. Teaching and learning new words and expressions
2. Word competition
3. Dictation
4. Teaching the dialogue by listening to the tape twice
5. Student pair work
6. Students acting out by reading the dialogue aloud at their seats and in the front
7. Oral practice between the teacher and the students
8. Explaining the grammar and language points

Table 5.2 Sequencing of Lesson 30 – reading: 'Food Around the World'

1. Reviewing Lesson 29 by word and expression testing, acting out the dialogue, guided conversation
2. Reciting the dialogue
3. Learning Lesson 30 by asking the students to listen to the tape twice, then the teacher read out the text sentence by sentence and the students followed the teacher
4. Explaining the language points of the text, giving out some examples and having the students do translation from Chinese into English and vice versa
5. Teaching the attributive clause
6. Oral practice

Table 5.3 Sequencing of Lesson 31 – grammar: revision of attributive clause

1. Reviewing Lesson 30 by asking students some questions
2. Doing exercises on the textbook and workbook orally: pair work, group work
3. Having the students make up the attributive clause sentences by using their daily life experiences
4. Doing translation from Chinese into English and vice versa

Table 5.4 Sequencing of Lesson 32 – listening, word study and writing

1. Dictation
2. Doing translation from Chinese into English and vice versa
3. Word study
4. Listening to the tape and listening comprehension training
5. Writing

According to Miss Wu, as soon as she became a teacher at that school, the Teaching and Research Group of Foreign Languages assigned her an experienced teacher as her mentor to help her prepare lessons, and answer her questions. Following this apprenticeship, Miss Wu attended her mentor's lessons almost every day. However, according to Miss Wu, when she designed her lesson plans, she did not merely copy her mentor's lesson models; instead, she read different kinds of teaching resources extensively and searched for some lesson plans available on the Internet. She said she wrote detailed lesson plans including each possible step, even the sentences she wanted to say and the exercises she wanted her students to do in class:

I think I benefit a lot from attending my mentor's lessons. Although her teaching style is different from the promoted communicative language teaching method, she encourages me to try out whatever method I believe is appropriate for my two classes. With her encouragement, I adopt more CLT method than grammar-translation method. Being a novice teacher, I prefer to write the detailed teaching plans to guide my teaching though I don't completely follow them all the time.

According to Miss Wu, her more communicative teaching plan was strongly influenced by her beliefs and her education background. When she studied at college, Miss Wu received rather systematic and Westernized training in teaching methods and subject matter knowledge, through which she became well informed of the latest English language teaching theory and classroom practice. She believed that English learning should be for the purpose of oral communication and that one should start to learn English by speaking it. According to Miss Wu, if one could speak English well, he or she should have no problems in learning how to read and write English well later. The study of Miss Wu's lesson plans and logs showed that she was determined to help her students work in that direction. However, in the follow-up interview with Miss Wu, she commented that the real situation in the classroom was different from what she planned. Many problems emerged in practice; therefore the sequencing described above was compromised and adjusted.

5.3.2 Content and focus

As discussed in Chapter 4, content and focus refers to the textbook materials in each unit, such as dialogue, reading, listening, writing, grammar, exercises on the students' workbooks, word study, language points and so on. The study of Miss Wu's lesson plans showed that she intended to cover Lesson 29 (the dialogue), Lesson 30 (the reading), Lesson 31 (grammar) and Lesson 32 (the listening, word study and writing) in four teaching periods, to be more exact, within 180 minutes. She also planned to cover all the exercises in the workbooks. According to the videotaped lessons, it is clear that Miss Wu had three foci when she taught Unit 8: 1. listening and speaking; 2. language points and grammar; and 3. practice with different types of exercises. According to Miss Wu's lesson plans, she originally planned to spend 100 minutes on listening and speaking. However, due to the pressures of teaching the attributive clause, Miss Wu had to cut 20 minutes from listening and speaking training so that she could devote adequate time to explaining grammar. Miss Wu spent about 50 minutes handling grammar and about 50 minutes doing translation, and exercises on the students' workbooks. Table 5.5 summarizes Miss Wu's major foci, content and time allocation in practice.

Table 5.5 Miss Wu's major foci and content in practice

Time (minutes)	Content and focus
80	Listening and speaking to understand the dialogues and the texts, word competition, performance and other activities
50	Language points, grammar and practice
50	Doing translation to consolidate sentence patterns, key words, collocations, revision, checking homework
Total time 180	

5.3.3 Teacher's roles

As demonstrated in Chapter 4, teacher's roles refers to the types of functions teachers are expected to fulfil, the degree of control the teacher has over how learning takes place, the degree to which the teacher is responsible for determining the content of what is taught and the interactional patterns that develop between teachers and learners. From the videotaped lessons, a striking feature was Miss Wu's way of handling the whole-unit teaching with a more communicative language teaching orientation. When she taught the lessons, Miss Wu felt comfortable speaking English all the time to her students although she sometimes used Mandarin to explain grammar briefly. When she handled the lessons, no matter what kind of content she was dealing with, Miss Wu acted as an organizer rather than a knowledge transmitter. She tried to help her students learn by arranging different kinds of activities. For example, to help her students learn new words and expressions in Unit 8, she organized a word competition, in which they were asked to say as many words as possible which related to drink, meat, fruit and vegetables. The students were seen to be active in learning the new words and expressions by reviewing the old words and expressions they had learned previously. During this process, Miss Wu acted as a helper and marker. She explained less in order to create more opportunities for her students to get involved in the learning process. As teaching and learning moved to the dialogue, Miss Wu worked as a controller and manager. She first had her students read the dialogue loudly, then she arranged for them to listen to the tape to imitate the pronunciation and intonation, and next she had them work in groups and in pairs. At this point, Miss Wu walked around to supervise their activities and also joined their discussion. When teaching and learning moved to the reading part, she started the lesson by asking some questions relating to the students' daily lives:

Miss Wu:	Do you like vegetables?
Student A:	Yes.
Miss Wu:	What kinds of vegetables do you like?
Student A:	Cabbages, tomatoes, p . . .
Miss Wu:	Peas?
Student A:	No, beans, French beans.
Miss Wu:	Do you eat corn?
Student A:	Yes, I do.
Miss Wu:	Well, do you happen to know where corn is grown?

By asking questions, Miss Wu naturally moved her teaching from the daily conversation to the text, in which corn was the key topic for discussion. Her role in reading was first as an activator, organizer and then as a resource provider and knowledge transmitter. Being an activator, Miss Wu used many questions to help her students understand the general ideas of each paragraph. After making sure that her students understood what the text was about, Miss Wu organized her students to discuss the text in detail. Observation showed that the students were separated into small groups to discuss the following topics:

1. When was corn first brought to China?
2. Why was corn grown a lot in Tibet and Sichuan?
3. How is corn cooked in the West?
4. What other plants were found in America?
5. Why is the potato thought to be a very useful plant?
6. What fruits are shipped from China to other countries?

Miss Wu walked around to monitor the discussion, and at the same time controlled the pace and timing. She encouraged her students to present their ideas about the discussion. The observation showed that from time to time, Miss Wu nodded her head or made comments such as 'wonderful' and 'excellent' to express her opinions of her students' performances. After that, Miss Wu started to act as a knowledge transmitter, that is, she started to explain some language points and grammar that occurred in the text. Handling the language points and grammatical items, Miss Wu only gave very brief and concise explanations. Then she gave out many exercises for her students to practise in both oral and written forms. For example, in order to help her students learn the phrase 'by the end of', Miss Wu designed two exercises for them to translate: 1. '到了上个学期之前，我们已经学了800个单词' (By the end of last year, we had already learned 800 words); and 2. 'By the end of last year, they had already planted thirty hectares of trees in the remote hills'. According to Miss Wu, it was necessary for the teacher to give some explanation, but it was more important for the students to have more practice. When she handled the listening, word study and writing, Miss Wu tried to act as a helper rather than a knowledge transmitter or resource provider, in other words, she tried her best to help her students identify the key words, the general meanings of the content, and how to use certain words appropriately in certain contexts. Table 5.6 summarizes Miss Wu's roles in teaching Unit 8.

Table 5.6 The teacher's role in Miss Wu's class

---

1. Organizer   2. Helper   3. Controller   4. Activator   5. Manager
6. Knowledge transmitter   7. Resource provider   8. Marker

5.3.4 Students' roles

As described in Chapter 4, students' roles refers to their contribution to the learning process, which is seen in the types of activities they carry out, the degree of control they have over the content of learning, the patterns of student groupings adopted, the degree to which they influence the learning of others, and the view of the student as processor, performer, initiator and problem-solver. In Miss Wu's classroom, according to the videotaped lessons, one could see that the students were active in participating in all kinds of activities that Miss Wu organized. Their chief contribution to the learning process was their keen cooperative spirit, which helped to create the communicative atmosphere, kept the speaking energy flow moving, and made Miss Wu's communicative language teaching method possible. For example, Miss Wu requested her students to work in pairs by asking each other about what they had had for their breakfast. The students in her class were seen to work in pairs for about three minutes and then Miss Wu had two students come to the front to act out what they had done:

> Miss Wu: Could you please act out the conversation you have just made?
> Student A: What did you have for your breakfast this morning?
> Student B: I had an egg, a piece of bread, a glass of milk and some pork.

(The whole class was very noisy when hearing this. Someone's voice could be heard: 'Wow, such a big breakfast!')

> Student A: Did you cook it yourself?
> Student B: No, I went to bed very late last night. My mum prepared the breakfast this morning.
> Student A: Was the pork del . . . del . . .?

Miss Wu:	It should be delicious. The whole class, please say the word delicious after me three times. Delicious.

(The whole class: Delicious, delicious, delicious.)

Miss Wu:	Good! Go on with your dialogue, please.
Student A:	Was the pork delicious?
Student B:	Oh, yes, very delicious. It was sweet and sour.
Student A:	Really? I'd love to learn how to prepare the pork as your mum did.
Student B:	That is easy. Come to my place this weekend. I am sure my mum is happy to show you how to do it.
Miss Wu:	Well done! Thank you.

When these two students finished, more students were invited to give their performances in the front. Miss Wu organized the activities. She stood to listen and watch and occasionally she cut in to give one or two words to help them carry on their conversation. In her interview, Miss Wu said that she wanted to leave more time for her students to practise, explaining her teaching principle: '以教师为主导, 以学生为主体', which means '[in the learning process], the students should be the main participants under the guidance of their teachers'. Their active participation was not only observed in giving performances in the front as described above, but also seen throughout the whole lesson process in terms of doing other activities, such as reading the dialogue aloud, asking and answering questions about the text, and doing translation work. When she started to explain the language points and grammatical items, Miss Wu deliberately gave very brief and short explanations. To Miss Wu, thorough explanation was not practical:

> I believe clear and brief explanation of some grammatical rules is necessary, but it is more important to leave time and chances for my students to learn through practice. If I keep on talking, it seems as if my students were busy keeping notes, but as a matter of fact, they are inactive in thinking. Bit by bit, they will feel bored and they will forget everything. That is why I minimize my explanation as much as possible and maximize the students' interaction as much as possible.

To be more exact, it is obvious from the observation that these students had more than one role to play in the learning process: we can see that they were knowledge acceptors when Miss Wu explained the language points and grammar; participants and collaborators when she had them discuss or present in groups and pairs; problem-solvers when she asked them to tackle exercises in the workbook; and rote memorizers when she had them go to the front to recite parts of the dialogues and texts. Table 5.7 summarizes the students' major roles in the learning process.

Table 5.7 The students' major roles in Miss Wu's practice

1. Collaborators   2. Participants   3. Knowledge receptors   4. Problem-solvers 5. Listeners   6. Rote memorizers

5.3.5 Organization

As pointed out in Chapter 4, organization refers to the way a method handles the presentation, practice and feedback phases of teaching. According to Miss Wu, she did not follow a fixed organization when she conducted her lessons. During her apprenticeship, Miss Wu attended her mentor's lessons regularly. To some extent, her mentor's organization, which was mainly a five-step approach, influenced Miss Wu's design. According to the data, Miss Wu mainly used revision, presentation practice, practice presentation and consolidation procedure. In each step, although she had to cover the content required by the curriculum, explain the language points and grammar, do translation, and train listening and speaking, Miss Wu paid great attention to leaving her students plenty of time and chances for practice. Table 5.8 summarizes Miss Wu's organization in practice.

Table 5.8 Miss Wu's teaching organization in practice

1. Revision   2. Presentation-practice   3. Practice-presentation   4. Consolidation

5.3.6 Activities

As mentioned in Chapter 4, activities refer to kinds of tasks and practice activities employed in the classroom through the organized and directed interactions of teachers, students and materials. According to the videotaped data, Miss Wu commenced her unit teaching by handling the vocabulary. She organized her students to learn the new words and expressions collectively and individually by listening to the tape, reading after her or reading the words aloud by themselves. She laid emphasis on their pronunciation and intonation; for instance, she had a number of students read the words and expressions aloud and corrected their pronunciation and intonation from time to time. She also tried to help her students review some old words and expressions while they were learning the new ones; for example, when they were learning the new word 'discover', Miss Wu helped them revise the word 'invent', a word they had learned previously. Miss Wu asked them to explain the different meanings of these two words. The students were divided into groups to discuss the meanings of these two words for a minute or so, then some answered Miss Wu's questions:

Miss Wu:	Could you tell me the meaning of the word 'discover', Tian Ye?
Tian:	Er . . . I think it means that we find out something that has existed.
Miss Wu:	Well done, Tian Ye. Thank you and sit down. What does the word 'invent' mean, Lei Yu?
Lei Yu:	'To invent' means to make or design something that did not exist before.
Miss Wu:	Very good. Could you use these two words to make up some sentences, class?

After they finished this activity, Miss Wu reminded her students of the different uses of the word 'room' in the new lesson. She mentioned that the word 'room' is an uncountable word in the dialogue which meant 'space'. Then she listed some more words that belonged to the uncountable noun category such as *coffee, tea, soup, beer* and so on by telling her students that some measure words should be used with them:

Miss Wu:	When we say '一杯啤酒', we should say 'a glass of beer'. Are you clear? Now how do we say '一杯咖啡'?
The whole class:	'A cup of coffee.'
Miss Wu:	'一块豆腐'?
(The whole class:	'A piece of beancurd.')
Miss Wu:	. . .

With all these done, Miss Wu believed that her students must have known how to pronounce the new words and expressions clearly and what their meanings were. Then she organized a word competition and a dictation test which were used as a consolidation measure to support her students to memorize the new words and expressions, including some old words.

When Miss Wu moved on to teach the dialogue, she first organized her students to listen to the tape three times, then asked them to work in pairs and groups. Miss Wu walked around the groups to give her students advice, then asked them to stand up to read the dialogue aloud. From time to time, she corrected their pronunciation and intonation. Later, Miss Wu encouraged some of her students to act out the dialogue at the front. Although some of them at the very beginning were a bit shy, with Miss Wu's encouragement, such as 'I am sure you can do it well', and 'Don't worry, you can refer to your book if you need to', they became more active in role-playing the dialogue. After she was sure that her students were able to read the dialogue smoothly and clearly, Miss Wu selected some useful phrases or sentences for them to practise in both oral and written forms. She called this kind of pattern drills intensive practice which could enhance her students' understanding of the key sentences in the dialogue; for instance, she asked them to identify the differences between 'Do you like . . . ?' and 'Would you like . . .?':

Miss Wu:	Shanshan, can you tell me what the difference between 'Do you like . . . ?' and 'Would you like . . . ?' is?
Shanshan:	Er . . . sorry, Miss Wu.
Miss Wu:	Well, sit down. Helen, please.
Helen:	Mmm . . . I think 'Do you like . . . ?' is a general question and 'Would you like . . . ?' is a kind of invitation, which means 'Do you want . . . now?'
Miss Wu:	Very good. Do you like tea, Helen?
Helen:	Yes, I do.
Miss Wu:	Would you like to have some tea with me in my office after this class?

(The whole class burst into laughter when they heard this.)

Helen:	Yes, please, Miss Wu.

With these completed, Miss Wu had her students separate into small groups to do more oral and written practice. Before the class was over, she asked some of them to recite the dialogue. According to Miss Wu, she used recitation as a kind of monitor to encourage her students to read the dialogue as much as possible outside class. At the end of the term, the students' final score would consist of their written examination plus their oral presentation and their recitation performance in class.

Miss Wu started Lesson 30 by reviewing the dialogue that they had learned the day before. Two students were seen to act out the dialogue without referring to the textbook; another two were asked to act out their own conversation based on the dialogue. Then Miss Wu had a conversation with some students, which aimed at guided/controlled drilling. After this was done, Miss Wu asked her students to follow this pattern and role-play their conversation in groups or in pairs. A conversation between Miss Wu and a student called Mary was recorded as follows:

Miss Wu:	Do you like meat, Mary?
Mary:	Yes.
Miss Wu:	What kinds of meat do you like?
Mary:	Well, pork, mutton and beef.
Miss Wu:	How do you like to prepare the meat?

| Mary: | I'd like to stew the beef, roast the mutton and boil the pork with soy sauce and sugar. |
| Miss Wu: | Mmm . . . it sounds very nice, Mary. |

After the revision, Miss Wu started to teach Lesson 30, entitled 'Food Around the World'. First, Miss Wu had her students listen to the tape of the text three times and then she asked them to read the text as quickly as possible in order to find out the key sentence of each paragraph. After the interaction between Miss Wu and her students on the general themes of Lesson 30, Miss Wu asked the following questions in order to help her students to understand the detailed information from the lesson:

1.   When and where did Christopher Columbus and his friends find corn?
2.   When was corn grown in China? Particularly in which parts of China?
3.   Which plant needs more water to grow, corn or rice?
4.   How do people in the West prepare corn for food?
5.   When corn first appeared in England, how was it called?
6.   Besides corn, what other plants were brought back to Europe by early European travellers to China?
7.   Why is the potato thought to be a very useful plant?
8.   What fruits are shipped from China to other countries?

When the oral practice aiming at understanding the general meaning and detailed information was finished, Miss Wu started to handle the language points and grammatical items they came across in Lesson 30. According to the data, she did not explain the attributive clause in detail; instead, she handled the attributive clause by discussion with her students:

Miss Wu:	Can you tell me one sentence with the attributive clause in paragraph one, Yang Min?
Yang:	Oh, yes, Miss Wu. Corn is a useful plant that can be eaten by both people and animals.
Miss Wu:	Right. What does the word 'that' mean?
Yang:	'That' refers to the word 'plant'.
Miss Wu:	Can we use 'which' to replace 'that'?
Yang:	Yes, I think so.
Miss Wu:	Can we omit the word 'which' or 'that'?
Yang:	Er . . . I am not quite sure.
Miss Wu:	No, we can't. If we take it away, there is no subject in the attributive clause. It won't do.
Yang:	Oh, I see.

When she was sure that her students had understood the conversation described above, Miss Wu asked them to try to find all the sentences with attributive clauses in Lesson 30 and then discussed with them the use of relative pronouns. Next, with her prepared slides, she asked her students to join the subordinate sentences with the main sentences first in oral form and then in written form:

1. The factory is at the end of the street. You are looking for it.
2. Have you ever visited the place? Comrade Zhou Enlai used to live there.
3. The nurse said that he could leave the hospital the next day. She was looking after him.
4. The eggs were not fresh. You had them for breakfast.
5. The man sells vegetables. He lives next to us.
6. The tomatoes were expensive. I bought them yesterday in the supermarket.
7. I don't like the people. They smoke a lot.
8. The pancakes were made of corn. We ate them just now.

Although Lesson 31 was a revision lesson in which plenty of written grammar work was designed to help students consolidate the attributive clause, Miss Wu continued to use a communicative orientation to handle all the items. According to the data, Miss Wu first asked her students to describe their daily life by using the attributive clause:

Miss Wu:	I'd like you to make up a sentence by using the attributive clause to describe your own life. You can talk about anything or anybody you know about. John, please?
John:	I take the bus whose number is 810 to school every day.
Miss Wu:	Good. Rose?
Rose:	The TV programme my mother and I watched together last night was about World War II.
Miss Wu:	Fine. Any volunteers? OK, good. Bob, please.
Bob:	The football match I watched last weekend was wonderful.
Miss Wu:	Excellent! . . .

After this activity, Miss Wu asked her students to do some translation from Chinese into English and vice versa. According to Miss Wu, she intended to use this activity to help her students consolidate one or two key grammatical items in the text. For example, Miss Wu asked the whole class to translate this sentence from Chinese into English: '到了上学期末, 我们已经学习英语三年了', which meant 'By the end of last term we had learned English for three years'. When she was sure her students had understood clearly that the past perfect tense should be used in this sentence pattern, Miss Wu asked her students to do more exercises by showing her prepared slides on which there were more translation sentences. Finally, she asked her students to read out the assignment and she made comments or corrected the mistakes her students had made.

Miss Wu spent one teaching hour on Lesson 32, which consisted of three parts: listening comprehension, word study and writing. The listening comprehension was about the different prices of fruits and vegetables at London and Beijing markets. Miss Wu first organized her students to read through the information about the markets and then gave out a few questions as reminders:

1. Are prices of fruit and vegetables always the same?
2. Why do prices go up and down?
3. Why do farmers need to know the market prices of things which they are going to sell?

Before she asked her students to fill out the prices forms, Miss Wu had her students go through the table and make sure how to fill in the information. According to the data, she played the tape twice, using the Pause button to stop here and there as necessary. After her students had finished the exercise, Miss Wu asked them to check their answers in pairs and then with the whole class. In order to help her students understand the listening text better, she replayed the tape one more time to confirm the answers. Miss Wu believed that the listening training needed her students' cooperation:

> In class, I can only show them the way to improve their listening comprehension, such as how to remember some key words, numbers, names of places, time and so on. The most important thing for them to do is to spend more time after class doing two kinds of practice: intensive listening and extensive listening. The former requires them to listen to the same short passages repeatedly until they can fully understand every single word of the content, and the latter requires them to listen to BBC, VOA or CCTV English news programmes at random as much as possible. Only by doing so can they improve their listening comprehension. Classroom practice is far beyond enough.

When she did the Word Study, Miss Wu first went over the words in the box and made sure her students knew all the meanings of the words. Then, she checked the answers by asking the students to fill in the blanks with the right words in their right positions. After that, Miss Wu had some of her students translate each sentence into Chinese:

> I think translation is very necessary because it helps my students understand the sentences exactly and clearly in both Chinese and the target language. It also helps my students to write correct English sentences when they write passages, which are requested in the national entrance examination.

Table 5.9 Different types of activities Miss Wu used in practice

1. Learning new words and expressions by listening to the tape
2. Pronunciation and intonation practice
3. Questions and answers
4. Oral practice in groups and pairs; presentation in class
5. Acting out the dialogue
6. Grammar practice
7. Translation both orally and in written form
8. Completing sentences
9. Retelling and reporting
10. Making up sentences by using some new words and key patterns linking to school life or personal life
11. Reading aloud

Writing in this lesson required students to complete some sentences by using the words given to them. Miss Wu first organized the whole class to do some examples orally so that they would understand how to join these sentences correctly. Then she let her students start to work on their own, in their exercise books; later, she asked some of the students to arrange the sentences in a correct order so that they read like a meaningful short passage. Miss Wu corrected some grammatical problems that her students made. Table 5.9 summarizes different types of activities Miss Wu used in her teaching practice.

5.3.7 Materials

As mentioned in Chapter 4, materials refer to the primary goal of materials (e.g. to present content, to practise content, to facilitate communication between learners or to enable learners to practise content without the teacher's help), the form of materials (e.g. textbooks, audiovisuals, computer software) and the relation of materials to other sources of input (i.e. whether they serve as the major source of input or only as a minor component of it). Miss Wu chiefly used the following materials in her teaching: 1. Senior English for China (Students' Book 1A), Senior English for China (Teacher's Book 1A); 2. some additional grammar materials and handouts; and 3. a tape recorder, tapes, and ready prepared slides.

Senior English for China (Students' Book 1A) was used as the main source of input in Miss Wu's teaching although the additional materials, handouts and prepared slides also served as a part of the input. According to Miss Wu, when she prepared her lessons, she referred to Senior English for China (Teacher's Book 1A) from time to time, but it was not her only source of reference; she also used websites and the Google search engine to look for more

Table 5.10 Materials Miss Wu used in practice

1. Students' Textbook (SEFC, Book 1A)
2. Teacher's Book 1A (Reference Book)
3. Slides (some commercial products and some self-prepared)
4. A tape recorder
5. Some listening tapes
6. English Accessorial Exercise Book for Senior One by local publishing house

information. When designing her lesson plan, Miss Wu said that the content and focus, the time and her students' needs were the most important factors for her consideration. In order to suit the real situation in class, she prepared some slides, on which there were mostly grammar and translation exercises. The tape recorder was frequently used as an aid to help her students hear the native speakers' pronunciation and intonation and other listening comprehension materials. Table 5.10 summarizes the materials that Miss Wu used in practice.

5.3.8 Summary

According to the above description, Miss Wu had a clear plan to cover the content set by the 1993 English Curriculum. In order to fulfil its objectives, she tried to use different kinds of methods in the hope of laying a solid foundation for her students in four basic skills, that is, listening, speaking, reading and writing. In her practice, Miss Wu had specific focus, to get her students involved in the teaching and learning process as much as possible. Therefore, she organized different activity types in order to provide her students with opportunities to practise listening, speaking, reading and writing. During the teaching process, although her roles were dominant, Miss Wu's students were heavily involved in all activities. Miss Wu's practice was a complicated and dynamic entity because, as discussed in Chapter 3, a teacher's pedagogy is greatly influenced or shaped by his or her beliefs and other social, cultural and political factors in her environment. Miss Wu's beliefs and other factors which influenced her practices will be explored in the next section.

5.4 Relationship between Miss Wu's beliefs and practices

As described above, Miss Wu's teaching was characterized by getting her students fully involved in the learning process. Her own learning experiences had a strong influence on her conception of what language learning involved, the basis on which she formulated her own practical theories of teaching:

My college education laid me a very solid foundation in pedagogic content knowledge and subject matter knowledge. I would like to say this systemic knowledge influenced my classroom practice greatly. When I started to teach in the first year, I was very eager to put what I had learned, both pedagogic content knowledge and subject matter knowledge, into the real classroom practice. I was also very enthusiastic to adopt the new teaching approaches, for example, the communicative method, which was strongly recommended by the 1993 syllabus to encourage teachers to devote more time to training students' listening and speaking skills.

Another important factor which influenced Miss Wu's practice was her professional development. She was able to benefit from her mentor's guidance, emotional support from her colleagues and her students' appreciation, which helped her to clear her many doubts as a novice teacher:

Most of my students liked the way I conducted the class because they liked the active atmosphere and they were happy to have many chances to speak English in class. When I had my demonstration classes to other teachers from my own school and other schools, I received positive feedbacks on my teaching approach. Some of my colleagues even said they would follow my way to conduct their teaching innovation.

In fact, her professional development was not very smooth. According to Miss Wu, as soon as she became a teacher, she followed the syllabus, and the promoted method, which encouraged teachers to give more time to train students' listening and speaking skills. Miss Wu allocated more time to train her students' speaking and listening skills, but this did not mean she chose not to develop her students' other skills at all, such as reading and writing. However, as mentioned in Section 5.2, at the end of the first school year, Miss Wu felt that she had fallen into a hole in that her students did not do well in the written examination as compared with the students in other classes at the same grade. She said that in her school the students' result in written examination was one of the most important factors to evaluate teachers' teaching performances. Immediately, Miss Wu came under very strong pressure from her school headmaster and the parents. She thought language teaching should pay more attention to speaking and listening, but her performance could not be understood. This led to self-reflection:

I believed I had done nothing wrong to follow the new teaching approaches. Most of my students liked the way I taught. The problem was that the assessment system remained unchanged though the curriculum had changed. This is where conflict and tension come from.

As a result, Miss Wu started to observe the lessons conducted by other experienced teachers and she gradually realized that they used the grammar-translation method. Although the students did not have many chances to speak English, it seemed that those experienced teachers' ways of teaching proved effective at the end of the term in the examination, with many of their students scoring very highly in the written examination. Miss Wu was very perplexed but felt she had no other choice but to adjust her teaching method, from a communicative approach towards a grammar-translation approach:

> I felt very disappointed by this dramatic change. There were no creative things to add to my landscape as well as to my students'. I was really tired of this teaching, but I had no other choice. What I cared about at that moment was not if my students liked my teaching, nor if I taught English in the scientific way so that my students could get the best developments in four language skills. What I was concerned about was whether I could hand in a satisfactory answer sheet to my headmaster and the parents at the end of the school year. If I didn't work hard to improve the students' scores in the written examination, my headmaster and others would deny everything I had done.

Miss Wu said that after a year's great effort, her students' scores reached or even surpassed the average level in her grade. Although she felt a heavy weight was lifted from her heart, she was not happy. She was aware that she had helped her students to obtain this good score in the written examination at the cost of sacrificing their listening and speaking training:

> I became very dominant in class. I kept on explaining the language points and giving out many exercises for my students to do, chiefly including the sentence translation, word test and grammatical choices. Everything I attempted to do was meant to achieve my students' higher and better scores in the written examination. My students became unhappy about my adjusted teaching method by asking me why the active and vivid teaching method had gone. After some self-reflection, I thought I should not be totally led by the leaders, the parents or the examination system. The students' needs must also be appropriately considered. I should insist on doing what I believe was right to do.

This self-reflection encouraged Miss Wu to study the syllabus and curriculum in greater detail and make more careful lesson plans in order to decide what should be taught and what could be left for her students to learn by themselves. Only by doing so, Miss Wu believed, was she able to squeeze in some time for listening and speaking. As described in the previous sections, it is apparent that Miss Wu became more confident about her communicative teaching method after one year's professional development. From the recorded data, we can see that she spoke English to her students all the time in her practice because she believed it was very important for a language teacher to create a good language environment for students. When she conducted her lessons, Miss Wu tried her best to organize her students to do oral practice and had her students get involved in the learning process as much as possible.

This conception, however, was not rootless. Miss Wu strongly believed that learning English was not simply for the sake of sitting for the national college entrance examination, though many people in China do treat English language teaching and learning in a utilitarian way. She knew that not all her students were able to go to college; some of them would find jobs right after they left secondary school in local restaurants, hotels, travel agencies, estate agents, department stores, McDonald's or KFC, where English would probably be used as a working language. Therefore, Miss Wu made every effort to meet her students' practical needs, by trying to build up their speaking and listening abilities in everyday English through appropriate guidance, and giving them as much speaking and listening practice as possible. In fact, Miss Wu was fully aware of the risks she had taken, especially since the experience of being pressured one year before still bothered her from time to time. Yet, some other overwhelming factors also influenced her beliefs in teaching:

> I believe currently China is still practising examinationism. If this system exists, teaching and learning for the purpose of examination is unavoidable. Being teachers, it is impossible that we are unaffected by this system as we don't live in a vacuum. However, if I realize and believe my practice and effort can benefit my students for their long-term development, I won't hesitate to do it, even though there is risk ahead. No matter how much pressure there is, I won't care because I am doing something good for my students.

With this belief in her mind, Miss Wu struggled to step out of the dilemma she was in and gave attention to improving students' overall communicative abilities. According to the data, she laid more stress on listening and speaking training; at the same time, she also gave enough attention to grammar and language points. Her way to maintain this balance was to combine oral practice with language and grammatical points, in other words, to teach grammar in context. Miss Wu's approach to handling grammatical and language points was not simply to dominate with teacher talk, but to encourage many interactions between the teacher and the students:

> One reason why I wanted to get my students involved in the activities was that I could get feedback in due course of time so that I could judge

and decide what support my students needed, what I should cut down, what I needed to discuss more and what my students needed to practise more.

With regard to translation and grammar teaching, given the harsh lesson she had had in her first year, Miss Wu never dared to ignore it, but unlike other experienced teachers in her school, she only explained grammar briefly, then intended to use it orally or in writing to help her students consolidate and apply their knowledge:

> I believe my students can't remember the rules well by just listening to me, no matter how clearly and in how much detail I have explained. Rules are just rules to them – they will forget them without practice. If I give them enough practice, allow them to correct mistakes through practice, as far as I am concerned, they will learn better.

Besides these methods, Miss Wu realized rote memory was also one effective way for her students to learn English. Therefore, she uncompromisingly encouraged her students to read the dialogue or the lesson aloud in class and work in pairs or in groups to recite some key sentences or parts of the dialogues and lessons:

> I believe reading aloud in front of other people and reciting some key sentences or parts of the dialogue or lessons will do good for my students as it can help them to overcome their shyness and encourage them to open their mouths to speak. At the same time, they can memorize some useful sentence patterns, which are useful in helping to convey their ideas to other people.

About modern technology as applied to teaching, Miss Wu believed that it was very important for her to use the Internet resource frequently as it could provide her with the information about the latest pedagogical development and change in ELT both domestically and internationally, which was something badly needed. She believed that if she was equipped with the latest developments on language, and language learning and teaching, she could approach her teaching in a more systematic and effective way. At the same time, there were a lot of teaching materials that she could download, which she believed was good for her teaching plans and could save her time and increase the efficiency in class. For example, the slides Miss Wu used in her practice came mainly from downloaded files. Miss Wu edited them and made some necessary changes to meet her particular needs:

> I usually visit some ELT websites when I prepare for my lessons and download some materials relevant to my teaching. I believe at least I benefit two

things: first, I get well informed about the latest developments of different kinds of pedagogical methods and different ideas of ELT teachers throughout the country or even all over the world; second, it helps me to save lots of time in designing the exercises. I can make use of the materials available, some of which include some interesting animated cartoons. But using the Internet in China now is still very expensive. Our school doesn't provide us with free access currently; I have to pay for it myself.

5.5 Discussion and summary

As discussed above, Miss Wu believes that language should be used as a tool for communication. Therefore, she attempts to treat English language learning as a process rather than a product. Miss Wu thinks teachers should not merely be knowledge transmitters, but also guides who can cultivate students to think independently and creatively. Influenced by her own learning experiences and things that she learned at college, Miss Wu dedicates more time training her students' speaking and listening abilities. Her students showed much interest in learning and speaking English both inside and outside class, and with her guidance and encouragement, spent much time reading English aloud. They were able to recite some dialogues and some parts of long lessons fluently. They were even brave enough to chat with foreigners in English who visited their school or their communities. However, at the end of the term examination, the students' written results were not up to standard. This evoked very strong reaction from Miss Wu's school authorities and the students' parents, which created strong pressure for change on Miss Wu. She realized that although the government and social media repeatedly encourage schools and teachers to carry out educational reform and teaching innovation, the examination and assessment systems remain unchanged. She also realized that her personal effort in this kind of educational environment is relatively insignificant. Miss Wu now understood that what she needed to do was to go with the stream; although this was a very painful mental struggle, she had no other choice. She had to adjust her teaching methods by spending more time focusing on grammar and language points in order to help her students to obtain good scores. One semester later, Miss Wu found that her students' written result in term examination had improved, but incredibly they had lost their interest in learning English because to them this was now tedious and boring. After lengthy self-reflection, Miss Wu decided that her teaching method should not be oriented only to the examination system, but should seek to meet her students' needs, demands and interest as well. In order to achieve these conflicting expectations, on the one hand, Miss Wu tries to minimize teaching of grammar and language points, that is, she only explains the most useful grammatical and language points and designs focused exercises for her students to consolidate their grammatical knowledge; on the other hand, she tries to make use of every possible chance to initiate, encourage and help her students to communicate in English both inside and outside class. At the same time, she encourages them to use recitation to reinforce their rote memory, which she believes can help them to remember a number of useful sentence patterns that can foster and nurture their listening and speaking abilities. Miss Wu also tries to use the Internet as much as possible, from which she believes she can obtain the latest information about the pedagogical change and materials that are helpful for her practice. Table 5.11 summarizes the prominent teaching features in Miss Wu's four teaching lessons.

To summarize, Miss Wu's pedagogy is closely associated with the weak form of communicative language teaching method with a mix of the grammar-translation method. Much influenced by her beliefs and her learning experiences, Miss Wu strongly holds that English should be taught and learned through ample communication and that it should be taught and learned for the purpose of real communication, particularly listening and speaking abilities.

Table 5.11 Prominent features of Miss Wu's teaching

1. Grammar and language points were clearly explained, but were minimized as much as possible so that time could be squeezed out to do more listening and speaking.
2. Oral communication and listening comprehension were strenuously emphasized; every possible effort was carried out to maintain these goals.
3. English was the main medium of instruction; however, when necessary, Chinese was also used as medium of instruction, for example to explain some rules of grammar.
4. Students were treated as the main participants in class; the teacher served as a guide or a helper.
5. About 27% of total time was spent learning grammar, language points, on translation into and out of the target language; about 45% of the total time was spent on oral communication in group work, pair work or the whole-class activity; about 28% of the total time was spent consolidating the knowledge, such as sentence patterns, key words, collocations, revision, checking homework and commenting on the students' writing on the blackboard.
6. Rote memory was used to assist, enhance and consolidate learning. Students were encouraged to learn by heart some structure-based dialogues and useful expressions.
7. Translation in both oral and written forms from Chinese into target language and vice versa was practised in order to achieve accuracy.
8. Oral practice was first guided/controlled, then students were encouraged to develop free talk by connecting what they had learned from the dialogues and texts with real-life experiences.

Nevertheless, her pedagogy has met with strong resistance from different sources, particularly school authorities and students' parents, due to the rigid national college entrance examination. Being a novice teacher, challenged and perplexed, Miss Wu has no other choice but to adjust to mainstream expectations. She has to compromise her pedagogy and follow suit in terms of imitating other teachers' practice, although she is fully aware that what she does goes against her beliefs and her original intention. After one year's struggle and practice, Miss Wu has accumulated certain experiences and has built up more confidence in herself in terms of professional development. She knows her school culture better, the complicated sociopolitical context, and the real demands of her students. Her self-reflection persuades her to adopt a pragmatic approach, but not to yield to conventional teaching methods totally. One prominent feature of Miss Wu's pedagogy is to select and explain clearly and thoroughly the grammatical items and language points which she believes her students need, leaving the rest of the general grammatical items and language points to be acquired through practice. After repetitive drilling and practice, Miss Wu believes her students are able to draw a conclusion themselves with some of her inductive scaffolding. Thus, it seems that this method greatly enhances the effect of teaching and learning and at the same time it creates the time to make listening and speaking training possible. Another notable feature of Miss Wu's pedagogy is to devote adequate time and energy to develop her students' comprehensive abilities, including speaking and listening, which are congruent with her beliefs. Miss Wu tries her best to help them make use of what they have learned in the real context, which greatly arouses their interest in learning. She believes that the 'deaf and dumb' national college entrance examination makes English language teaching and learning boring. Many students are not able to speak English well enough to introduce themselves after six years of learning. In order to break through this barrier, Miss Wu overcomes many difficulties, such as time pressure and sociopolitical factors, to create a more flexible language environment for her students. This effort substantially leads Miss Wu's pedagogy from a teacher-centred towards a more student-centred orientation.

Chapter 6

Ms Ma's pedagogy

6.1 Introduction

In this chapter, we focus on describing and analysing Ms Ma's beliefs, design and practices. Following the same format that we used in Chapter 4 and Chapter 5, we will first provide a brief biographical profile of Ms Ma, introducing her personal life story, learning experience, teaching experience and professional development. Next, we will describe the teaching and learning processes, content and focus, teacher's roles, students' roles, organizations, types of activities, and resources in Ms Ma's classroom teaching. Then we will identify the relationship between Ms Ma's beliefs and her practices. Finally we will discuss how Ms Ma's beliefs influenced her design and affected her practices and also how issues emerging from practices refined, expanded and transformed her beliefs.

6.2 Ms Ma's biographical profile

Like Mr Yang, our final case study teacher, Ms Ma, was a senior teacher of English. She was 35 years old when she joined this study, having graduated from an average university in Fuzhou with a Bachelor's Degree. She had taught for twelve years with two different series of textbooks; one was relatively grammar focused and the other was relatively communicative oriented. She was a bit unusual in that she had worked in a UK secondary school for one year on a government exchange programme some years before the study started. We approached Ms Ma to participate in this research as an informant when we attended her class on an Open Day in her school. We talked with her informally, and showed our keen interest in interviewing her about her view of language teaching and learning. She accepted our request to involve her and we had a chance to conduct a preliminary interview with her. From what she said and from our observation of her lesson, we strongly believed Ms Ma's teaching method would add broader and deeper understandings to the dimension of the implemented pedagogy of secondary school teachers of English in the PRC.

In contrast to Miss Wu's school, Ms Ma's was a key middle school, which received more privileges and funding from the local government and more attention from local education officers. The school campus was located in the inner-city area, and consisted of two eight-storey teaching buildings, an administrative building, a library building, a laboratory building, a stadium and a track and field playground. Each year university graduates with Honours Degrees were assigned to teach in this school. After three years of study in this school, about 95 per cent of the students were admitted to universities and colleges through the rigorous national college matriculation examination. Ms Ma's school was very happy to cooperate in our study and promised to provide every possible assistance, including rearranging her timetable and reorganizing her classroom for the videotaping.

Ms Ma came from a working-class family and did not start to learn English until she went to secondary school in 1981. At that time English Curriculum innovation and change was just under way in China. As discussed in Chapter 2, the 1982 version textbooks compiled by PEP promoted a mix of functional and notional approach with the audiolingual method and the grammar-translation method. Ms Ma recalled that her teacher of English tried to achieve a balance between the functional/notional approach and the grammar-translation method. Ms Ma said that she benefited a lot from that mixed teaching approach because she felt that she laid a very good foundation of grammar and that she received good training in listening and speaking as well. This learning experience was deeply embedded in her epistemic beliefs, which became a dominant element in her belief system. In 1996, Ms Ma was chosen to work in an English secondary school on an exchange programme in England, where she taught Chinese culture and Chinese history for a year. Ms Ma said that during the time she was in England, she had many opportunities to sit in to observe her colleagues teaching. She was very interested in the notion that during instruction, awareness of the structure and function of language developed by using it socially. Her overseas teaching experience helped her to gain a better understanding of 'inner circle' ELT theory and practice and influenced her choice of pedagogy in her own classroom. The following section will focus on Ms Ma's practice.

6.3 Ms Ma's practice

6.3.1 Processes of teaching and learning

As demonstrated in the previous chapters, processes of teaching and learning indicate the way a teacher handles the presentation, practice and feedback phases of teaching and learning in the classroom (Richards and Rodgers, 2001). From the recorded classroom teaching, the following procedures were observed when Ms Ma handled Unit 8, which consisted of four lessons (see Table 6.1, Table 6.2, Table 6.3 and Table 6.4).

A study of Ms Ma's lesson plans and teaching logs shows that when she prepared her lessons, she referred to the Teacher's Book, published by PEP, which was the only authoritative teaching reference book available for her at

Table 6.1 Sequencing of Lesson 29 – dialogue

1. Teaching new words and expressions
2. Teaching dialogue by asking the students to read the dialogue aloud
3. Listening to the tape sentence by sentence three times
4. Asking questions and having the students do pair work and group work
5. Discussing the dialogue
6. Having students recite the dialogue and asking some of them to act the dialogue out at the front
7. Explaining the grammar and language points by inviting her students to work together with her, doing exercises designed for this dialogue
8. Doing some translation from Chinese into English and vice versa

Table 6.2 Sequencing of Lesson 30 – reading: 'Food Around the World'

1. Reviewing Lesson 29, asking the students to do translation from Chinese into English and vice versa
2. Conversation, making up a similar dialogue with the words from Lesson 29
3. Reciting
4. Acting out the dialogue
5. Reading the text aloud, listening to the tape sentence by sentence, asking questions about the text
6. Explaining the language points of the text, doing translation from Chinese into English and vice versa
7. Discussing the food
8. Making comments on classroom exercises

Table 6.3 Sequencing of Lesson 31 – grammar: revision of attributive clause

1. Reviewing language points of Lesson 30
2. Doing translation, putting Chinese into English and vice versa
3. Explaining attributive clause in Chinese
4. Doing exercises about attributive clauses

Table 6.4 Sequencing of Lesson 32 – listening, word study and writing

---

1. Reviewing grammar: attributive clause
2. Listening to the tape and doing listening comprehension training
3. Writing
4. Summarizing the whole unit

---

hand, and she made some use of the recommended methods from the book. In her teaching plans, Ms Ma only sketched out the general layout, which served as a guide to the whole unit teaching:

> I have been teaching this series of textbooks for more than eight years. I am very clear that the promoted pedagogy is to encourage us teachers to pay attention to the cultivation of [students'] communicative competence and performance in English rather than merely knowledge of the language. I am also quite aware of the recommended teaching sequence, which is called the Five Steps (revision, presentation, controlled practice, production, consolidation). Generally speaking, I follow this sequence. However, in practice, I have to adapt myself to the emergent situations that occur from interactions between my students and me. Therefore, I think teaching plan is only a plan which highlights the focus of contents, key language points and some additional materials that I want to use in teaching. In regard to sequence, I believe my teaching experience will tell me what to do and how to do it in practice. It is unnecessary for me to write them down specifically and definitely. It is impractical to do so.

In a follow-up interview, we showed Ms Ma her teaching sequence of Unit 8, which we tidied up from her recorded lessons in order to make sure that it was correctly transcribed. She told us that her sequence basically matched the recommended sequence, namely, presentation-practice-product, which was promoted in Western books on communicative language teaching (e.g. Hubbard *et al.*, 1983). However, she pointed out that although the new text-books enhanced listening, speaking and reading training, they also emphasized grammar teaching:

> Facing this kind of challenging situation, I need to adjust myself. The allocated time for teaching is very tight. I must figure out how much time I can devote to training my students in speaking and listening, and, at the same time, I must also make sure to maintain enough time to handle grammar and language points which are tested in our national matricula-tion examination. What is more, my students in this key school have very high expectation from teachers. They want to go to the top universities in

China or go to study abroad, which requires them not only writing ability and grammar knowledge, but also speaking and listening competence.

It is obvious that the sequence Ms Ma chose to teach was based on the different factors that she faced: the influence of the new curriculum, the pressure of the national matriculation examination, the needs from her students, and her own belief in teaching and learning a foreign language.

6.3.2 Content and focus

Content and focus refers to the textbook materials in each unit, such as dialogue, reading, listening, writing, grammar, exercises on the students' workbooks, word study and language points. A study of Ms Ma's lesson plans indicated that she intended to spend four hours teaching Unit 8, roughly, one hour on each lesson. However, the recorded lessons showed that although she spent four hours teaching the whole unit, she did not spend the time evenly on each lesson. Instead, she adjusted her plan and focused on grammar teaching. Spending more time than she planned originally, she set out to explain the attributive clause carefully in detail in Chinese and tried to consolidate this knowledge by getting her students to do a lot of translation exercises. It was clear that grammar talk was Ms Ma's main focus as the classroom observation showed that she spent 70 minutes out of the total 180 minutes in explaining grammar and the language points. Speaking and listening was also Ms Ma's focus as she spent about 60 minutes in training her students on speaking and listening points. Grammar consolidation by translation in both oral and written forms was Ms Ma's third focus. In the remaining 50 minutes the students did translation from Chinese into English and vice versa, which was designed to help them learn how to use the phrases, idiomatic expressions and the attributive clause they had learned in Unit 8. Table 6.5 summarizes Ms Ma's major focus, content and time allocation in practice.

6.3.3 Teacher's roles

As discussed in the previous chapters, teacher's roles refers to the types of functions teachers are expected to fulfil, the degree of control the teacher has over how learning takes place, the degree to which the teacher is responsible for determining the content of what is taught and the interactional patterns that develop between teachers and learners (Richards and Rodgers, 2001). In her practice, Ms Ma was confident and comfortable with her role as a knowledge transmitter. During the lessons, when she came across grammatical items, for example the attributive clause, Ms Ma tried to explain them in English as much as possible. Nevertheless, sometimes she also tried to reinforce

Table 6.5 Ms Ma's major foci and content in practice

Time (minutes)	Content and focus
70	Grammar, language points and written and oral activities
60	Listening and speaking to understand the dialogue and the texts, students' recitation, performance and other activities
50	Doing translation to consolidate sentence patterns, key words, collocations, revision, checking homework, commenting on the students' writing on the blackboard
Total time	
180	

the explanation in Chinese briefly and concisely. After explaining the rules, Ms Ma made use of the relevant exercises from the workbooks and some additional exercises designed by herself to have her students practise. When doing so, according to the videotaped data, Ms Ma served as a controller and consultant. She went around the classroom, stopping here and there, answering her students' questions, giving advice and discussing with them. When students stood up to present their work, Ms Ma worked as a helper, organizer, assessor and feedback provider. When she saw some tricky problems emerging from the interactions, she became a decision-maker in terms of cutting down some easy content and focusing on the more difficult part for her students. For example, when commenting on a translation sentence on the blackboard written by a student, Ms Ma realized that it was necessary for her to explain more thoroughly the use of the relative pronouns. The original Chinese sentence was: '所有来自农村的人工作都努力得多.' The student translated this sentence like this: 'All the people who come from the countryside work much harder.' Ms Ma pointed out that the relative pronoun in this sentence should be *that* instead of *who*. Then she made the following remarks:

> Well, class, usually speaking, when the antecedent in an attributive clause refers to a person, the relative pronoun we use could be *who, whom* or *that* and when the antecedent in an attributive clause refers to a thing, the relative pronoun we use could be *which* or *that*. However, in the following situations, we had better use *that* as the relative pronoun to connect the main clause: 1. when there are words such as *all, any, every, no* before the antecedent; 2. when the superlative degree of adjectives are used to modify the antecedent; 3. when the words such as *only, very, the first* and *the last* are used to modify the antecedent.

> (Observed from the video picture, 23 December 2003)

Next Ms Ma wrote down some examples on the blackboard to further demonstrate how to use the relative pronouns accordingly. Later, she read a number of Chinese sentences aloud and requested her students to put them into English. When interviewed, Ms Ma said that originally she did not plan to introduce so much to her students in one lesson. However, in response to the unexpected problem, she decided to spend more time on this grammatical item as she thought it was very important for her students to master the rules of the attributive clause.

From the videotaped data, it was obvious that Ms Ma encouraged the students to speak English as much as possible. When teaching dialogue, she was an organizer, group process manager and activator/catalyst. She asked her students to read the dialogue aloud first, then listen to the tape several times, imitate the pronunciation and intonation carefully, act out the dialogue with peers, and finally she asked several pairs of her students to act out the dialogue at the front of the classroom. The students were each a bit nervous before going to the front, but Ms Ma offered encouraging remarks to them, such as 'I trust you can do it well!' and 'Just have a try and don't worry too much'. When the students finished their performance, Ms Ma said, 'Well done!', 'Excellent!' and 'Great!' To sum up, according to the data, Ms Ma's role in the practice can be described in Table 6.6.

Table 6.6 The teacher's role in Ms Ma's class

1. Knowledge transmitter   2. Resource provider   3. Helper   4. Controller 5. Consultant   6. Organizer   7. Assessor   8. Feedback provider   9. Manager 10. Activator   11. Decision-maker

6.3.4 Students' roles

As demonstrated in Chapters 4 and 5, students' roles refers to the their contribution to the learning process, which is seen in the types of activities they carry out, the degree of control they have over the content of learning, the patterns of student groupings adopted, the degree to which they influence the learning of others, and the view of the student as processor, performer, initiator and problem-solver (Richards and Rodgers, 2001). According to the observation, the students in Ms Ma's class played multiple roles. First, they were the knowledge receptors. One major focus that Ms Ma had in practice was to explain grammar and language points, so the students listened to her very carefully and made notes for their future references. Some of them were not quite able to catch what she said, so they asked their classmates about the points or borrowed their notes to copy them down. Another focus that Ms Ma had in practice was to help her students with speaking and listening. In this learning process, the students were seen to take an active part in carrying out the activities that Ms Ma arranged. Most of the time, they followed what she asked them to do; for instance, from the recorded classroom teaching, they read the dialogue aloud, tried to recite it in class, acted it out in different groups, and discussed with peers about the main ideas of the text. They worked collaboratively to solve problems. To some extent, their interactions and performances in practice influenced Ms Ma's teaching plan, which led her to adjust her teaching plan and focus significantly. For instance, as mentioned in Section 6.3.3, when she realized that a student could not clearly understand the relative clause from his translation, Ms Ma decided to deepen and widen the exploration of this grammatical item in class. A third focus of Ms Ma's teaching was to consolidate what had been taught in class. The students acted as problem-solvers when she was leading them to that direction. From the observation data, we can see that their keen participation evoked an active learning atmosphere. The students' roles in Ms Ma's class can be best summarized in Table 6.7.

Table 6.7 The students' roles in Ms Ma's class

1. Knowledge receptors   2. Collaborators   3. Participants   4. Problem-solvers 5. Negotiators   6. Rote memorizers

6.3.5 Organization

As demonstrated in the previous chapters, organization refers to the arrangement of the presentation, practice and feedback phases of teaching. According to the data, Ms Ma mainly adopted the recommended procedure from Teacher's Book, that is, revision, presentation, drill, practice and consolidation. When she followed these steps, Ms Ma used different kinds of activities to organize her teaching, such as teacher talk, and interactions between the teacher and students. Teacher talk was the primary mode observed in her lessons; by using this, she transmitted the grammar, explained the language points and commented on different kinds of exercises and writing. Another mode that Ms Ma used to control her students' behaviours was to do question and answer exercises; by using this, she helped her students with listening and speaking, and at the same time, she had an immediate chance to get feedback from her students about how well they understood her instruction. A third mode that Ms Ma applied in her practice was to use social interactions among students, such as pair work, group work, group competition and performance by the students collectively and individually at the front of the classroom. By using this mode, Ms Ma intended to get her students to speak English through more encouraging communication with their peers, thus more students could make the best use of the limited time to practise speaking in class. Table 6.8 summarizes Ms Ma's teaching organization in practice.

Table 6.8 Ms Ma's teaching organization in practice

1. Revision   2. Presentation   3. Drill   4. Practice   5. Consolidation

6.3.6 Activities

As mentioned previously, activities refer to kinds of tasks and practice activities employed in the classroom through the organized and directed interactions of teachers, students and materials. According to the videotaped data, the first lesson Ms Ma taught was Lesson 29, which was a dialogue about food and cooking. The first thing she set out to do was to get her students to learn the vocabulary, as she believed that vocabulary was the bricks used to build language. Before she started to teach a unit, Ms Ma asked her students to pronounce every single word carefully and clearly, and, at the same time, she asked them to remember the Chinese meanings of the words and expressions they learned; from the data, she appeared to put much emphasis on this process. For example, after reading the words and expressions several times, Ms Ma gave their Chinese meanings in order to have the students use them in English and vice versa. She believed that this activity would lay a good and solid foundation for her students and enhance their speaking, listening and reading abilities.

Next Ms Ma started to teach the dialogue by playing the tape several times for the students to listen and follow. Then she requested her students to read the dialogue silently. After that, she asked them to practise it in pairs. The videotaped data showed that while students acted out the dialogue in pairs, Ms Ma was walking around to serve as an observer and helper. Later she tried to encourage some students to go to the front and act the dialogue out voluntarily, but no student did so. Finally, Ms Ma had to tell two pairs of students to give the performance by calling their names. They were allowed to take their textbooks, but were discouraged from referring to these as much as possible. With these activities done, she started to explain the language points in the dialogue. The focus of the dialogue was about measure words, such as *a piece/cup/bowl/glass/bottle of.* After explaining, Ms Ma asked the students to translate those measure phrases from Chinese into English, such as 一碗汤 (*a bowl of soup*), 一瓶啤酒 (*a bottle of beer*), and 一杯咖啡 (*a cup of coffee*). Then she got the students to use a correct phrase for each food from the exercise book and did the exercise orally with the whole class. Here are some examples which requested the students to find the correct phrases on the left for the different foods:

a/an/another	noodle	beef
some . . . (s)	beer	pancake
some more . . . (s)	pork	chicken
a piece of	carrot	beancurd
a cup of	water	milk
a bowl of	mutton	cake
a glass of	coffee	egg
a bottle of	ice cream	soup

Lesson 30 in Unit 8, entitled 'Food Around the World', mainly introduced how corn was discovered and how it was prepared in many different ways for food. According to the videotaped data, before asking the students to skim the text, Ms Ma prepared a general question on the blackboard for the students to think about: in which part of the world the tomato, the potato and corn were first discovered? Then she asked the students to read the text as quickly as possible in order to answer this question, then she played the tapes three times for the students to follow and imitate. Next, Ms Ma asked her students some further questions, such as: When was corn first brought to China? Why was corn grown a lot in Tibet and Sichuan? How is corn cooked in the West? What other plants were found in America? Why is the potato thought to be a very useful plant? What fruits are shipped from China to other countries? She asked these questions in order to make sure that her students had fully understood the general meaning of the lesson. With this done, Ms Ma separated her students into small groups to discuss the main idea of each paragraph in their own words. Some students represented their groups to report their ideas in class. Ms Ma listened to their reports carefully and also made some comments on their reports. Finally, based on the general discussion, Ms Ma summarized the main idea of the whole lesson briefly for her students' reference.

Till then, much exercise about speaking and listening of the lesson had been done. Seeing her students understood the general meaning of the lesson pretty well, Ms Ma then started to explain some grammatical items and language points from the lesson. Evidence from the videotaped data showed that she only picked out some key language points to explain. Those key language points include:

1. There was not enough room = There was not enough space. Room here is an uncountable noun which is different from a place to live in.
2. The comparison between the words discover and invent.

3. Some examples of the restrictive attributive clauses (language focus for this lesson):

> a useful plant *that can be eaten*; a plant *which didn't need as much water*; not the only food *which was taken*; another traveller *who went to America*; people *who bought them*; another plant *that was taken back*; the seeds of fruit trees *that they hadn't seen*; fruit trees *which once grew*.

After Ms Ma explained these language points to her students, she asked them to point out the functions of the relative pronouns in the sentences and translate each of them from English into Chinese. Then she wrote four sentences which contained the attributive clauses on the blackboard and had her students translate them into English. Four students were asked to do these sentences on the blackboard while the rest were asked to do the translation in their exercise books. Later, Ms Ma commented on the students' jobs by giving detailed assessment.

Lesson 31 in Unit 8 was a revision of the attributive clause. The textbook specifically designed a number of exercises to consolidate and enhance the students' understanding of the attributive clause. The videotaped data showed that Ms Ma first asked her students to make sentences from the given material or join sentences using *who, whom, which* or *that* in written form. Then she asked them to exchange their points of views in pairs or in groups. Next Ms Ma had some students practise at the front of the class by reading out their sentences. This kind of activity was deliberately used to train their listening comprehension by listening to different kinds of speakers' pronunciation. Later Ms Ma had ten pairs of students do reading and translating practice, that is, one student read out his or her English sentence, and the other translated it into Chinese. For example, from the videotaped data, we could see one student stood up and read out: 'Put the eggs which you bought yesterday in water.' Then his partner translated this sentence from English into Chinese like this: '把你昨天买的蛋放在水中'. Ms Ma then asked the whole class whether the relative pronoun in this sentence could be omitted or not and why, and whether the relative pronoun *which* in this sentence could be replaced by the word *that* and why yes or not. Receiving the feedback from her students in chorus, Ms Ma set out to answer the questions herself in detail and then allowed the second pair to carry on the activity. This kind of activity was not uncommon in her practice. Ms Ma felt that the exact understanding of target language in Chinese was very important for her students in the learning process.

Lesson 32 in Unit 8 was designed to train the students' listening comprehension, which required them to identify the prices of fruits and vegetables at London and Beijing markets, to do word study, such as *allow, taste, feed, fetch, supply, prepare, boil, discover* and *offer*, and to do writing by completing the sentences using the words given. Ms Ma started to review the attributive clause before she handled the listening comprehension. According to the videotaped data, Ms Ma wrote four sentences in Chinese and four sentences in English on the blackboard, then she asked her students to translate them accordingly. When her students finished doing that, she encouraged several students to read out their translation for comment. After this, Ms Ma asked her students to take out their workbooks to do the listening exercises. She explained the purpose of this exercise clearly to the students: to listen to the two market reports in order to find out the prices in the correct part of a given table. The students had three chances to listen to the same tape. While they listened to the tape, they were filling in the blanks. After that, Ms Ma asked some students to report the prices that they had heard over the tape. When she found the reports were incorrect, Ms Ma played the tape back and forth to make sure that her students could understand the content clearly and exactly.

A third focus of Lesson 32 was writing, with activities arranged in two steps. First, Ms Ma asked her students to complete the sentences designed in the textbook orally; and second, she asked her students to write the sentences in their exercise books. According to the data, after finishing this, some of the students were asked to read sentences aloud and translate them into Chinese. With all these done, Ms Ma spent about five minutes to summarize the key points of Unit 8 by reminding the students of some useful phrases and patterns and the rules of the attributive clause. Table 6.9 summarizes the types of activities Ms Ma used in practice.

Table 6.9 Different types of activities Ms Ma used in practice

---

1. Vocabulary learning by listening to the tape; pronunciation practice
2. Making up sentences by using the new words and expressions both orally and in written form
3. Reading aloud and reciting parts of dialogue
4. Acting out the dialogue
5. Oral practice in groups and pairs; presentation in class
6. Grammar talk and practice
7. Translation both orally and in written form
8. Retelling the story that students learn from the text and reporting their discussion
9. Learning how to write by joining sentences
10. Making up sentences by using key patterns linking to school life or personal life
11. Checking homework

6.3.7 Materials

As discussed in Chapters 4 and 5, materials refer to the primary goal of materials (e.g. to present content, to practise content, to facilitate communication between learners, or to enable learners to practise content without the teacher's help), the form of materials (e.g. textbooks, audiovisuals, computer software) and the relation of materials to other sources of input (i.e. whether they serve as the major source of input or only as a minor component of it). The textbook series called Senior English for China (Students' Book 1A) and the teacher's book series called Senior English for China (Teacher's Book 1A) were the chief materials that Ms Ma used in her practice. According to Ms Ma, she and her colleagues in the same grade also used an additional exercise book entitled English Accessorial Exercise Book for Senior One, which consisted of many multiple-choice exercises, translation and reading materials. Using this could save Ms Ma's energy for looking for materials, and editing exercises herself. A tape recorder, some listening tapes and the ready prepared slides were used in Ms Ma's practice. No computer aid or language laboratory was used.

According to the observation, Students' Book 1A served as the major source of input in Ms Ma's practice. She tried to cover all the objectives and linguistic content designed by the textbook, adding materials such as translation exercises to suit students' needs. The learning activities and the teacher's role recommended by the Teacher's Book were Ms Ma's major references. However, she said that the time was too limited but the content was too much so it was impossible for her to cover everything. In order to spend more time on the difficult part of the content, Ms Ma had to handle easy content briefly and quickly. She believed that the attributive clause was one of the most difficult grammatical items in Senior English for China:

> If they learn attributive clauses well, it will be easy for them to learn other noun clauses. It will also be easy for them to learn adverbial clauses. If they learn attributive clauses well, they will for sure learn the present participles and past participles well.

Therefore, Ms Ma made every possible effort to emphasize attributive clause teaching by explaining the rules clearly, doing as many exercises as possible including the additional exercises designed by herself. According to the observation, the teaching aids Ms Ma used were the overhead projector and a tape recorder; she used the tape recorder to play the dialogue, the text and the listening materials, which enabled the students to be exposed to the target language atmosphere. Ms Ma used the overhead projector to drill sentence patterns and provide keys to the answers so that the students could see them

Table 6.10 Materials Ms Ma used in practice

---

1. Students' Book (SEFC, Book 1A)
2. Teacher's Book 1A (Reference Book)
3. Slides (most of the which were prepared by Ms Ma)
4. A tape recorder
5. Some listening tapes
6. English Accessorial Exercise Book for Senior One by local publishing house

---

clearly. She believed slides would help her save time in class but they took her more time to prepare beforehand. It was not possible for her to use slides every lesson as she taught two classes, having many papers to mark, lessons to prepare and meetings to attend. Table 6.10 summarizes the materials that Ms Ma used in practice.

6.3.8 Summary

To summarize, Ms Ma's practice was a dynamic entity, in which she attempted to cover the content required by the curriculum. She tried to employ different kinds of methods to accomplish her objectives. She had a specific focus in her teaching. She organized different kinds of activities in order to help her students develop their grammar, listening, speaking, reading and writing abilities. In her practice, she played multiple roles in terms of organizer, knowledge transmitter, helper, consultant and assessor. However, as discussed in the literature review, what a teacher does in the practice is greatly influenced or shaped by his or her beliefs and other social, cultural and political factors in the environment. The following section will explore what Ms Ma's beliefs were and which other factors were to influence her practices.

6.4 Relationship between Ms Ma's beliefs and practices

According to the videotaped data, Ms Ma's lessons were characterized by a focus on grammar teaching and language explanation with teacher and students' interaction and students' participation in both oral and written activities. Ms Ma articulated her guiding principle in helping her students to maintain grammar knowledge as follows:

> Grammar is a very important component in my teaching in a sense that it gives clear rules for my students to follow. My teaching experience tells me that learning some specific rules day by day, my students feel comfortable

and confident when they do their speaking, reading and writing. Grammar really tells them concrete and substantial things that can help them learn faster and more solidly.

This conception came partly from Ms Ma's own learning experience in school and partly from the professional experience she gained in teaching. When she started to learn English in the early 1980s, Ms Ma said her secondary school teachers taught the lessons by reading out each sentence, explaining and analysing the grammatical items in great detail. She felt this teaching method helped her accumulate solid grammar knowledge and helped her write more accurately in her later study of the language. In the mid-80s, Ms Ma became an English major. With the Open Door Policy, more and more Western teaching approaches were introduced into China at that time, among which the communicative language teaching method was the most popular. Ms Ma's teachers at college, most of whom had been overseas, encouraged students to improve their listening and speaking by listening to BBC or VOA English programmes and speaking to both native speakers and Chinese peers as much as possible. Nevertheless, her teachers never gave up teaching grammar to Ms Ma and other students. Ms Ma believed the rigid grammar training in her learning process laid her a very solid foundation for her later academic improvement and professional development.

When she became a secondary school teacher of English herself, Ms Ma's view of language and language learning, which was gradually accumulated and formed through her own learning experience, influenced her teaching practice greatly. She thought that the grammar of the target language should be explicitly taught because she perceived language as knowledge as well as abilities. For example, when handling the attributive clause, she elaborated the rules by presenting some typical examples and had her students translate a number of sentences from Chinese into English and vice versa until she was sure her students could understand this grammatical item well. Ms Ma taught phonology, syntax and lexis in the same way as knowledge:

> I believe the ultimate goal for our students in learning a foreign language is to be able to translate the target language into their mother language and translate their mother language into the target language. In order to maintain this, they should learn phonology, lexis, grammar and discourse. However, there is something else for them to learn, such as communication strategies and strategies for the four language skills.

Ms Ma's overseas teaching experience gave her some reflection in treating language as abilities:

> When I taught at an English secondary school on an exchange programme

in the late 1990s, I had some chances to sit in the language classes. Teachers there tended to use different kinds of activities to help students learn language through socialization. The students were organized to sit in groups or in a big circle so that they could see one another face to face while the teachers were able to move around easily to scaffold them. Teachers there did not emphasize the accuracy or fluency of the language learning at the initial stage. They were very tolerant to the mistakes or errors their students made. But I think the situation in China is a bit different. Our basic education now is still directed by the examination orientation. We emphasize the accuracy and fluency of the language learning from the very beginning. I think that is the dilemma I face.

Ms Ma called her way of teaching 精讲多练、讲练结合, which means in order to provide students with sufficient opportunities to practise, the teacher should select the key points to address, and [the teacher] should get students involved in practice while he or she lectures. Guided by this norm, when she taught dialogue, the attributive clause and word study, the first thing Ms Ma set out to do was to go over the content by giving the necessary explanation and illustration. At this point, her role approximated to a knowledge transmitter. However, very often, Ms Ma found out that she was unable to carry out her norm ideally:

> We have only four teaching periods each week. Time is very limited. In order to achieve a better result in the national entrance examination in three years' time, the first thing I need to do is to cover all the content required by the curriculum. This is the first priority. I have no other choice. Everyone around me is doing so. Only when this is completely done can I start to consider about other things. To be more exact, I have to pay sufficient attention to the language explanation and grammar learning. There are so many things to cover. It is obvious if I put more effort into those aspects, I cannot find much time to do others, for instance speaking and listening. Though I want very much to enhance listening and speaking, yet I really can't find the time. Sometimes, I even cannot find enough time to complete the lessons. I know I should have followed the communicative ways, but the examination pressure there is awfully strong.

With regards to reading and writing, Ms Ma had the same opinions:

> One of the biggest problems to teach reading and writing, I strongly feel I don't have enough time to handle them thoroughly. If I treat reading in the same way as I did with the old series of textbook, it is impossible for me to finish them in due course. Reading takes a lot of time in my class. In order to solve this problem, I have to adopt some new teaching methods. My way

of handling reading now is to let my students get a general understanding of the text, answer some simple questions, find out the key sentences, or the main idea of the text. I also have to minimize the explanation of the language points, say, in each lesson, at most from three to five language points. In fact, I am really worried if my students could understand the rest of the language points left unexplained due to the time limit.

This worry came from the pressure of the national college matriculation examination, a term frequently repeated in Ms Ma's interview. She felt that this examination cast a strong influence on her classroom teaching:

> Although the curriculum has changed towards a more student-centred mode, yet the national matriculation examination has not changed too much. It still follows the stereotyped format to test students' language proficiency; for example, the 25 multiple choices are the grammar-based testing. In order to help my students prepare for the examination, I have to explain the language points. I have to use some teaching methods that we used in teaching the old series of textbooks although the promoted methods seem to be good and reasonable. If I don't spend enough time explaining grammar and language points, I find my students will make 30 per cent mistakes out of the 25 multiple choices. What is more, if my students cannot master the language points, when they do writing, it is likely that they will also make a lot of mistakes.

However, influenced by the promoted methods, and also driven by her overseas teaching experience which had shaped her beliefs, Ms Ma realized that she should involve her students in the teaching and learning process as much as possible by using different activity types to develop the four language skills, i.e. listening, speaking, reading and writing. Otherwise, she believed that her students might become 'lame ducks' in terms of speaking or listening. This was something she really didn't want to happen. In order to provide the students with sufficient opportunities for practising listening and speaking, Ms Ma had to overcome the time pressure by cutting down teacher talk and presentation. Very often she found it extremely difficult to make a choice between what to do and what not to do because she felt any kind of deletion of material was not a gain but a loss to her students. She said that it was very hard to make the best of both worlds. From the data, it is obvious that Ms Ma applied the communicative language teaching method to handle the dialogue, reading, and even grammar teaching. For example, when she taught Lesson 30, 'Food Around the World', Ms Ma had the following conversation with her students:

Ms Ma: Have you ever had corn, John?
John: Yes, I have.

Ms Ma: How did you cook it?

John: Er . . . I really don't know . . . my mum cooked it.

(The whole class burst into laughter.)

Ms Ma: Well, do you happen to know when corn was first brought to China?

John: Oh, yeah. According to our lesson, it was brought into China at least 450 years ago.

Ms Ma: Good! Now class, please do pair work to find out why corn was grown a lot in Tibet and Sichuan and how corn is cooked in the West.

When she started to direct her students to do practice, Ms Ma's role shifted from a knowledge transmitter to organizer, helper and assessor.

From the description earlier in this chapter, we can see Ms Ma stressed the importance of rote memory in learning English. She recognized that the environment in which her students lived provided very little opportunity for them to speak English. Even inside class, due to reasons such as the bulk of content to cover, the large number of the students and so on, opportunities were limited. A possible way to remedy this deficiency was to encourage them to memorize some useful sentence patterns:

> Bearing in mind a number of good sentences and some necessary information, particularly for those who were timid and shy, it helped my students to build up their confidence and courage to face speaking activities in class or even have authentic conversation in their real lives. I have quite a few successful examples to support this behaviour.

Observation from video-recorded data showed that Ms Ma encouraged her students to use their deep memorization both inside and outside class. For example, when handling the dialogue, Ms Ma first organized her students to listen to the tape, then read the dialogue after the tape recording; from time to time she helped them with pronunciation and intonation. When she was sure that her students could read and understand the dialogue, Ms Ma asked them to read the dialogue aloud individually, trying to memorize it within five minutes. After that, Ms Ma had some students go to the front and act it out. Seeing those who could perform pretty well, Ms Ma praised them by saying 'Well done!'; seeing those who were unable to recite the dialogue well, she was very encouraging by saying 'You could refer to the textbook for the key words if you like', or 'It doesn't matter. You can certainly do it better next time.' She believed that doing this would stimulate and encourage her students as much as possible to read aloud the dialogue or the other part of the lesson; hence, recitation was a part of their routine homework every day. Ms Ma regularly checked this when they returned to class the next day: those who did a good job were highly praised, and those who failed to do the job well were encouraged to do it better later. Ms Ma told her students that a positive attitude in recitation was much appreciated, which was regarded as diligence – an important moral value in study.

Ms Ma was aware of the advantage and benefit of using multimedia aid in teaching in terms of introducing sight and sound – the real world to the students, and this could help save time that the teacher spends writing on the blackboard and improve teaching efficiency in class. Ms Ma commented that she wanted to use the language laboratory and video or audio materials to conduct her teaching in order to solve the time pressure and increase her teaching efficiency within the prescribed time. However, the school administrative management made her feel disappointed:

> I really want to use the multimedia method. However, maybe most of my colleagues also have this kind of feeling, the facilities that our school can provide are very, very limited. Our school is a key middle school at the provincial level, but we only have one multimedia classroom. There are more than 30 classes in our school. The application procedure is complicated and the chance of using it is limited, say, it is even hard to get one chance to have our lesson there per week. Another problem is that the multimedia software at present is not something that fits our classroom teaching. This is my personal feeling. We don't lack multimedia software, but we lack the good software that can help us teachers to save the preparation time as well as the stuff we need to solve our students' problems. Personally speaking, it is very hard to promote the multimedia teaching at the moment in China. As far as I know, most of the teachers in the different schools in Fuzhou designed their own multimedia software when they gave the demonstration class. It would take them a lot of time preparing this. A teacher needs to spend two weeks preparing one lesson's multimedia software. If teachers use multimedia methods to teach every day, it is almost impossible or incredible. I believe the best things for me to use now in my classroom teaching are the textbook, the Teacher's Book, a tape recorder, the blackboard and some chalk though sometimes I use slides.

Ms Ma strongly believed that in teaching English in *gaozhong*, or senior middle school, although teachers should transmit knowledge clearly, it is not necessarily teacher dominated. Ms Ma worked hard to place her students in the centre of the teaching. For example, according to the videotaped lesson, she encouraged her students to imitate pronunciation and intonation in the dialogue, and once familiar with the text, she asked them to create new conversations from existing dialogues. This was an opportunity for her students to develop their creativity. While they were doing pair work, Ms Ma was walking around to assist them when necessary; when she found some pairs could not create dialogue, she reorganized pairings, in other words, mixing a 'good' student with a 'slow' student:

> By using peer collaboration, the slow students gradually gain their confidence and after some time, they start to open their mouths to speak! I feel it is very useful and effective. Sometimes my students do pair work by using the topics from the dialogue and sometimes I encourage them to design their own topics which are closely connected with their own life. This helps to arouse their interests and they won't feel bored. If I keep on talking too much, I can see the atmosphere in class is very dull. When I use different activity types, they become active. I can walk around to supervise them. If necessary, I scaffold them by giving some key words or some hints.

In Ms Ma's classroom one could hear English used nearly all the time. She held that a teacher should use the target language in class as much as possible in order to create the language atmosphere. She encouraged her students to use English in group work and pair work and would remind her students from time to time that they should not use Chinese. However, Ms Ma sometimes used some Chinese when she explained grammar:

> Grammatical terminologies are hard. When I explain grammar, if I feel I can use a few Chinese words to explain it clearly, I will definitely use the Chinese. It saves time. If it is more direct and easier for my students to understand in Chinese, why do I bother to explain it in English with long and difficult sentences?

6.5 Discussion

According to what has been described in the previous section, judging from her articulated beliefs, it is clear that Ms Ma, first of all, treats English language learning as knowledge accumulation. Therefore, she believes that to learn a foreign language well, one ought to lay a very solid foundation in phonology, lexis and grammar. She requires her students to have a good command of pronunciation and intonation by listening to the tape as much as possible, imitating the native speakers' accent. To Ms Ma, language is used as a tool for communication. When expressing ideas, one should first express them clearly and accurately. In order to maintain this, it is necessary for her students to grasp English grammar systematically. The significance of learning grammar well is not only for getting high scores in the examination, but also for developing accuracy in speaking, reading, listening and writing, which are the four principal abilities for future academic and career development. Second, according to the previous account, it is clear that Ms Ma treats English language learning as ability cultivation. The limited teaching time handicaps Ms Ma in her practice. On the one hand, she must cover the content required by the curriculum in order to help her students prepare for the national college matriculation examination, but on the other hand, she thinks the ultimate goal of secondary schooling should help students not only to prepare for the examination, but also to develop their overall abilities, especially speaking and listening. To handle this tension, Ms Ma tries to avoid lengthy teacher talk or presentation and leaves some easy parts of the lessons for her students to study themselves outside class. To cultivate their overall abilities, according to the observation, Ms Ma tries to make them aware of certain communication strategies, notably cooperative methods, and importance of these in facilitating oral production, as well as providing her students with opportunities to use such strategies consciously. She also helps her students become more confident and fluent communicators and risk-takers. Third, Ms Ma tries to encourage them to employ every possible way to learn English. For instance, Ms Ma believes that deep memorization is a very effective way to learn English. She thinks that before her students open their mouths to speak, they need to memorize some useful sentence patterns; once they know these sentence patterns thoroughly, they will certainly be able to speak and understand well in real-life communication. Fourth, it is obvious that social, cultural and political factors also influence Ms Ma's beliefs, design and practice explicitly and implicitly. She knows that multimedia or interactive multimedia, which is the use of multiple types of media (audio, video, graphics, animations and text) within a single desktop computer program, can support student understanding by providing appropriate and immediate feedback, be integrated into the context of the course of study, and provide a high level of interactivity. Ms Ma very much wants to use this new technology to help solve her time problem, and enhance learning opportunities for her students within the total context of their studies. However, she feels that her school administrative management fails to meet her needs:

> It is funny that our school leaders show their great concern to acquire new facilities for the purpose of impressing society – the first rate school owns the first rate facility. When they show officials and visitors around to see the resources available, the school's fame would be increased because those people believe the first rate facilities will certainly cultivate outstanding

students. In regard to how to make the best use of those facilities, they don't really care. Although we have made many suggestions for their consideration, they just don't care and little effort has been made to improve this situation. This reveals that we common teachers can't control what we want to do with teaching innovation freely. What we want to do in class is also partly controlled and constrained by our school cultural and social environment. Time and again, when we teachers find it hard to have the access to the use of these new facilities, our enthusiasm dies down. Eventually, we have to stick to our old ways – textbook, Teacher's Book, blackboard, chalk and a tape recorder or slides. Only those who need to conduct a demonstration lesson start to consider using multimedia teaching to prove that they are following the tide. But I think this is for the sake of demonstration only! Besides this, I also feel our school leaders show their personal preference to some subjects. For instance, Chinese and mathematics are given the priority in terms of more time allocation. Some teachers of mathematics are only assigned to teach one class because the school leaders think their workload is heavier than other disciplinary courses. In contrast, some teachers of English have to teach three classes. As far as I understand it, these phenomena reflect that our teaching here is by no means apolitical.

The prominent features of Ms Ma's teaching are summarized in Table 6.11.

From what has been discussed above, it can be concluded that Ms Ma's pedagogy is closely associated with the grammar-translation method with a mix of the weak form of communicative language teaching method. Deeply embedded in her beliefs, she holds that grammar teaching should be explicitly upheld and that in grammar teaching it is important that the teacher should conduct the instruction in such a way that will help her students to become aware of the grammatical items. Another significant feature is that Ms Ma tries to help her students use the target linguistic structures appropriately in meaningful contexts. She tries not only to represent grammatical concepts and usage to her students in an interesting way, but also to make them relevant to her students in terms of connecting grammar teaching with the context of school life and real life. Due to the pressure of the national college matriculation examination, Ms Ma believes the grammar-translation method is the safest way to help her students prepare for the examination because it is still based on testing linguistic accuracy. However, Ms Ma feels that she should not merely teach English for the sake of the national matriculation examination. Her students would eventually be faced with the manifold uses of English in the real world, which would require comprehensive skills in speaking, listening,

Table 6.11 Prominent features of Ms Ma's teaching

---

1. Great effort was made to cover the content required by the curriculum; simple and easy content were left unexplained in order to squeeze some time to focus on difficult grammar and language points.
2. English was the main medium of instruction; however, when necessary, Chinese was also used as part of the medium of instruction; for example, Chinese was used to explain the hard core of grammar.
3. About 44% of total time was spent learning grammar, language points, doing translation into and out of the target language; about 33% of the total time was spent doing oral communication in group work, pair work or the whole-class activity; the remaining time was spent consolidating knowledge, such as sentence patterns, key words, collocations, revision, checking homework, commenting on the students' writing on the blackboard.
4. Rote memory was used to assist, enhance and consolidate learning. Structure-based dialogues and some idiomatic speech were required to be learned by heart.
5. Grammar and language points were explicitly taught in a systematic way.
6. Oral communication and listening comprehension were considerably emphasized, which were conducted by using group work and pair work, as compared with grammar and language points.
7. Translation in both oral and written forms from Chinese into target language and vice versa was highly emphasized and accuracy was the desired goal.
8. Oral practice was first guided/controlled, then students were encouraged to have free talk by connecting what they had learned from the dialogues and texts with real-life experiences.

---

reading and writing. This sociolinguistic view of English is in tension with her beliefs about the primacy of grammar. Ms Ma does not want to chain herself to her beliefs, nor does she want to make a big change in her teaching. As a compromise, she follows the requirements of the examination oriented system by spending approximately half of her teaching time going over the language points, grammar and doing translations, which is congruent with her beliefs, and then she helps her students to develop their skills in speaking, listening, reading and writing. To achieve the last, Ms Ma tries to employ different kinds of teaching methods. In this regard, she benefits from her one-year overseas teaching experience, from which she gains some knowledge about sociocultural theory.

Chapter 7

The interplay of complex forces

7.1 Introduction

The previous three chapters described the teachers' beliefs and practices and the factors which influenced them to develop their pedagogy. The relationships between the beliefs and practices of Mr Yang, Miss Wu and Ms Ma have been examined and explored in detail. The salient features of their personal pedagogies have also been described. Based on the descriptive findings of those three chapters, and guided by the view of ELT and pedagogic change reviewed in Chapter 2 and Chapter 3, this chapter explores to what extent and why the pedagogy of the three English language teachers in the secondary schools in the People's Republic of China has changed as a result of curriculum innovation and changes.

Within this chapter, Section 7.2 describes the key features of teachers' implemented pedagogy identified by this research; Section 7.3 examines the external forces that have created various tensions for the three case study teachers of English and describes how they cope with these tensions; Section 7.4 discusses how the teachers' beliefs have influenced their classroom practices; Section 7.5 examines how teachers negotiate with their situated contexts when they handle their classroom practices; and the final section (Section 7.6) attempts to provide a conceptualization of a tentative model of pedagogical innovation and change in the People's Republic of China based on the findings and discussion arising from this research study.

7.2 General impressions

As discussed in previous chapters, the salient pedagogical features of the three case study teachers of English in this research study can be best described as 'blended pedagogy', the characteristics of which can be summarized in Table 7.1, Table 7.2 and Table 7.3.

The complicated and dynamic features of this 'blended pedagogy' of these three case study teachers appear to have been significantly influenced and

Table 7.1 The three case study teachers' beliefs

	Mr Yang	Miss Wu	Ms Ma
Belief statements	The ultimate goal for learning is the outcome; teaching and learning are constrained by public examinations; reading aloud and rote memory are imperative	Listening and speaking should be given attention at the initial stage; authentic and real communication is the desired goal; teaching and learning is not for the sake of public examination	New teaching methods, such CLT and TBLT, are worth trying; however, traditional method, e.g. grammar-translation, should not be discarded; high stakes exam strongly influences classroom teaching
Learning objectives	Use vocabulary correctly; have a good command of grammar knowledge; use key sentences and patterns in speaking and writing smoothly; establish sound reading ability	Be able to use vocabulary correctly; good pronunciation and intonation; fluent spoken English; good reading efficiency within certain time limit; clear writing	Enhance reading and writing development; translation is an important method in language acquisition; have a good common base of language points; good listening
Priorities in teaching and learning	Grammar; vocabulary	Listening and speaking	Grammar; translation; reading for understanding
Designs of activities	Good for transmitting knowledge; teacher and student interaction should be considered	Try every possible way to engage students in different types of activities	Provide students with more practices in reading and writing
Teacher's roles	Knowledge transmitter, resource provider and helper	Organizer, helper and activator	Knowledge transmitter and manager
Students' roles	Knowledge receptors, listeners and participants	Collaborators, participants and learners	Knowledge receptors, listeners and problem-solvers
Types of activities	Vocabulary competition, oral translation, recitation, drill, dialogue in groups or pairs	Vocabulary, recitation, story retelling, performance and translation in pairs or groups	Translation, grammar, recitation, story retelling in pairs or groups

continued

Table 7.1—continued

	Mr Yang	Miss Wu	Ms Ma
Materials	Students' Book (SEFC, Book 3A), Teacher's Book 3A, self-prepared slides, a tape recorder, tapes	Students' Book (SEFC, Book 1A), Teacher's Book 1A, slides, a tape recorder, tapes, self-prepared materials	Students' Book (SEFC, Book 1A), Teacher's Book 1A, slides, a tape recorder, tapes

Table 7.2 The three case study teachers' designs

	Mr Yang	Miss Wu	Ms Ma
Organization	Revision, presentation, drill, practice and consolidation	Revision, presentation, drill, practice and consolidation	Revision, presentation, drill, practice and consolidation
Sequencing	Vocabulary, grammar, dialogue, reading, language points, translation, listening, exercises, writing	Vocabulary, language points, grammar, translation, speaking	Vocabulary, dialogue, reading, grammatical and language points, translation, listening, writing
Content and focus	Vocabulary, grammar, language points, translation, reading, speaking, writing	Vocabulary, language points, grammar, translation, speaking	Vocabulary, translation, grammar, speaking, reading, writing
Teacher's roles	Knowledge transmitter, resource provider, helper	Organizer, helper, activator, marker	Knowledge transmitter, manager, scaffolder
Students' roles	Knowledge receptors, listeners, participants	Collaborators, participants, learners	Knowledge-receptors, listeners, problem-solvers
Types of activities	Translation, recitation, reporting in pairs or groups	Recitation, story retelling, translation in pairs or groups	Translation, grammar, recitation, story retelling in pairs or groups

continued

	Mr Yang	Miss Wu	Ms Ma
Materials	Students' Book (SEFC, Book 3A), Teacher's Book 3A, self-prepared slides, a tape recorder, tapes, no IT	Students' Book (SEFC, Book 1A), Teacher's Book 1A, slides, a tape recorder, tapes, self-prepared materials, no IT	Students' Book (SEFC, Book 1A), Teacher's Book 1A, slides, a tape recorder, tapes, no IT

Table 7.3 The three case study teachers' practices

		Mr Yang	Miss Wu	Ms Ma
Medium of instruction		English as the main medium of instruction, Chinese as part of medium of instruction	English as the main medium of instruction, Chinese when necessary	English as the main medium of instruction, Chinese as part of medium of instruction
Organization		Revision, presentation, drill, practice and consolidation	Revision, presentation, drill, practice and consolidation	Revision, presentation, drill, practice and consolidation
Sequencing		Vocabulary, grammar, dialogue, reading, language points, translation, listening, exercises, writing	Vocabulary, language points, grammar, translation, speaking	Vocabulary, dialogue, reading, grammatical and language points, translation, listening, writing
Content and focus	Grammar, language points and translation	Attended carefully and in detail, lots of translation in written form	Attended concisely, practised both orally and in written form	Attended carefully, translation highly demanded
	Listening and speaking	Adequately emphasized, different types of activities, such as pair work and group work, used to maintain this goal	Strenuously emphasized; different types of activities, such as group work and pair work, used to achieve this goal	Adequately emphasized, different types of activities, such as pair work and group work, used to maintain this goal

continued

Table 7.3—continued

		Mr Yang	Miss Wu	Ms Ma
	Reading	For understanding general meaning, grammar and key patterns; translation and explanation	For understanding general meaning and some language points; oral practice	For understanding general meaning; oral translation
	Writing	Correct grammar, simple sentences, clear ideas	Express whatever students want to express in simple sentences	Correct grammar, clear ideas
Types of activities	Learning strategies	Rote learning; pair and group work	Peer collaboration; rote memory	Peer collaboration; rote learning
	Time allocation	50% on grammar and translation; 25% on speaking and listening; 25% on exercises and writing	35% on speaking and listening; 35% on reading and writing; 30% on grammar, translation and exercises	40% on grammar and translation; 30% on speaking and listening; 30% on exercises and writing
	Language as forms	Linguistic accuracy required as a desired goal	Accuracy is a desired goal for examination	Linguistic accuracy required as a desired goal
	Language as abilities	Encouraged students to speak as much as they could	Encouraged students to use English socially and linked it to school life	Encouraged students to use English communicatively
Teacher's roles		Teacher dominated	Teacher supportive	Teacher dominated
Students' roles		Student supportive	Student supportive and student collaborative	Student supportive
Materials		Mainly adopted the mandated teaching materials; cut some easy parts and added some self-prepared materials	Mainly adopted the mandated teaching materials; made some necessary adaptation by using some self-prepared materials	Mainly adopted the mandated teaching materials; cut some easy parts and added some self-prepared materials

shaped by three forces, that is, external forces, internal forces and situated forces (see Davison, 2001; Fullan, 1991; 2001; Wideen, 1994). First, as discussed in Chapter 3, teachers have to understand the intended curriculum, take into account the demands of the national assessment system, and try to adapt themselves to the intended communicative methods (see Adamson and Davison, 2003; Calderhead, 1984; Doll, 1996; Goodson, 2003; Hargreaves, 1994). Teachers are then confronted with a series of challenges from within their own teaching environment, coping with school authorities' expectations, parental expectations, students' learning aptitudes and attitudes, the school cultures, available resources and collegial interaction (see Berman and McLaughlin, 1975; Fullan, 2001; Halsey *et al.*, 1980; Hargreaves, 1994; Jarzabkowski, 2002). Third, as teachers are reflective practitioners (Dewey, 1933; Schön, 1973), they constantly and continually ask themselves why they are doing what they do and always are ready to debate and discuss different viewpoints, at the same time holding often entrenched opinions and attitudes as a result of their experiences of learning and teaching as well as their professional education, conceptions of teaching and learning, and life stories (see Freeman, 2002; Johnson, 1994; Tsui, 2003). The findings of this research study show that these three forces clash and twist in a host of subtle ways, which ultimately helps to mould the salient features of implemented ELT pedagogy described in the tables above. In the following sections, we will separately elaborate how these three forces help to foster the 'synthesized implemented pedagogy' identified in this research.

7.3 External forces

This section focuses on the discussion about how the external forces that Mr Yang, Miss Wu and Ms Ma confronted gave impetus to the process of their pedagogical innovation and change in terms of beliefs, designs and practices. Based on the findings, we have identified three significant factors which have noticeably influenced Mr Yang's, Miss Wu's and Ms Ma's teaching practices. They are the 1993 English Curriculum, the national college entrance examination and the intended communicative methods.

The 1993 English Curriculum is arguably the most comprehensive, fundamental and controversial attempt to promote systemic curriculum innovation with the purpose of teaching English in China's secondary schools as training of listening, speaking, reading and writing skills among students to enable them to acquire the foundation of the English language and to use English for communication (see Adamson, 2004a; Ng and Tang, 1997). The message about learning English for communication is very clear and teaching is described as 'a training process' which aims to develop students' ability to communicate. However, according to the findings of this research study, the 1993 English Curriculum has given a different stimulus to different sorts of teachers. For Mr Yang, who has more than 20 years of teaching experiences, the 1993 English Curriculum seems to be an idealized blueprint which demands too much radical change from teachers:

> I think the new curriculum sets up too high goals with too much expectation from our teachers. Although we feel the desired goals sound nice, we worry a lot about its feasibility as we are fully aware that our own teaching proficiencies are not good enough to face the challenges and the complex situations that we have to confront. However, no matter how difficult it might be, we are also fully aware that we must follow the trend, otherwise, we will fall behind.

According to the findings of this study, the content and goals promoted by the 1993 English Curriculum have significantly influenced Mr Yang's lesson design and practices. Mr Yang tried very hard to fulfil the content, and endeavoured to achieve the goals set by the curriculum, which shows the fact that the underlying ideology of the national curriculum has been embedded in teachers' beliefs for a long time. Teachers treat the intended curriculum as a 'must' to follow because the existing national assessment system still has much to do with it (see Gao and Watkins, 2001; Zheng and Adamson, 2003). The findings also show that the intended methods have extensively influenced Mr Yang's personal pedagogy, which will be illustrated later in detail.

Compared to Mr Yang, Miss Wu, a young and inexperienced teacher, treats the 1993 English Curriculum as a lively source of ideas which, she believes, can help to bring about change to traditional conceptions and help to transform the stagnant teaching situation, which is regarded as producing 'deaf and dumb' learners who are relatively weak in communicative skills such as listening and speaking:

> I believe that the curriculum is a positive and natural response to the foreign language teaching and learning need of our country as China is more open to the outside world. We need to absorb new conceptions from the West and it is necessary to make them best suit our own teaching and learning. The revised 1993 Curriculum is just the very trigger for us to do so. On the one hand, we young teachers treat it as a chance to alter our teaching and learning pattern in practice; on the other hand, the new curriculum imposes great demand on our own language ability, cultural knowledge as well as our pedagogical knowledge.

As for Ms Ma, who once taught in the UK on an exchange programme for one year, she believes that curriculum renewal is a complex process, which needs to match what is planned (the intended curriculum) and what actually occurs in the language classroom (the implemented curriculum) (see Figure 7.1):

> The curriculum has set up a platform for us teachers of English to practise, experience and reflect. We teachers are placed right in the centre of the tensions. In my opinion, the new curriculum can be used as a guide which is directed towards an objective yet to be realized. However, we must also be fully aware of our actual tasks and contextual situations. If the methods we used in the past still work, why don't we stick to them? If the methods promoted are good, why don't we accept them?

As discussed in Chapter 3, educational change occurs along several dimensions including changes in curriculum and revised materials, use of new teaching approaches and possible alteration of beliefs (Fullan, 2001). Based on the research findings, we can see that the 1993 English Curriculum has given a noticeable impetus to Mr Yang, Miss Wu and Ms Ma in terms of enacting their personal pedagogies, determining their professional development, and conducting their classroom practices, although some other underlying factors might have also influenced them.

As suggested in Chapter 3, apart from the influence from the 1993 English Curriculum, another influence on English teachers is the assessment system, i.e. the national college entrance examination that students take at the end of their six years' secondary schooling (see Gao and Watkins, 2001; Scovel, 1995). The examination in English language comprises a multiple choice section that focuses on discrete grammar items (presented in communicative contexts) and a cloze test, worth 30 per cent in total; reading comprehension, worth 27 per cent; an error correction exercise and a written composition, worth 23 per cent in total; and (since 2002) a listening comprehension test, worth 20 per cent. There is no oral component and, prior to the introduction of the listening comprehension, the examination was nicknamed the 'deaf and dumb' test. The implicit view of language and language learning underpinning the examination (and consequently determining the general flow of backwash effects on teachers' pedagogical choices) is a weak form of CLT in which the detailed bottom-up processing of language receives more attention than the holistic construction of meaning (Zheng and Adamson, 2003). Constrained by this orientation, teachers have to make every effort to meet the demand of the task.

The findings of this research do not suggest that Mr Yang, Miss Wu and Ms Ma were recalcitrant, conservative or unwilling to change. Mr Yang commented several times that he did not merely want to train his students to become 'examination machines'. Miss Wu was very innovative in that she spent a lot of time paying much attention to her students' listening and speaking. As for Ms Ma, she tried to adopt a broad-based view of assessment through the use of tasks, and formative assessment to cater for her students' individual differences. Nevertheless, eventually all three teachers had to face the premium on high stakes testing for selective purposes and they have to be pragmatic in terms of helping their students score high grades in the examination.

A third influence on the English language teachers in this research study was the promoted methods. As reviewed in Chapter 2, Senior English for China (SEFC) compiled by PEP and Longman reflects a synthesis in terms of the structural approach (with a linear grammatical progression and a focus on sentence patterns) and audiolingualism (with behaviourist drills to aid memorization). The methods to develop reading skills, for instance, emphasize reading for meaning – rather than the grammar-translation method of analysing the linguistic composition of the passage, which has been traditionally popular in the PRC. In the Teacher's Books accompanying SEFC, teachers are encouraged to pay attention to the cultivation of communicative competence and performance in English rather than merely knowledge of the language. As discussed in Chapter 2, the intended teaching sequence is called the Five Steps (revision, presentation, controlled practice, production, consolidation), which is a meshing of the PPP (Presentation-Practice-Production) sequence that was promoted in Western books on communicative language teaching (CLT) (Hubbard *et al.*, 1983) with existing practices in the PRC (Adamson, 2004a). The Five Steps envisages teachers playing a range of roles as language models, instructors, orchestrators and scaffolders of students' learning. Students acquire the language through gradual mastery of predetermined language forms and functions, with some opportunities for self-expression.

The findings of this research study show that Mr Yang believes grammar is central to language learning. He believes that if his students can grasp the usage of grammatical items or structures, they will be able to use them correctly in the appropriate context and even score highly in the public examinations. Mr Yang also believes that learning should be outcome oriented and that there should be evidence to show that learning has taken place. He feels that grammar teaching is an area where it is relatively easy to see the outcome of learning as compared to teaching other language skills. Constrained by the national college entrance examination, Mr Yang has to give first priority to cover the content required by the intended curriculum. In doing so, he chooses the methods which he feels comfortable with to explain the grammatical points. However, this does not mean Mr Yang ignores other skills. Influenced by the promoted methods and his colleagues' practices, Mr Yang is willing to expand his repertoire rather than stick to his traditional ways of teaching. The findings of the research also show that under the influence of the 1993 English Curriculum and its promoted methods, Miss Wu, a novice teacher with keen innovative ideas, feels strongly that English should be taught and learned through ample interactions, and that it should be taught and learned for the purpose of real communication. The findings show that Ms Ma feels that the grammar-translation method is the safest way to help her students prepare for the public examinations because they are still based on testing linguistic accuracy. However, stimulated by the promoted methods and other theories, for instance the sociocultural theory discussed in Chapter 2 (see Donato, 2000; Lantolf, 2000), Ms Ma feels that she should not teach English merely for the sake of the national college entrance examination. Instead, she thinks that teaching and learning should be treated in terms of linking social action with cognition, and that covering the curriculum should require students' active collaboration.

To sum up, based on the above discussion, we can see that external forces, that is, the 1993 English Curriculum, the national college entrance examination and the promoted methods, have brought about a number of tensions in English language teaching in the PRC. On the one hand, the 1993 English Curriculum and the promoted methods extend the parameters of ELT classroom teaching to focus on holistic communication-oriented constituents, and on the other hand, the continuing premium on selection and the testing-oriented view of assessment, i.e. the national entrance examination, prevent teachers of English from changing radically. The task of reconciling these competing and contradictory tensions is thus left to grassroots teachers of English in the PRC to resolve.

7.4 Internal forces

As noted above, the previous section argues that external forces have significantly influenced English teachers in their classroom instruction in the PRC. This section focuses primarily on the discussion of internal forces identified by this research study that have also caused much influence on teachers' classroom practices. As described in Chapter 3, many researchers have described the link between teaching and previous learning (see, for example, Freeman and Richards, 1996). Other studies (see for example, Calderhead and Robson, 1991; Richardson, 1994; Tsui, 2003; Yung, 2000) have shown that teachers' conceptions of teaching and learning have a powerful influence on their classroom practices. Elbaz (1983) characterizes teacher knowledge as practical knowledge – practical in the sense of its being closely tied to teachers' experience and the specific contexts of the classroom and in the sense of its action and decision-oriented nature. Connelly and Clandinin (1994) affirm that teachers' personal values and beliefs are very much shaped by their personal experiences. Therefore, in understanding teachers' personal pedagogies, it is important to understand their conceptions of teaching and learning and the sources of influence that shape such conceptions (Tsui, 2003).

The findings of this study indicate that in their practices Mr Yang, Miss Wu and Ms Ma have been strongly influenced by their beliefs in terms of their personal experiences, their experiences of learning, and their conceptions of learning and teaching. The three case study teachers grew up in entirely different environments, had different learning experiences, and accumulated different conceptions of learning and teaching. The findings demonstrate clearly that the individual disparities in the life histories and experiences of the three case study teachers have affected their educational judgements and decision-making in their classroom practices tremendously.

As described in Chapter 4, we can see that at the time when Mr Yang learned English, grammar was systematically taught, and translation and linguistic accuracy was strongly emphasized. All his teachers focused almost exclusively on helping their students to attain this goal. As demonstrated in Chapter 1, due to political reasons, English was treated as a pro-imperialistic tool at that time (see, for example, Dzau, 1990; Ross, 1993). Few people dared to speak English in public; to some extent, speaking and listening were over-looked. This learning experience was deeply embedded in Mr Yang's belief system and thus dominated his teaching. Mr Yang believed that the teacher should lead in teaching while students needed to cooperate with the teacher in learning. He thought that materials from the textbooks were adequate for his teaching although he felt it necessary to add some supplementary materials, for instance grammar exercises, in order to provide his students with more system-atic practice. Mr Yang thought that the types of activities that he designed should be used for strengthening knowledge delivery.

In contrast to Mr Yang, as described in Chapter 5, Miss Wu had an entirely different college education. She received a good training in listening, speaking, reading, writing and translation. Besides the subject matter knowledge (SMK), Miss Wu was also well informed about the latest development of pedagogical content knowledge (PCK) both inside and outside China. To Miss Wu's advantage, her department had two teachers of English from Canada and Australia. They often introduced information about the latest trends in teaching methods to students, and they also demonstrated how to apply those teaching strategies to their classroom practices. This learning experience added a plus to Miss Wu's belief system. Once she began teaching after graduation, Miss Wu was immediately keen and enthusiastic to teach communicatively. She strongly believed that learning should be a process of knowledge co-construction between the teacher and students. Her guiding principle was that in the teaching and learning process, students should be the main participants under the guidance of the teachers, and that the types of activities should be designed to serve for this purpose. Her focus was to help her students to establish an overall comprehension in using English for the communicative purpose in their further life in particular.

As noted in Chapter 6, Ms Ma's learning experience was neither similar to Mr Yang's nor similar to Miss Wu's. At the time when she started to learn English, the school curriculum in China was in a transitional stage. Teachers used a blended method: compassing elements of the audiolingual method and the grammar-translation method. Grammar was systematically taught, and speaking and listening were also emphasized. Influenced by her learning experiences, when she went into teaching, Ms Ma paid sufficient attention to grammar teaching; at the same time, she also paid attention to developing her students' holistic abilities, such as listening, speaking and reading. Her guiding principle was that learning a foreign language, one should understand its exact meaning in his or her mother tongue. She believed that the teacher must play a major role in the teaching and learning process. However, she also believed that the teacher should try his or her best to engage students in all types of activities, and that students should be active in participating in a range of collaborative and interactive tasks both inside and outside the classroom.

In summary, the three case study teachers' pedagogies were strongly influenced by their different learning experiences, based on their different knowledge of linguistics, knowledge of teaching in general and communicative language teaching in particular, knowledge of the students, knowledge of language learning strategies, and knowledge of specific contexts in which they operated, Although all three case study teachers taught vocabulary; explained grammatical items; trained their students in speaking, listening, reading and writing; organized interactive tasks, such as group work and pair work; there were obvious qualitative differences in the way they made sense and implemented these practices. Below, we will describe how the different beliefs and understandings of Mr Yang, Miss Wu and Ms Ma made their teaching distinctive. We will focus on the three case study teachers' practices in teaching vocabulary, grammar and reading respectively to demonstrate that the complexity of a pedagogical innovation change is a characteristic of the individual teacher, a result of the discrepancy between the state of existing practice and beliefs of the individual teacher and the innovation itself (Fullan, 2001).

All three case study teachers started their lessons by teaching vocabulary. As pointed out in Chapter 4 and Chapter 6, both Mr Yang and Ms Ma stressed the importance of vocabulary learning. In response to the fact that most of their students thought vocabulary was one of the biggest obstacles in their language learning and that their living environment was not conductive to studying at home, both Mr Yang and Ms Ma set out to help their students pronounce words and expressions clearly and correctly. They focused on the linguistic content rather than on the communicative use of the vocabulary. In order to help their students remember words better they used different types of activities to enhance the effectiveness of the students' understanding of the meanings of the set phrases and collocation. Both Mr Yang and Ms Ma developed the vocabulary consolidation routine in each subsequent lesson by engaging their students in different kinds of activities. The knowledge geared by this experience helped them to understand further the importance of con-solidation in teaching, for example in grammar teaching. By contrast, as noted in Chapter 5, when Miss Wu taught vocabulary, although she also helped her students with pronunciation and to understand the meaning of the new words and expressions, she focused on how to help her students use those words and expressions communicatively in certain contexts. She used different types of activities, from guided/controlled oral practice to some free communication, to achieve this goal. The difference between Mr Yang, and Ms Ma, and Miss Wu is due to the powerful influence of their different conceptions of teaching and learning deeply embedded in their beliefs. For Mr Yang and Ms Ma, linguistic accuracy is the primary goal, while for Miss Wu, communicative competence is the first priority. We can see clearly that Mr Yang and Ms Ma perceive students' interests and instructional objectives as an integrated whole in their enactment of the 1993 English Curriculum, and their focus of attention is on linguistic accuracy. In contrast, Miss Wu gives communicative expression priority over linguistic accuracy. The underlying reasons are very complex, however. Both Mr Yang and Ms Ma are experienced teachers. They are clearly aware of the public examinations and they try their best to use different types of activities to retain the balance. However, Miss Wu is a relatively young, inexperienced teacher. Although she is aware of the public examinations, stimulated by her innovative conception of teaching and learning, Miss Wu is bound to try out something new.

The research findings demonstrate that both in the interviews and in their classroom performance Mr Yang, Miss Wu and Ms Ma all considered grammar teaching as the most important area of English language teaching. However, due to their different understanding and interpretation of the 1993 English Curriculum, and the constraints embedded in it and the way in which they related it to their specific context of work, their implementation of grammar teaching differed dramatically.

According to Ellis (1997), there are four theoretically motivated options in grammar teaching. The first option is called 'structured input'. In the teaching process teachers present the target structure in written or oral texts in a way in which students can identify its salient features. The psycholinguistic rationale, as noted in Chapter 2, is that getting students to attend to rather than produce the target structure assists acquisition. The second option is 'explicit instruction'. Teachers explain rules directly and explicitly; sometimes teachers have students work out rules for themselves. The third option is referred to as 'production practice'. Teachers elicit the production of the target structures, usually going from sentence level to text level creation. The fourth option is 'negative feedback'. Teachers provide feedback to students when they have made mistakes. Some research studies (see, for example, Tanaka, 1996, cited in Ellis, 1997) show that mixed use of the four options is more effective in helping students understand and command grammar.

As mentioned in Chapter 4, Mr Yang felt that grammar still has an important place in the 1993 English Curriculum, but it is less systematically organized than that in the previous curriculum. For Mr Yang, grammar permeates everything – dialogues, texts and composition. He believed that grammar affects students' learning enormously because he found that in his students' writing and tests, grammatical inaccuracies often hindered the proper expression of meaning and therefore affected their learning effectiveness and their academic scores. Mr Yang's major concern in grammar teaching was how to represent grammatical concepts and grammatical points to his students clearly. He mainly used the materials from the textbook (SEFC), but he also selected some materials from other sources that he believed could enrich his students' knowledge of grammar. As shown in Chapter 4, Mr Yang used the 'structured input' approach to start with his grammar teaching. Typically, his structured input consisted of several examples in which he kept the target form constant and varied the rest of the sentence in order to help his students to notice it. Explicit instruction was followed in which Mr Yang explained the rules explicitly. After providing explicit instruction, Mr Yang let his students do some drills in order to consolidate the learned objectives. Then he proceeded to ask them to do translation from English into Chinese and vice versa in pairs or groups followed by individual work.

Unlike Mr Yang, Miss Wu is critical of the exercises in the textbook, which consist merely of manipulation of forms. Miss Wu preferred to present meaningful contexts for the use of the target structure by arranging different types of activities to engage her students in grammar learning processes. She did not teach grammar for the sake of it; instead, she tried to relate her grammar tasks to current events, including social and political figures, and even to students' own daily lives, for example Western fast food in China. As shown in Chapter 5, Miss Wu used 'explicit instruction' to teach attributive clauses by asking her students to point out and explain when and where the attributive clauses were used in the texts. Then she moved to 'structured input' by giving them an activity to join the subordinate sentences with the main sentences in oral form. Next Miss Wu proceeded to 'production practice' by giving her students an activity about their daily life, such as taking the bus to school and watching TV at home. For this activity, students were required to produce statements using the attributive clauses that they had just learned. Due to the pressure of the examination, Miss Wu also had her students do translation in order to focus on form.

Like Mr Yang, as described in Section 7.3, Ms Ma believes that grammar learning is of vital importance in learning a foreign language. She attached a great deal of importance to accuracy. Her guiding principle was to use translation to attain and enhance this goal, but it does not necessarily mean that her grammar teaching was monotonous. In her practices, Ms Ma started her grammar teaching by asking her students to make sentences from the given material or join sentences by using *who, whom, which* or *that* in written form. Then she asked her students to exchange their points of views in pairs or in groups. Next Ms Ma had some students practise at the front of the class by reading out their sentences. The combination of 'structured input' and 'negative feedback' methods aroused her students' great interest in grammar learning in terms of problem-solving, collaboration and consolidation. After this, Ms Ma used 'production practice' to reinforce the learning. Ms Ma asked her students to present their work in English with some other students translating the sentences from English into Chinese. Ms Ma strongly believes that exact understanding of target language in Chinese was very important for her students in the learning process.

As shown above, we can see clearly that Mr Yang, Miss Wu and Ms Ma have demonstrated considerably different ways in grammar teaching in terms of guiding principles, selections of materials and design of activities. Mr Yang taught grammar inductively for form. He articulated that grammar was everything and he organized different types of activities in order to attain the linguistic accuracy. By contrast, Miss Wu taught grammar deductively for meaning. She was able to see grammar teaching not as the teaching of discrete knowledge and skills, but as all interrelated in using English for the purpose of real communication. Compared with Mr Yang and Miss Wu, Ms Ma was determined to teach grammar for linguistic knowledge based on her personal experience, but at the same time, based on her own experience of the exchange programme in the UK, she felt that grammar teaching must also be inextricably linked with interactive, collaborative studies in the learning and teaching process.

The research findings demonstrate that teaching reading is also a very important area which all three teachers focused on. As described in Chapter 4, Mr Yang's learning experience of reading was very traditional. According to Mr Yang, in his school day, his teachers usually had students read the text aloud, corrected their pronunciation, and explained grammar and structure sentence by sentence. Thus, the complete text was broken into discrete fragments. According to the findings, in teaching reading Mr Yang did not completely rely on his past learning experience. In asking his students to listen to the tapes, he went through a passage once or twice to get the main idea for a general comprehension. He sought to integrate reading with speaking and writing by engaging his students in different kinds of activities he designed. However, although he tried to minimize the detailed grammatical analysis and translation work as much as possible, Mr Yang still emphasized linguistic knowledge and accuracy. He saw the main objective of teaching reading as understanding the content of a piece of text. According to Mr Yang, teaching reading was also a process for vocabulary learning and consolidation. Underlying the way he handled reading as integrated training were his compromises, as he responded to time limits, too much content, variable student interest, perhaps unrealistic objectives and promoted methods. This approach is coherent with his approach to the teaching of vocabulary and grammar.

Like Mr Yang, in coping with the teaching of reading, Miss Wu tried to integrate listening, speaking and writing in the process. She asked her students to listen to tapes three times and then she asked them to use skimming and scanning strategies to find out the topic sentences or key sentences for a general understanding of the passage. In the teaching of reading, Miss Wu was most concerned about whether she could arouse her students' enthusiasm for participating in the discussion. She organized different types of activities, such as individual brainstorming, pair work, group presentation and class presentation. According to Miss Wu, the purpose of these activities were aimed at helping her students understand the passage better. Unlike Mr Yang, Miss Wu maintained a very positive and open-minded attitude to teaching reading. What she tried to do was to relate her students' existing knowledge to new knowledge presented in the text. She asked them to use the attributive clauses that they had just learned to describe orally the food they preferred to cook at home. Because they were familiar with the food and cuisine they had, the students were very eager to get involved in the oral discussion. As a result of her growing teaching experience and consultation with her mentor and colleagues, which will be discussed in Section 7.5 as one of the situated forces, Miss Wu was also aware of the linguistic components in the reading, such as set phrases, useful verbal phrases, vocabulary and so on. As described above, we can see the approach Miss Wu adopted in teaching reading was congruent with the approach she used to teach vocabulary and grammar, that is to say, her teaching of reading articulated with her personal conceptions of teaching and learning, and the values embedded therein.

As mentioned above, we can see Ms Ma's learning experience was neither the same as Mr Yang's, nor the same as Miss Wu's. Her most salient conception of teaching and learning was that one could not learn English well without the exact understanding of the target language in his or her mother language. In handling teaching of reading, Ms Ma asked her students to skim the text and answer some questions written on the blackboard to form some general impressions. Then she asked them to read it as quickly as possible in order to answer some specific questions. Next Ms Ma had her students express their comprehension of the text in their own words in pairs and groups. She went around the class and joined in one or two groups to discuss with them as a peer. Later she had some students go to present at the front of the classroom. Occasionally Ms Ma made some comments or gave necessary feedback. When she was sure that her students were able to understand the text well, and express themselves fluently in their own words, Ms Ma proceeded to tackle the linguistic elements. She picked out some key sentences to explain in greater detail because she believed that these were important for a full understanding and useful as good models in writing. Ms Ma had some students read these sentences out aloud and had others translate these sentences into Chinese. From time to time, she gave feedback to them. As described above, it is clear that Ms Ma had two distinct differences in coping with teaching of reading. One is that she participated in the group discussion as a peer, which shows that being a teacher, Ms Ma was much more willing to share her ideas with her students and provided necessary scaffolding for them in the context. The other is that she attached a great deal of importance to her students' exact understanding of the message both in the target language and in their mother language. The former shows that the knowledge of Vygotskian sociocultural theory (see Chapter 2) that she held through her overseas teaching experience has been embedded in her belief system. Consciously or unconsciously, in the implementation of the 1993 English Curriculum, she was able to link it with her specific contexts of work. Her conception of teaching and learning as well as her learning experience made her teaching of reading distinctive from Mr Yang's and Miss Wu's.

Nevertheless, perhaps because they shared similar beliefs most likely influenced by Chinese culture (see, for example, Lewis and McCook, 2002), all three case study teachers also showed clear similarities in their practices. For instance, each attached importance to recitation and memorization, which was a key feature of their personal histories in their childhood, early secondary schooling and college education. They believed that in an environment where English was used as a foreign language, having some input by rote memory could help their students to use the language in the manifold contexts of their daily life, including taking part in high stakes tests. To return to the findings of the earlier literature review (see Chapter 3), we can see that the kind of stage of concern framework proposed by Hall and Hord (2000) appears to be rather simplistic. The findings of the three case study teachers show not only a strong awareness of change, but also their desire to change though constrained.

In summary, from what has been discussed above, we can see that Mr Yang, Miss Wu and Ms Ma had their own personal conceptions of teaching and learning, which were dramatically influenced by their own life experiences, their personal education background, their learning and teaching experiences, their professional training and their beliefs and values. As discussed above, those conceptions, or the internal forces, have a powerful influence on the way all three teachers made sense of their work in their contexts. However, it is unlikely that those conceptions were fixed or unchanged. When they encountered tensions and challenges, they had to modify, or even to change and update their conceptions of teaching and learning in order to suit the real situation. From the above discussion, we can also see that instead of adopting the fidelity approaches the three case study teachers adopted mutual adaptation approaches in the curriculum implementation to suit their contexts (Clandinin and Connelly, 1992). The next section will discuss about how Mr Yang's, Miss Wu's and Ms Ma's pedagogies were mediated by particular situated forces, namely, their school authorities' expectations, collegial inter-action, students' learning attitudes, the school culture, parents' expectations and the availability of resources.

7.5 Situated forces

As discussed in Chapter 3, situated forces including principals, school culture and collegial interaction affected teachers' pedagogical innovation and change (see Davison, 2001; Fullan, 2001; Hargreaves, 1994; Jarzabkowski, 2002; Wideen, 1994). From what has been discussed in the previous sections, we can see that both external and internal forces have created very powerful influences on Mr Yang's, Miss Wu's and Ms Ma's practices. The findings of this study indicate that the contexts in which the three case study teachers work have also a role to play in shaping their personal pedagogies. This section focuses on the situated forces that the three case study teachers encountered and how these factors have affected their classroom practices.

As discussed in Chapter 2, we can see that ELT is by no means apolitical. Pedagogical choices about content, materials, classroom processes and language use are inherently ideological in nature (see Auerbach, 1995; Canagarajah, 1999; Hall and Eggington, 2000; Phillipson, 1992; Tollefson, 2000). The classroom functions are a kind of microcosm of the broader social order, or to be more exact, the political relationships in the world outside the classroom are reproduced within the classroom (Pennycook, 2000). As demonstrated in Chapter 2, Pennycook (2000) points out that we can perceive that everything we do in the classroom is social and political. Lave and Wenger (1991) state that knowledge that teachers develop is jointly constituted by their specific contexts of work and their own understanding of and responses to the contexts (see also Putnam and Borko, 1997). This kind of knowledge has been referred to as situated knowledge (Fenstermacher, 1994). Benner and his associates (1996) point out that being situated means that one is neither totally determined nor constrained by the specific context, nor is one radically free to act in whichever way one wants (see also Fullan, 1991; 2001; Hargreaves, 1994; Wideen, 1994).

As reviewed in Chapter 3, collegial practices in schools are activities in which culture is being developed (see Hargreaves, 1994). According to the research findings, we can see that Mr Yang, Miss Wu and Ms Ma had to navigate a range of stipulating and changed situated forces in their contexts on top of addressing the demands for a more communicative and task-based approach to teaching. In his professional development, the most striking thing for Mr Yang was the interaction with his younger colleagues. As mentioned in Chapter 4, influenced by his conceptions of teaching and learning and the national college entrance examination, Mr Yang was cautious and traditional in terms of using the grammar-translation method too much, and he was rather teacher dominated in his teaching. In the interview, Mr Yang said that his original pedagogical intention was to help his students to acquire linguistic accuracy – learning grammar well and writing good English. However, in the foreign language group where he worked, there were a number of young teachers who were innovative with the latest academic input from their postgraduate studies. Observation of their vivid communicative performances stimulated Mr Yang to critically reflect about his teaching. He took advantage of these opportunities and others to renew his pedagogical content knowledge and subject matter knowledge, which helped him to realise a more multi-dimensional interpretation of his pedagogical choices. In his self-reflection, Mr Yang said that he realised that language learning was an interactive and communicative process as well, and in this process the teacher should use every possible means to engage students in diverse interactions. As observed in Chapter 4, as a result of this collegial interaction, Mr Yang was motivated to change from a rather teacher-centred to a more student-centred approach although it was a slow and incremental change. A second factor that affected his teaching came from his school's curriculum innovation and change, which aimed to offer more subjects to students by cutting off five minutes from a 45-minute lesson. The tight timetable gave Mr Yang a significant challenge, as he had to manipulate the contradiction between the originally planned design and adjusted design in terms of content and focus, activities, teacher's role, and students' role. To solve this problem, on the one hand, Mr Yang worked out how to minimize knowledge delivery, even though it formed a core component of his beliefs and practices he did not want to jettison, and on the other hand, he judiciously picked up the aspects of innovative method that he felt comfortable with. A third factor that influenced his teaching was the large class size, with quite a few students having a significant gap in their studies compared with the average. Mr Yang felt that he should be responsible for every student. In order to meet different kinds of students' needs, he had to adopt different kinds of approaches. Apart from the three major factors that affected his decision-making, Mr Yang also had to cope with many other issues, such as negotiating for resources and venues, and responding to different complaints from his students and their parents. In fact, his responses to all these factors mentioned above showed that in dealing with the challenges emerging from his context of work, Mr Yang had to modify or change his instructional design based on his conceptions of teaching and learning in order to suit the real situation and achieve more effective class-room instruction. The discussion above suggests that the form of culture is a very powerful and significant element in the life and work of teachers in school.

As mentioned in Chapter 5, Miss Wu's professional development was not a very smooth one. In her teaching immediately after graduation, she was keen to teach communicatively. As pointed out in Chapter 5, Miss Wu strongly believed that students should be fully engaged in the teaching and learning process, and that listening and speaking should be substantially emphasized at the initial teaching stage; therefore, she devoted most of the time to training them in speaking and listening. Her students were very active in acting out different kinds of communicative performances. Her way of teaching, labelled as innovative, was much talked about and commented on by her colleagues. To her great disappointment, at the end of the school year, the academic results of her students in the examination were lower than those of other classes. The school authorities and parents immediately pressured her to change. Without investigating in any depth, the school authorities officially informed Miss Wu that for the benefit of the school and students in the national entrance examination, in the new semester she must remain in the same grade for another year to learn how to teach well. This was considered a serious warning and a punishment because this kind of situation only took place when a teacher was considered 'incapable' of teaching.

Miss Wu was thus thrown into perturbance – a kind of confusion as described by Shaw *et al.* (1991). This perturbance made Miss Wu think and reflect because she realized her current practice might be problematic, which is the crucial point for teachers to change (Cobb *et al.*, 1990). Miss Wu was very disappointed about what she perceived as unfairness and she even considered quitting her job. It was Miss Wu's mentor who came to her assistance; after a lengthy discussion, Miss Wu started to reflect on what she had done. She believed that she had done nothing wrong in advocating speaking and listening since many of her students showed a positive attitude towards her teaching. However, she realized that linguistic competence was also a desired goal required by the intended curriculum and the national college entrance examination as well. She figured out that the key point was how to achieve a sound balance between the four skills. Miss Wu's experience demonstrated that the role of principal and peer interaction are very important for teachers in the process of change (see Berman *et al.*, 1979; Fullan, 2001; Wideen, 1994).

As reviewed in Chapter 3, the ethic of practicality among teachers is a powerful sense of what works and what does not (Hargreaves, 1994). Miss Wu's frustration and reflection marked the turning point of her professional development. She started to sit in to observe the lessons conducted by other, experienced teachers and held more talks with her colleagues in the common room in order to share their experiences. She strengthened her grammar teaching by giving necessary explanations of the structural patterns followed with some language production practice. In her grammar lessons, there were many contexts in which the target structures were re-presented in order to help her students understand how they were used. Miss Wu tried hard not to dominate the teaching, but to get her students involved in language production. As described in Chapter 5, although she shifted back to teach grammar, Miss Wu still motivated her students to work together collaboratively in pairs or in groups to complete the tasks. As discussed above, it is clear that Miss Wu's shifting back to strengthen grammar instruction was not only a compromise to the realistic world, but also an intention to arouse her students' awareness and interest that having a good command of grammar could help them communicate better and more efficiently, which, as we have seen in the previous discussion, was deeply rooted in her conceptions of teaching and learning. Miss Wu's experiences revealed that pragmatism, one of three clusters of indicators identified by Fullan (1991; 2001), is associated with the decision to adopt a pedagogical innovation and change in different contextual situation.

As reviewed in Chapter 3, resource availability involves financial means, time, equipment and appropriate materials related to the intended change (Louis and Miles, 1990). Readiness involves the school's capacity to initiate and develop the innovation and being prepared to use new equipment, activities, behaviours or practices. Furthermore, readiness also involves the availability of the prerequisite knowledge and skills at the individual teacher level, needed for a successful implementation of the educational change (Fullan, 1991). As described in Chapter 6, the school multimedia teaching resources available for Ms Ma were relatively limited. According to Ms Ma, to some extent it was a problem not of resources, but of school management. She was fully aware of the advantage and benefit of using multimedia aid in teaching in terms of bringing sight and sound – the real world – to the students. She understood that it could help her to save time that she spent writing on the blackboard and improve teaching efficiency in class, and Ms Ma further expressed that she wanted very much to use the language laboratory and video or audio materials to conduct her teaching in order to solve the time pressure. However, reality made her feel rather disappointed, for two reasons. First, the ratio of the multimedia equipped classrooms to the huge classes was unbalanced. There were more than 30 classes in Ms Ma's school, but there was only one multi-media equipped classroom available. Besides, the application procedure was so complicated that most of the teachers felt it very troublesome to use it. Second, the school multimedia software available was unfit for her specific classroom teaching. If she wanted to use PowerPoint slides and transparencies, Ms Ma had to spend many hours drawing pictures and charts, downloading materials and so on. She felt that it was not practical for her to do this in present circumstances, and the inconvenience significantly prevented her from applying IT to her classroom teaching. In addition, according to Ms Ma, one unpleasant aspect of her school culture was that many teachers were not happy to have others sit in to observe their lessons, which she felt was an unhealthy academic atmosphere for her professional development. The phenomenon discussed above demonstrates that school effectiveness, school improvement and staff development are increasingly accepted wisdoms that schools should have a mission or a sense of mission which mitigates the guilt-inducing uncertainties of teaching by forging common beliefs and purposes among the teaching community (Hargreaves, 1994: 163).

To summarize, the above discussion reveals that it would be one-sided to see only the powerful influence of conceptions of teaching and learning on teachers' classroom practices. In fact, based on the above discussion, we can see that teachers' pedagogical choices were in a dialectical relationship with external and situated forces. As teachers responded to their contexts of work and reflected upon their practices, they came to a new understanding of teaching and learning. In return, this kind of new understanding of teaching and learning could also help them to reshape and change their practices.

7.6 A model of pedagogical innovation and change in the PRC

English language teaching itself is very complex because it involves many factors that affect instruction. Based on the above discussion, we have argued that in the process of pedagogical innovation and change in English language teaching in the People's Republic of China, there are three key forces involved, that is to say, internal, external and situated forces (see Figure 7.1). The internal forces, including teachers' learning experience, teaching experience, their life stories, professional education, conceptions of teaching and learning, and meta-cognitive thinking processes, have a crucial role to play in their classroom practices in terms of lesson design, teacher's roles, students' roles, selection of materials, types of activities, choices of teaching methods and so on. However, the external forces, such as the implementation of the new curricula, national college entrance assessment and intended methods, as identified in this research, have also been a powerful influence on teachers' practices. Although the new curricula identified pedagogy as a major area for change, and the textbooks co-compiled by PEP and Longman promoted communicative methods which treated language learning as an interactive activity, the big dilemma that teachers confronted was that the national college entrance assessment remained unchanged. Moreover, the school authorities and parental expectations, two major elements of the situated forces, were focused on observable outcomes like some public examinations, the national entrance examination in particular. Teachers are fully engaged in the process of change in which they need to probe and understand the meaning of multiple dilemma (see Fullan, 1991). Therefore, influenced by their own conceptions of teaching and learning, teachers had to set out to make changes in pedagogy in ways that are more aligned with the intended methods, and at the same time, teachers had to negotiate with the situated forces in order to adapt to the real world in their teaching practices. It is those complexities that constitute the process of pedagogical innovation and change in the People's Republic of China – which fosters the very dynamic development and interplay of teachers' personal pedagogies. As argued above, it is suggested that the framework of these forces for pedagogic change illustrated in Figure 7.1 can serve as a tentative model of pedagogical innovation and change in the PRC for further relevant research studies.

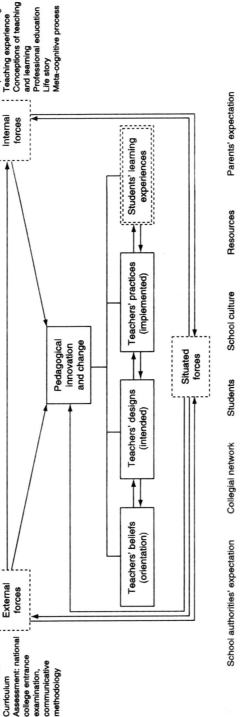

Figure 7.1 The conceptual framework for implemented ELT pedagogical innovation and change in the PRC (Zheng, 2005)

7.7 Conclusion

This chapter has systematically explored and examined the complicated relationships between the diverse factors that influenced or shaped the dynamic entities of teachers' implemented pedagogy. Based on the case study findings, which show three major forces influencing the beliefs and practices of secondary school teachers of English in the PRC, a tentative model of classroom pedagogical innovation and change in the PRC is proposed, which can be used to demonstrate that curriculum implementation is a series of decisions and adaptations according to particular circumstances. The conceptual model can serve as a theoretical framework to explore and examine the genesis, the nature and the impact of the implemented pedagogy by the secondary school teachers of English in the PRC from different perspectives. Since this tentative model provides a three-dimensional view, that is to say, the external forces, the internal forces and the contextual conditions, to examine the dynamic entities of teachers' implemented pedagogy, it therefore adds to our knowledge of the complex act of teaching and how teachers go about it, enhances our understanding of ELT pedagogical change and implementation of curriculum in the PRC, gives assistance to teacher-educators and publishers in providing teacher support, and provides curriculum planners with information in designing future curricular reform.

Chapter 8

Conclusions and implications

8.1 Introduction

In previous chapters, we examined three teachers' classroom practices by observing their process of teaching and learning, content and focus, their roles, their students' roles, organization, activities and materials. We also analysed these three teachers' beliefs by investigating their personal life stories, their personal experiences of learning, their teaching experience, their conceptions of teaching and learning, their professional education and development and their contextual conditions. We show that the pedagogy of these three secondary school teachers of English in the PRC does appear to include these three levels and it is obviously a very dynamic and complex entity.

8.2 The teachers' beliefs

As defined earlier, belief represents implicit views of language and language learning and teachers' personal knowledge. Belief is often tacit and unconsciously held. Moreover, belief has a cognitive and affective component. Belief is also a co-construction and a product of dynamic and evolving socioculture, hence, it is also value-laden and inherently political (see Borg, 2001; Davison, 2001; Kagan, 1992; Nespor, 1987; Rust, 1994). In practice, belief serves as a mediator for experiencing, negotiating and responding to the environment (Tsui, 2003). Furthermore, as beliefs are generally contextualized and associated with a particular situation or circumstance, it is not surprising that systems of beliefs may contradict each other (Ennis, 1994). Our study shows that beliefs held by the three secondary school teachers of English in the PRC played a very important role in their classroom practices, although some of their beliefs also contradicted one another. The common fundamental beliefs held by the three secondary school teachers of English in the PRC can be summarized as follows:

- Grammar is primary in teaching and learning English as it helps to lay a solid foundation of linguistic knowledge for Chinese students, who do not have an ideal target language environment.
- Translation is helpful for students to understand the target language accurately in both form and meaning.
- Vocabulary, including lexical and semantic learning, is a very important input, without which speaking, listening, reading and writing become unsustained.
- Teachers should first help students with speaking and listening through social interactions both inside and outside class, which can help to nurture students' skills in sharing experiences and conducting authentic communication in their real life and eventually help to arouse their interests and build up their confidence.
- Great attention should be attached to reading and writing as they serve as the chief means for Chinese students to get information, to sit for examinations, to look for jobs and so on.
- Teachers should dominate the teaching while students need to be supportive, and all types of activities should be designed to assist the knowledge delivery.
- In the learning process, students should be the main participants under the guidance of the teachers, and the types of activities should be designed to serve for this purpose.
- Teachers should help students to develop healthy and effective learning habits for their future study, that is to say, teachers should work together with students to sort out certain learning strategies that are fit for them.
- Reading aloud and recitation help students to consolidate what they have learned and store some necessary target language codes for use.
- Classroom teaching is very pragmatic; for instance, it is mainly directed by public examinations, high stakes examinations in particular and students' needs.
- It is worthwhile trying out new methods, such as communicative methods, but traditional teaching methods, such as grammar-translation, should not be discarded completely.
- Teachers should learn how to make best use of the resources available in their work environment, including IT in order to make teaching and learning more effective and help to solve constraints, such as time pressure and big class size.
- Teachers should be flexible about the content and foci of the textbooks and should select some materials themselves to adapt to students.

However, there were also differences in the teachers' beliefs. For example, although Mr Yang, Miss Wu and Ms Ma believed that grammar teaching was important to language learning, they addressed grammar teaching in different ways. For Mr Yang, grammar teaching could enable his students to achieve concrete and observable learning outcomes in terms of written results. For Miss Wu, grammar teaching was treated as a complementary strategy to enhance her teaching. As for Ms Ma, grammar teaching could enable her students to speak better and communicate more smoothly in different sorts of social activities in terms of school life.

8.3　The teachers' designs

Our study also demonstrates that the beliefs summarized above have considerably influenced the case study teachers' designs for teaching and learning. As discussed in both Chapter 2 and Chapter 3, design includes the general and specific objectives of the method, subject-matter content, organization, types of learning and teaching activities, learners' roles, teacher's roles and materials. Our study shows that the designs for teaching and learning prepared by the three case study secondary school teachers of English in the PRC have the following common features:

- Senior English For China (SEFC), together with its students' workbooks and supplementary grammar and reading exercises prepared by teachers themselves, is the main teaching material that teachers use to teach; self-made transparencies and audio tape recorders are used in practice.
- The grammar-translation method and a weak form of communicative language teaching method are the two chief teaching methods identified in teachers' design and their logs.
- Revision, presentation, drill, practice and consolidation is the major organization pattern that teachers consider in their design for practices.
- Vocabulary, grammar, dialogues, reading, listening, writing, comprehensive exercises in SEFC and its students' workbooks are the foci for teachers to cover in their lesson plans.
- Individual, pair, group and whole-class activities are designed for different purposes; for example, pair work and group work are used for dialogue and reading discussions; individual work is used for brainstorming and translation; whole-class activities are used for oral presentation, grammar explanation, translation comment, and listening comprehension.
- Teachers appear to juggle a variety of roles: knowledge transmitter,

presenter, demonstrator, organizer, controller, helper, resource provider, memory activator, helper, consultant, marker/assessor, prompter, feedback provider, manager and decision-maker.

- In teachers' designs, students are considered performers, participants, knowledge receptors, problem-solvers, listeners, supporters, collaborators, rote memorizers and negotiators.

However, there were also differences in the teachers' designs. For example, Mr Yang and Ms Ma were senior teachers. When they designed their lesson plans, Mr Yang and Ms Ma only outlined the key points that they wanted to cover, such as the grammatical points, main ideas of the texts, and the types of activities applied to solve certain problems. When Miss Wu designed her lessons plans, she prepared detailed ones. Miss Wu wrote each step or procedure clearly and carefully, including the content and focus, questions and answers, teacher's roles, students' roles and even grammar and translation exercises (with keys to two different languages). With regard to teaching strategies, Miss Wu tried to explain them clearly in her lessons as to why and how she wanted to apply them. However, Mr Yang and Ms Ma did not write those steps in detail. The findings demonstrate that the more experienced teachers of English in the PRC were more flexible when they prepared their lesson designs while the younger teacher tended to be more dogmatic and cautious due to lack of experience.

8.4 The teachers' practices

When teachers apply their designs to their classroom practice, they have to negotiate with their environment and adapt their teaching designs to real situations. As discussed and analysed in Chapter 7, the chief features of these teachers' practices are summarized as follows:

- The grammar-translation method is used to deal with grammatical/language points that emerge in dialogues and reading.
- Communicative language teaching approaches in their weak form are applied to teaching dialogues and texts in order to help students engage in asking and answering questions, collaborative discussion and oral presentation.
- Revision, presentation, drill, practice and consolidation is the usual sequence that teachers follow in classroom practices.
- Teachers mostly follow the sequences of content arrangement by the textbooks, that is, vocabulary, dialogues, reading, grammar, grammar exercises, listening and writing are conducted respectively; teachers some-

times cut off or add some content according to the situations of their time available, students' needs and so on.

- Activities as such dictation, individual work, pair work, group work/ discussion, teacher's scaffolding, recitation and oral presentation are used to get students involved in the learning process.
- Teachers are knowledge transmitters, organizers, activators, helpers/ scaffolders, controllers, resource providers, memory activators, consultants, markers/assessors, feedback providers, managers and decision-makers in their practices.
- Students are first of all knowledge receptors and listeners, and then performers, participants, problem-solvers, supporters, collaborators, rote memorizers and negotiators.
- Audio tape recorders are used to train students' listening, and transparencies are used to explain grammar, translation, vocabulary and questions and answers; sometimes transparencies are used to add supplementary materials that teachers design themselves.
- English is the main medium of instruction; however, when necessary, Chinese is also used as part of the medium of instruction. Chinese is used to explain new items and to enable comparisons to be made between English and Chinese.
- Attention is also paid to consolidating the knowledge, including sentence patterns, key words, collocations, revision, checking homework and commenting on the students' writing on the blackboard.
- Linguistic competence is the desired goal; translation in both oral and written forms from Chinese into the target language and vice versa is highly emphasized and accuracy is the desired goal.
- Rote memory is used to assist, enhance and consolidate learning; structure-based dialogues and some idiomatic ways of saying are required to be learned by heart.

However, there were also some differences in practices. For example, when students raised questions in his class, Mr Yang tended to answer all those questions himself, whereas when Ms Ma's and Miss Wu's students asked questions, the teachers tended to discuss with them or arranged them into small groups to discuss those questions themselves first and then presented their ideas in class.

8.5 The influences on teachers' beliefs, designs and practices

As demonstrated in Chapter 7, there are three forces that are influencing and shaping the three case study teachers' beliefs, designs and practices. The three forces are external forces, including the intended curriculum, national college entrance examination and promoted communicative methods; situated forces, including school culture, collegial network, resources, school authorities' expectations, parental expectations and students' learning attitudes; and teachers' internal forces, such as teachers' experiences of learning, teaching experiences, professional development, and conceptions of teaching and learning. Obviously, in the conflict between the three forces, teachers' classroom practices are not merely a matter of pedagogical choices, but also a matter of responding to and negotiating with different factors inside and outside the classrooms, including political and social factors.

The findings of the three case study teachers show that their pedagogies are complicated, dynamic and evolving entities. Their beliefs guide them in how to design their lessons and how to engage in their practices. However, the three case study teachers met with many unforeseen issues that arose in teaching. With the rigid national college entrance examination pulling them to one direction, and promoted communicative methods pulling them to the other, the three case study teachers have to cope with their teaching pragmatically. On the one hand, they are open to the promoted methods, they negotiate with the intended curriculum in context, and they adapt to pedagogical change, but on the other hand, they have to put every possible effort into helping their students score high grades in the high stakes examinations. The findings of the three case study teachers also show that the complex interactions between students and between teachers and students help to shape or reshape teachers' beliefs. Moreover, the case study findings demonstrate that the school principals, school cultures and collegial network have a crucial impact in teachers' decision-making, renewal of their beliefs and professional development. As a result, the three case study teachers are totally bound neither by their existing beliefs, nor by the examination system – they are willing to incorporate new ideas. However, the findings highlight that the three case study teachers' pedagogical change is not radical, but incremental and pragmatic: they do not stick to only one teaching method; instead, they select different kinds of teaching methods to suit their needs, such as the grammar-translation method, audiolingualism and the communicative method in its weak form, to make teaching and learning comfortable, easy and effective so that they can address their own problems in different contexts.

8.6 Implications for practice

As stated above, teachers' pedagogy is not an isolated entity. It includes many constituent factors that interact with each other, such as curriculum, teacher education, teaching materials and contextual conditions. Therefore, we propose some suggestions to those concerned with improving pedagogy and practice in schools as follows.

- **Make the curriculum more suitable to practical needs**

As stated above, classroom practices are heavily influenced by different kinds of forces, including the intended curriculum and promoted methods. Therefore, when curriculum is designed, designers should consider the real contexts that teachers might face and provide appropriate flexibility and time for them to make their own pedagogic decisions to suit their contexts. As pointed out above, pedagogical innovation and change is an incremental and pragmatic process rather than a radical one. Therefore, when curriculum designers promote certain kinds of teaching methodologies, they should not overstate the superiority of one method to another. Teachers should be encouraged to adopt different kinds of methods that suit their teaching.

- **Make teacher-training programmes more effective**

Teacher-training programmes are carried out at different levels in the PRC from time to time every year. However, most training programmes attach great attention to transmitting subject matter knowledge to teachers. Few courses about educational research, such as action research, are offered to teachers. In future, training programmes should include more information about the latest pedagogic innovation and change and ongoing academic research both inside and outside China in order to help teachers to carry out more action research-based study so that they can explore their pedagogic spaces and reflect their beliefs and practices.

- **Make the assessment system more congruent with the intended curriculum**

As pointed out above, the national college entrance examination is one of the most important, influential factors that affect teachers' classroom practices. Nevertheless, the current assessment system is not congruent with the intended curriculum in that there is a discrepancy between what has been taught and what has been examined. In other words, the national college entrance examination still attaches great importance to grammar and linguistic accuracy. In contrast, the intended curriculum promotes a more practical and communicative teaching and learning. Given this dilemma, teachers have to compromise. To some extent, the national college entrance examination becomes a 'baton' for teachers to follow. In order to change this abnormal situation, experts from both curriculum and assessment fields should work together to find out some better solutions to solve this problem so that teachers will not be largely led by public examinations when they conduct their practices.

- **Improve teaching materials**

As discussed in Chapter 7, the three case study teachers felt that the content of SEFC was overloaded and there were big curves in grammar arrangement, that is to say, the grammar requirement in JEFC was minimized but the grammar requirement in SEFC was much enhanced, which made teaching and learning difficult. In addition, reading and listening materials in SEFC were highly demanding. Due to time pressure, teachers found it difficult to finish all the content. Instead, they had to cut down some part of the content and added something they felt useful and necessary for their students to learn. In future, when the textbooks are revised or re-printed, careful consideration should be given to the smooth transition and connection of each textbook and grammar needs to be more systematically arranged. Listening materials should be closely linked with the content of the textbooks because both teachers and students are comfortable with and interested in the familiar things that they have experienced in the textbooks, which is likely to achieve a better and more effective result in teaching and learning. Reading materials should not contain too many new words and expressions, which might hinder students' reading speed and mislead teachers into over-emphasizing or over-explaining language points.

- **Create more favourable contextual conditions**

As discussed in Chapter 7, contextual conditions are one of the most important forces that impact on teachers' practices. School authorities should create a more interactive and collegial school culture or atmosphere so that teachers can feel free to participate in different kinds of academic seminars and exchange their teaching experiences with peers. Supporting teaching should become the first priority in the school administrative agenda, not merely a slogan. School authorities should avoid judging teachers' achievements by merely evaluating how well their students do in public examinations.

8.7 Implications for future research

As discussed above, this research study has contributed to our understanding of what teachers' implemented pedagogy is all about in the PRC. However, in adopting a naturalistic qualitative approach as its research design, there were obviously some limitations. First, as this was a case study of only three teachers over a limited period of time, the findings might not fully address the complicated, dynamic and comprehensive pedagogy of English teachers in the PRC. The reason is that teachers do not use the same teaching methods even when they teach the same lessons in the same contexts, let alone when there are so many different lessons in the textbooks and teachers have to teach them in very different contexts. Therefore, many questions about why and how teachers use this method or that method remain unanswered. Thus, further studies of teachers' pedagogy in handling different kinds of linguistic content and skills in different contexts are necessary.

Second, as mentioned in Chapter 3, this research site was located in one province only, that is, Fujian province, so it can hardly reflect the full picture of teachers' implemented pedagogy in the PRC. China is a large country with enormous regional differences in terms of geographic characteristics, ethnicity, economic development, demographic density, culture and educational development. Thus, further studies should be conducted in different provinces, including coastal cities, remote rural towns or villages and minority autonomic regions, in order to gain a better and more thorough understanding of the implemented pedagogy.

Third, this study was limited in that data was collected several years ago. Currently secondary schools in the PRC are using a series of revised JEFC and SEFC textbooks, in which a more communicative teaching method – task-based instruction – is highly promoted. Thus, more longitudinal and related research is needed; for instance, a study examining the relationship between teaching strategy and learning strategy might help us to understand teachers' pedagogy better because many research studies have shown that teachers' pedagogy has much to do with students' independence and autonomy.

Finally, there need to be more studies of the teachers' experiences of innovation and change, and the dynamic role of teachers as mediators of change. As Hargreaves (1994) has emphasized, teachers are first and foremost social beings, but the contexts in which particular theories and strategies are developed are often ignored. Although this research study has probed the nature of innovation and change and teachers' roles in the development of ELT in the PRC to some extent, more research studies should be conducted in a wider range of contexts throughout the world to enhance our understanding of teachers' experiences and interpretations of innovation and change.

References

Abelson, R. P. (1979). The differences between belief and knowledge system. *Cognitive Science, 3*, 355–366.

Adamson, B. (1998). *English in China: The junior secondary school curriculum 1949–94*. Unpublished PhD dissertation, The University of Hong Kong.

Adamson, B. (2001). English with Chinese characteristics: China's new curriculum. *Asia Pacific Journal of Education, 21*(2), 19–33.

Adamson, B. (2002). Barbarian as a foreign language: English in China's schools. *World Englishes, 21*(2), 231–343.

Adamson, B. (2004a). *China's English*. Hong Kong: Hong Kong University Press.

Adamson, B. (2004b). Fashions in language teaching methodology. In A. Davies and C. Elder (Eds.), *The Handbook of Applied Linguistics* (pp. 604–622). Oxford: Blackwell.

Adamson, B. and Davison, C. (2003). Innovation in English language teaching in Hong Kong primary schools: One step forward, two steps sideways? *Prospect, 18*(1), 27–41.

Alexander, R. (2000). *Culture and Pedagogy: International Comparisons in Primary Education*. Oxford, UK; Malden, MA: Blackwell Publishers.

Alexander, R., Osborn, M. and Phillips, D. (Eds.). (2000). *Learning from Comparing: New Directions in Comparative Educational Research* (Vol. 2). Oxford: Symposium Books.

Allen, J. B. (1995). Friends, fairness, fun and the freedom to choose: Hearing student voices. *Journal of Curriculum and Supervision, 10*(4), 286–301.

Allwright, D. and Bailey, K. (1991). *Focus on the Language Classroom: An Introduction to Classroom Research for Language Teachers*. Cambridge: Cambridge University Press.

Anderson, J. (1993). Is a communicative approach practical for teaching English in China? Pros and cons. *System, 21*(4), 471–480.

Anthony, E. M. (1963). Approach, method and technique. *English Language Teaching, 17*, 63–67.

Auerbach, E. (1995). The politics of ESL classrooms: Issues of power in pedagogical choices. In J. Tollefson (ed.), *Power and Inequality in Language Education* (pp. 9–33). New York: Cambridge University Press.

Austin, J. L. (1962). *How to Do Things with Words.* Oxford: Oxford University Press.

Bachman, L. (1991). *Fundamental Considerations in Language Testing.* Oxford: Oxford University Press.

Bachman, L. and Palmer, A. (1996). *Language Testing in Practice.* Oxford: Oxford University Press.

Bailey, K. M. (1992). The processes of innovation in language teacher development: What, why and how teachers change. In J. Flowerdew, M. Brock and S. Hsia (Eds.), *Perspectives on Second Language Teacher Education* (pp. 253–282). Hong Kong: City Polytechnic of Hong Kong.

Bean, T. and Zulich, J. (1992). A case study of three preservice teachers' beliefs about content area reading through the window of student–professor dialogue journals. In C. K. Kinzer and D. J. Leu (Eds.), *Literacy Research, Theory, and Practice: Views from Many Perspectives* (pp. 463–474). Chicago: National Reading Conference.

Becker, J. R., Pence, B. J. and Pors, D. (1995). Building bridges to mathematics for all: A small scale evaluation study. In D. T. Owens, M. K. Reed and G. M. Millsaps (Eds.), *Proceedings of the Seventeenth PME-NA Conference* (Vol. 2, pp. 255–261). Washington, DC: Office of Educational Research and Development.

Bell, D. (2003). Method and postmethod: Are they really so incompatible? *TESOL Quarterly, 37*(2), 325–336.

Bell, J. and Gower, R. (1997). *Elementary Matters: Teacher's Book.* Essex: Addison Wesley Longman.

Benner, P., Tanner, C.A. and Chesla, C.A. (1996). *Expertise in Nursing Practice: Caring, Clinical Judgement and Ethics.* New York: Springer Publishing Company.

Benson, P. (1997). The philosophy and politics of learner autonomy. In P. Benson and P. Voller (Eds.), *Autonomy and Independence in Language Learning* (pp. 18–34). London: Longman.

Berman, P. and McLaughlin, M. (1975). *The findings in review* (No. 158914HEW). Rand Change Agent Study–Federal Programs Supporting Educational Change.

Berman, P., McLaughlin, M., Pincus, J., Weiler, D. and Williams, R. (1979). *An Exploratory Study of School District Adaptations.* Santa Monica, CA: Rand Corporation.

Bernstein, B. B. (1975). *Class, Codes and Control, Vol 3: Towards a Theory of Education Transmission.* London: Routledge and Kegan Paul.

Best, S. and Kellner, D. (2001). *The Postmodern Adventure.* New York: Guildford Press.

Bogdan, R. and Biklen, S. K. (1998). *Qualitative Research for Education: An Introduction to Theory and Methods* (3 ed.). Boston: Allyn and Bacon.

Bolton, K. (2002). Chinese Englishes: From Canton jargon to global English. *World Englishes, 21*(2), 181–199.

Bolton, K. (2003). *Chinese Englishes: A Sociolinguisitc History.* Cambridge: Cambridge University Press.

Bolton, K. (2005). Symposium on English today (Part II) Where WE stand: approaches, issues, and debate in world Englishes. *World Englishes, 24*(1), 69–83.

Borg, S. (2001). Key concepts in ELT: Teachers' beliefs. *ELT Journal, 55*(2), 186–188.

Borg, S. (2003). Teacher cognition in language teaching: A review of research on what language teachers think, know, believe and do. *Language Teaching, 38*, 81–109.

Boyle, J. (2000). A brief history of English language teaching in China. *IATEFL Issue 155, June–July.*

Brayan, L. A. and Atwater, M. M. (2002). Teacher beliefs and cultural models: A challenge for science teacher preparation programs. *Science Teacher Education, 86*(6), 821–839.

Breen, M. (1987). Learner contributions to task design. In C. N. Candlin and D. F. Murphy (Eds.), *Language Learning Tasks* (pp. 23–46). Englewood Cliffs, NJ: Prentice Hall International.

Breen, M. and Candlin, C. N. (1980). The essentials of a communicative curriculum in language teaching. *Applied Linguistics, 1*(2), 89–112.

Brooks, N. (1964). *Language and Language Learning: Theory and Practice* (2 ed.). New York: Harcourt Brace.

Brousseau, B., Book, C. and Byers, J. (1988). Teacher beliefs and the cultures of teaching. *Journal of Teacher Education, 39*(6), 33–39.

Brown, H. (1980). *Principles of Language Learning and Teaching.* Englewood Cliffs, NJ: Prentice Hall International.

Brown, H. (1994). *Teaching by Principles: An Interactive Approach to Language Pedagogy.* Englewood Cliffs, NJ: Prentice Hall International.

Brown, H. (2000). *Principles of Language Learning and Teaching* (4 ed.). New York: Longman.

Brumfit, C. J. and Johnson, K. (Eds.). (1979). *The Communicative Approach to Language Teaching.* Oxford: Oxford University Press.

Bruner, J. (1985). Vygotsky: A historical and conceptual perspective. In J. Wertsch (ed.), *Culture, Communication and Cognition: Vygotskian Perspectives* (pp. 21–34). Cambridge: Cambridge University Press.

Burnaby, B. and Sun, Y. (1989). Chinese teachers' views of Western language teaching: Context informs paradigms. *TESOL Quarterly, 23*(2), 219–238.

Burns, A. (1999). *Collaborative Action Research for English Language Teachers.* Cambridge: Cambridge University Press.

Bussis, A., Chittenden, F. and Armel, M. (1976). *Beyond Surface Curriculum*. Boulder, CO: Westview Press.

Cairns, H. S. (1999). *Psycholinguistics: An Introduction*. Austin, TX: Pro-Ed.

Calderhead, J. (1984). *Teachers' Classroom Decision-Making*. London: Holt, Rinehart and Winston.

Calderhead, J. and Robson, M. (1991). Images of teaching: Student teachers' early conceptions of classroom practice. *Teaching and Teacher Education, 7*(1), 1–8.

Canagarajah, A. S. (1993). Critical ethnography of a Sri Lankan classroom: Ambiguities in student opposition to reproduction through ESOL. *TESOL Quarterly, 27*(4), 601–626.

Canagarajah, A. S. (1999). *Resisting Linguistic Imperialism in English Teaching*. New York: Oxford University Press.

Canale, M. and Swain, M. (1980). Theoretical bases of communicative approaches to second language teaching and testing. *Applied Linguistics, 1*(1), 1–47.

Candlin, C. N. (1987). Towards task-based language learning. In C. N. Candlin and D. F. Murphy (Eds.), *Language Learning Tasks* (pp. 5–22). Englewood Cliffs, NJ: Prentice Hall International.

Carless, D. (2001). *Curriculum innovation in the primary EFL classroom: Case studies of three teachers implementing Hong Kong's target-oriented curriculum (TOC)*. Unpublished PhD, The University of Warwick.

Carless, D. (2002). Implementing task-based learning with young learners. *ELT Journal, 56*(4), 389–396.

Carter, K. (1990). *Handbook of Research on Teacher Education*. New York: Macmillan.

Celce-Murcia, M. (2001). Language teaching approaches: An overview. In M. Celce-Murcia (ed.), *Teaching English as a Second or Foreign Language* (3 ed., pp. 3–12). Boston, MA: Heinle and Heinle.

Celce-Murcia, M., Dörnyei, Z. and Thurrell, S. (1997). Direct approaches in L2 instruction: A turning point in communicative language teaching? *TESOL Quarterly, 31*(1), 141–152.

Chan, F. K. H. (2002). The cognitive element of curriculum change. In B. Mak (ed.), *Reflecting on Language in Education* (p. 227). Hong Kong: Hong Kong Institute of Education.

Chastain, K. (1988). *Developing Second Language Skills* (3 ed.). San Diego, CA: Harcourt Brace Jovanovich.

Chaudron, C. (1988). *Second Language Classrooms: Research on Teaching and Learning*. New York: Cambridge University Press.

Chen, S. (1988). A challenge to the exclusive adoption of the communicative approach in China. *Guidelines, 10*(1), 67–76.

Cheng, L. Y. (2005). *Changing Language Teaching through Language Testing: A Washback Study*. Studies in Language Testing: Volume 21. Cambridge: Cambridge University Press.

Cherland, M. (1989). The teacher educator and the teacher: When theory and practice conflict. *Journal of Reading, 32*, 409–413.

Chiang, O. K. K. (2002). *Dictation in a Local Primary School*. Unpublished MEd., The University of Hong Kong.

Chomsky, N. (1957). *Syntactic Structure*. The Hague: Mouton.

Chomsky, N. (1959). Review of B. F. Skinner: Verbal behavior. *Language, 35*, 26–58.

Chomsky, N. (1965). *Aspects of the Theory of Syntax*. Cambridge: MIT Press.

Cimbricz, S. (2002). *State-mandated testing and teachers' beliefs and practice*. Retrieved 9 June, 2003, from http://epaa.asu.edu/epaa/v10n2.html

Clandinin, D. J. and Connelly, F. M. (1992). Teacher as curriculum maker. In P. W. Jackson (ed.), *Handbook of Research on Curriculum* (pp. 363–401). New York: Macmillan.

Clark, C. (1988). Asking the right questions about teacher preparation: Contributions of research on teaching thinking. *Educational Researcher, 17*(2), 5–12.

Clark, C. M. and Peterson, P. L. (1986). Teachers' thought processes. In M. C. Wittrock (ed.), *Handbook of Research on Teaching* (pp. 255–296). New York: Macmillan.

Clark, J. L. (1987). *Curriculum Renewal in School Foreign Language Learning*. Oxford: Oxford University Press.

Cobb, P., Wood, T. and Yackel, E. (1990). Classroom a learning environment for teacher and researchers. In R. B. Davis, C. A. Maher and N. Noddings (Eds.), *Constructivist Views on the Teaching and Learning of Mathematics* (pp. 125–146). Reston, VA: National Council of Teachers of Mathematics.

Cohen, L. and Manion, L. (1994). *Research Methods in Education* (4 ed.). London: Routledge.

Cohen, L., Manion, L. and Morrison, K. (2000). *Research Methods in Education* (5 ed.). London; New York: Routledge/Falmer.

Connelly, F. M. and Clandinin, D. J. (1994). Telling teaching stories. *Teacher Education Quarterly, 21*(1), 145–158.

Cortazzi, M. and Jin, L. X. (1996). English teaching and learning in China. *Language Teaching, 29*, 61–80.

Coupland, N. and Jaworski, A. (1997). *Sociolinguistics: A Reader and Course-book*. Basingstoke: Macmillan.

Cowan, J. R., Light, R. L., Mathews, B. E. and Tucker, G. R. (1979). English teaching in China: A recent survey. *TESOL Quarterly, 13*(4), 468–482.

Creswell, J. W. (1998). *Qualitative Inquiry and Research Design: Choosing among Five Traditions*. Thousand Oaks, CA: Sage Publications.

Crystal, D. (1997). *English as a Global Language*. Cambridge, UK; New York: Cambridge University Press.

Crystal, D. (2003). *English as a Global Language* (2 ed.). Cambridge, UK; New York: Cambridge University Press.

Cumming, A. (1989). Student teachers' conceptions of curriculum: Towards an understanding of language teacher development. *TESL Canada Journal*, 7(1), 33–51.

Davison, C. (2001). Identity and ideology: The problem of defining and defending ESL-ness. In B. Mohan, C. Leung and C. Davison (Eds.), *English as a Secondary Language in the Mainstream: Teaching, Learning and Identity* (pp. 71–90). Harlow: Longman.

Denzin, N. (2001). *Interpretive Interactionism* (2 ed.). Thousand Oaks, CA: Sage.

Desforges, C. and Cockburn, A. (1987). *Understanding the Mathematics Teacher: A Study of Practice in First Schools*. London: Falmer Press.

Dewey, J. (1933). *How We Think: A Restatement of the Relation of Reflective Thinking to the Educative Process*. Boston: D.C. Heath and company.

Diller, K. C. (1978). *The Language Teaching Controversy*. Rowley, MA: Newbury House.

Doff, A. and Jones, C. (2000). *Language in Use Pre-Intermediate New Edition: Teacher's Book*. Cambridge: Cambridge University Press.

Doll, R. C. (1996). *Curriculum Improvement: Decision Making and Process* (9 ed.). Boston, MA: Allyn and Bacon.

Donato, R. (2000). Sociocultural contributions to undersanding the foreign and second language classroom. In J. P. Lantolf (ed.), *Sociocultural Theory and Second Language Learning* (pp. 44–7). London: Oxford University Press.

Donato, R. and McCormick, D. (1994). A sociocultural perspective on language learning strategies: The role of mediation. *Modern Language Journal*, 78, 453–464.

Dooley, D. (2001). *Social Research Methods* (4 ed.). Upper Saddle River, NJ: Prentice Hall.

Dzau, Y. F. (ed.). (1990). *English in China*. Hong Kong: API Press.

Edwards, D. and Mercer, N. (1987). *Common Knowledge: The Development of Understanding in the Classroom*. London: Methuen.

Edwards, T. (1994). *Using a model to understand the process of change in a middle school mathematics teacher*. Paper presented at the Annual Meeting of the National Council of Teachers of Mathematics, Indianapolis, IN.

Elbaz, F. (1983). *Teacher Thinking: A Study of Practical Knowledge*. London: Croom Helm.

Elliott, J. (1991). *Action Research for Educational Change*. Milton Keynes: Open University Press.

Ellis, R. (1994). *The Study of Second Language Acquisition*. Oxford: Oxford University Press.

Ellis, R. (1998). Teaching and research: Options in grammar teaching. *TESOL Quarterly, 32*(1), 39–60.

Ellis, R. (2003). *Task-Based Language Learning and Teaching*. Oxford: Oxford University Press.

Engestrom, Y. (1993). Developmental studies on work as a test bench of activity theory. In S. Chaikin and J. Lave (Eds.), *Understanding Practice: Perspectives on Activity and Context* (pp. 64–103). Cambridge: Cambridge University Press.

Ennis, C. (1994). Knowledge and beliefs underlying curricular expertise. *Quest, 46*(2), 164–175.

Erickson, F. and Shultz, J. (1992). Students' experience of the curriculum. In P. W. Jackson (ed.), *Handbook of Research on Curriculum: A Project of the American Educational Research Association* (pp. 465–485). New York: Macmillan Pub. Co.

Fang, Z. (1996). A review of research on teacher beliefs and practices. *Educational Research, 38*(1), 47–65.

Feikes, D. (1995). One teacher's learning: a case study of an elementary teacher's beliefs and practice. In D. T. Owens, M. K. Reed and G. M. Millsaps (Eds.), *Proceedings of the Seventeenth PME-NA Conference* (Vol. 2., pp. 175–180). Washington, DC: Office of Educational Research and Development.

Fenstermacher, G. D.(1994). 'The knower and the known: The nature of knowledge in the research on teaching'. In L. Darling-Hammond (ed.), *Review of Research in Education* (pp. 3–56). Washington D.C.: AERA.

Finocchiaro, M. and Brumfit, C. (1983). *The Functional-Notional Approach: From Theory to Practice*. New York: Oxford University Press.

Firth, J. (1957). *Papers in Linguistics: 1934–1951*. London: Oxford University Press.

Ford, D. J. (1988). *The Twain Shall Meet: The Current Study of English in China*. Jefferson, NC: McFarland and Company.

Frankfort-Nachmias, C. and Nachmias, D. (1996). *Research Methods in the Social Sciences* (5 ed.). New York: Oxford University Press.

Freeman, D. (1989). Teacher training, development and decision making model: A model of teaching and related strategies for language teacher education. *TESOL Quarterly, 32*, 27–45.

Freeman, D. (1991). To make the tacit explicit: Teacher education, emerging discourse, and conceptions of teaching. *Teaching and Teacher Education, 7*(5/6), 439–454.

Freeman, D. (2002). The hidden side of the work: Teacher knowledge and learning to teach. *Language Teaching, 35*, 1–13.

Freeman, D. and Richards, J. C. (1996). Prologue: A look at uncritical stories. In D. Freeman and J. C. Richards (Eds.), *Teacher Learning in Language Teaching* (pp. 50–78). Cambridge: Cambridge University Press.

Fu, K. (1986). *Zhong Guo Wai Yu Jiao Yu Shi (History of Foreign Language Education in China)*. Shanghai: Shanghai Foreign Language Educational Press.

Fullan, M. (1982). *The Meaning of Educational Change*. New York: Teachers College Press.

Fullan, M. (1991). *The New Meaning of Educational Change*. New York; London: Teachers College Press.

Fullan, M. (1993). *Change Forces: Probing the Depths of Educational Reform*. Bristol, PA: Falmer.

Fullan, M. (1995). *Successful School Improvement: The Implementation Perspective and Beyond*. Buckingham, UK; Bristol, PA: Open University Press.

Fullan, M. (2001). *The New Meaning of Educational Change* (3 ed.). New York; London: Teachers College Press.

Fullan, M. and Stiegelbauer, S. (1991). *The New Meaning of Educational Change*. New York; London: Teachers College Press.

Fullan, M. and Hargreaves, A. (1992). *What's Worth Fighting for in Your School? Working Together for Improvement*. Buckingham: Open University Press.

Gabrielator, C. (1998). Translation impossibilities: Problems and opportunities for TEFL. *TESOL Greece Newsletter, 60*.

Galton, M., Simon, B. and Croll, P. (1980). *Inside the Primary Classroom*. London: Routledge and Kegan Paul.

Gao, L. B. and Watkins, D. A. (2001). Towards a model of teaching conceptions of Chinese secondary school of teachers of physics. In D. A. Watkins and J. B. Biggs (Eds.), *Teaching the Chinese Learner: Psychological and Pedagogical Perspectives* (pp. 27–45). Hong Kong: Comparative Education Research Centre, The University of Hong Kong.

Geertz, C. (1973). Thick description: Towards an interpretive theory of culture. In C. Geertz (ed.), *The Interpretation of Cultures*. New York: Basic Books.

Glesne, C. and Peshkin, A. (1992). *Becoming Qualitative Researchers: An Introduction*. White Plains, NY: Longman.

Golombek, P. R. (1998). A study of language teacher's personal practical knowledge. *TESOL Quarterly, 32*(3), 447–464.

Gong, Y. F. (1999). To have a good grasp of communicative teaching. In PEP (ed.), *Foreign Language Teaching: Theory and Practice* (pp. 113–122). Beijing: People's Education Press.

Goodlad, J. I., Klein, M. F. and Keneth, A. T. (1979). The domains of curriculum and their study. In J. I. Goodlad and Associates (eds), *Curriculum Inquiry: The Study of Curriculum Practice* (pp. 43–76). New York: McGraw-Hill.

Goodson, I. F. (2003). *Professional Knowledge, Professional Lives: Studies in Education and Change*. Philadelphia: Open University Press.

Gumperz, J. J. and Hymes, D. (1972). *Directions in Sociolinguistics: The Ethnography of Communication*. New York: Holt, Rinehart and Winston.

Hall, G. E. and Hord, S. M. (1987). *Change in Schools: Facilitating the Process*. Albany, NY: State University of New York Press.

Hall, G. E. and Hord, S. M. (2000). *Change in Schools: Facilitating the Process*. Boulder, CO: netLibrary.

Hall, G. E. and Hord, S. M. (2001). *Implementing Change: Patterns, Principles, and Potholes*. Boston: Allyn and Bacon.

Hall, G. E. and Loucks, S. F. (1978). *Innovation Configurations: Analyzing the Adaptations of Innovations* (No. 3049). Austin: The University of Texas at Austin, Research and Development Center for Teacher Education.

Hall, J. K. and Eggington, W. G. (2000). *The Sociopolitics of English Language Teaching*. Clevedon: Multilingual Matters.

Halliday, M. A. K. (1973). *Explorations in the Functions of Language*. London: Edward Arnold.

Halsey, A., Heath, A. and Ridge, J. (1980). *Origins and Destinations*. Oxford: Oxford University Press.

Hargreaves, A. (1992). Foreword. In M. Fullan (ed.), *Understanding Teacher Development* (pp. ix–x). London: Routledge.

Hargreaves, A. (1994). *Changing Teachers, Changing Times: Teachers' Work and Culture in the Postmodern Age*. London: Cassell.

Hargreaves, A., Earl, L., Moore, S. and Manning, S. (ed.). (2001). *Learning to Change: Teaching Beyond Subjects and Standards*. San Francisco, CA: Jossey-Bass.

Hargreaves, A. and Evans, R. (1997). Teachers and educational reform. In R. Evans (ed.), *Beyond Educational Reform: Bringing Teachers Back In* (pp. 1–18). Buckingham; Philadelphia: Open University Press.

Harmer, J. (2001). *The Practice of English Language Teaching* (3 ed.). Harlow: Longman.

Herdina, P. (2002). *A Dynamic Model of Multilingualism: Perspectives of Change in Psycholinguistics*. Clevedon, UK; Buffalo, NY: Multilingual Matters.

Hitchcock, G. and Hughes, D. (1995). *Research and the Teacher* (2 ed.). London: Routledge.

Hodge, H. A. (1953). *Languages, Standpoints and Attitudes*. London: Oxford University Press.

Holliday, A. (1994). *Appropriate Methodology and Social Context*. Cambridge: Cambridge University Press.

Holmes, J. (1992). *An Introduction to Sociolinguistics*. Harlow: Longman.

Hord, S., Rutherford, W., Huling-Austin, L. and Hall, G. (1987). *Taking Charge of Change*. Alexandria, VA: ASCD.

Howatt, A. (1984). *A History of English Language Teaching*. Oxford: Oxford University Press.

Hsu, I. C. Y. (2000). *The Rise of Modern China* (6 ed.). New York; Oxford, UK: Oxford University Press.

Hu, G. (2002). Recent important developments in secondary ELT in the People's Republic of China. *Language, Culture and Curriculum, 15*(1), 30–50.

Hubbard, P., Jones, H., Thornton, B. and Wheeler, R. (1983). *A Training Course for TEFL*. Oxford: Oxford University Press.

Hudson, R. (1996). *Sociolinguistics* (2 ed.). Cambridge: Cambridge University Press.

Hui, L. (1997). New bottles, old wine: Communicative language teaching in China. *English Teaching Forum, 35*(4), 38–41.

Hymes, D. (1968). On communicative competence. In C. Brumfit and K. Johnson (Eds.), *The Communicative Approach to Language Teaching* (pp. 5–26). Oxford: Oxford University Press.

Hymes, D. (1972). Models of the interaction of language and social life. In J. Gumperz and D. Hymes (Eds.), *Directions in Sociolinguistics: The Ethnography of Communication* (pp. 35–71). New York: Holt, Rinehart and Winston.

Ireson, J., Mortimore, P. and Hallam, S. (1999). The common strands of pedagogy and their implications. In P. Mortimore (ed.), *Understanding Pedagogy and Its Impact on Learning* (pp. 213–232). London: Sage Publications.

Jarzabkowski, L. (2002). The social dimensions of teacher collegiality. *Journal of Educational Enquiry, 3*(2), 1–20.

Jin, L. and Cortazzi, M. (2003). English language teaching in China: A bridge to the future. In R. Y. L. Wong (ed.), *English Language Teaching in East Asia Today: Changing Policies and Practices* (2 ed., pp. 131–145). Singapore: Time Academic Press.

Johnson, K. (1992). The relationship between teachers' beliefs and practices during literacy instruction for non-native speakers of English. *Journal of Reading Behaviour, 24*, 83–108.

Johnson, K. (1994). The emerging beliefs and instructional practices of pre-service English as a second language teachers. *Teaching and Teacher Education, 10*(4), 439–452.

Johnson, R. K. (1989). A decision-making framework for the coherent language curriculum. In R. K. Johnson (ed.), *The Second Language Curriculum* (pp. 1–23). Cambridge: Cambridge University Press.

Kagan, D. (1992). Implications of research on teacher belief. *Educational Psychologist, 27*(1), 65–90.

Kelly, A. V. (2004). *The Curriculum: Theory and Practice* (5 ed.). London; Thousand Oaks, CA: Sage.

Kennedy, C. (1988). Evaluation of the management of change in ELT projects. *Applied Linguistics, 9*(4), 329–342.

Kumaravadivelu, B. (1994). The postmethod condition: (E)merging strategies for second/foreign language teaching. *TESOL Quarterly, 28*(1), 27–47.

Kumaravadivelu, B. (2001). Toward a postmethod pedagogy. *TESOL Quarterly, 35*(4), 537–560.

Kumaravadivelu, B. (2003). Critical language pedagogy: A postmethod perspective on English language teaching. *World Englishes, 22*(4), 539–550.

Labov, W. (1972). *Sociolinguistic Patterns*. Philadelphia: University of Pennsylvania Press.

Lam, A. (2002). English in education in China: Policy changes and learners' experiences. *World Englishes, 21*(2), 245–256.

Lam, A. (2005). *Language Education in China*. Hong Kong: Hong Kong University Press.

Lang, G. and Heiss, G. D. (1991). *A Practical Guide to Research Methods* (4 ed.). Lanham, ML: University Press of America.

Lantolf, J. P. (2000). Introducing sociocultural theory. In L. J. P. (ed.), *Sociocultural Theory and Second Language Learning*. Oxford: Oxford University Press.

Larsen-Freeman, D. (1986). *Techniques and Principles in Language Teaching*. New York: Oxford University Press.

Larsen-Freeman, D. (2000). *Techniques and Principles in Language Teaching* (2 ed.). Oxford: Oxford University Press.

Lave, J. and Wenger, E. (1991). *Situated Learning: Legitimate Peripheral Participation*. New York: Cambridge University Press.

Lee, S. M. C. (2002). *English teachers' conceptions of task-based learning*. Unpublished MEd, The University of Hong Kong.

Lewis, M. and McCook, F. (2002). Cultures of teaching: Voices from Vietnam. *ELT Journal, 56*(2), 146–153.

Li, J. P. (2003). *xin kecheng shiyan tuiguang paichu shijianbiao (The implementation of new curriculum is scheduled)*. Retrieved 4 May 2006, from http://www.tjjy.com.cn/pkuschool/teacher/kegai/kgfxb/16.htm

Liao, X. Q. (2000). What influenced teachers' adoption of the communicative approach in China? *TESOL Matters, 11*(1), 6.

Lincoln, Y. S. and Guba, E. G. (2000). Paradigmatic controversies, contradictions, and emerging confluences. In N. Denzin and Y. Lincoln (Eds.), *Handbook of Qualitative Research* (2 ed.) (pp. 163–188). Thousand Oaks, CA: Sage Publications.

Liu, D. Y. (1988). *EFL in schools in China*. Beijing: People's Education Press.

Liu, D. Y. (1995). *English language teaching in schools in China.* Paper presented at the International Language in Education Conference, The University of Hong Kong.

Liu, D. Y. (1996). *English language teaching in schools in China.* Paper presented at the English 2000 Conference, Beijing.

Liu, D. Y. (2001). Junior English for China geared to the times – the revised JEFC. *Zhong Xiao Xue Wai Yu Jiao Xue (Foreign Language Teaching in Schools), 24*(11), 20–24.

Liu, D. Y. (2002). English: The new curriculum leads to the textbook innovation. *Ke Cheng, Jiao Cai, Jiao Fa (Curriculum, Teaching Materials and Methods)* (9) (pp. 44–47).

Liu, D.Y. (2005). On English teaching assessment in basic education. *Ke Cheng, Jiao Cai, Jiao Fa (Curriculum, Teaching Materials and Methods)* 25(10), 56–60.

Liu, D. Y. and Adamson, B. (1998). *Progress and challenges in changing ELT in Chinese secondary schools.* Unpublished manuscript, Department of Curriculum Studies, The University of Hong Kong.

Liu, D. Y. and Adamson, B. (1999). Changing the English curriculum for secondary schools in China. *Curriculum Forum, 9*(1), 62–72.

Long, M. (1985). Input and second language acquisition theory. In S. M. Gass and C. G. Madden (Eds.), *Input in Second Language Acquisition* (pp. 377–393). Rowley, MA: Newbury House.

Long, M. and Crookes, G. (1992). Three approaches to task-based syllabus design. *TESOL Quarterly, 26*(1), 27–49.

Long, M. and Robinson, P. (1998). Focus on form: Theory, research, and practice. In C. Doughty and J. Williams (Eds.), *Focus on Form in Classroom Second Language Acquisition* (pp. 15–41). New York: Cambridge University Press.

Louis, K. and Miles, M. (1990). *Improving the Urban High School: What Works and Why.* New York: Teachers College Press.

McKay, S. L. and Wong, S. C. (1988). Language teaching in Nativist times: A need for sociopolitical awareness. *The Modern Language Journal, 72*, iv.

McLaughlin, M. W. (1998). Listening and learning from the field: Tales of policy implementation and situated practice. In A. Hargreaves, A. Lieberman, M. Fullan and D. Hopkins (eds.), *International Handbook of Educational Change* (pp. 70–84). London: Kluwer.

McNeil, J. D. (1996). *Curriculum: A Comprehensive Introduction* (5 ed.). New York, NY: Harper Collins.

Markee, N. (1997). *Managing Curricular Innovation.* New York: Cambridge University Press.

Marsh, C. J. and Willis, G. (2003). *Curriculum: Alternative Approaches, Ongoing Issues* (3 ed.). Upper Saddle River, NJ: Merrill.

Marshall, C. and Rossman, G. (1999). *Designing Qualitative Research* (3 ed.). Thousand Oaks, CA: Sage Publications.

Martens, M. L. (1992). Inhibitors to implementing a problem-solving approach to teaching elementary science: Case study of a teacher in change. *School Science and Mathematics, 92*(3), 150–156.

Marton, F. and Wenestam, C. (1987). *Qualitative differences in retention when a text is read several times.* Paper presented at the Second International Conference on Practical Aspects of Memory, University College of Swansea.

Marton, F. (2000). 'Afterword: the lived curriculum'. In B. Adamson, T. Kwan and K. K. Chan (eds). *Changing the curriculum: The impact of reform on primary schooling in Hong Kong.* Hong Kong: Hong Kong University Press.

Maxwell, J. A. (1996). *Qualitative Research Design: An Interactive Approach.* Thousand Oaks, CA: Sage publication.

Mei, D-M. (2004). *Dazhongxiaoxue yingyu jiaoxue xianzhuang diaocha* (A Survey on ELT at primary, secondary and tertiary schools in China). Shanghai: Shanghai Foreign Language Education Press.

Mercer, N. (1995). *The Guided Construction of Knowledge.* Clevedon: Multilingual Matters.

Mitchell, R. and Myles, F. (1998). *Second Language Learning Theories.* London; New York: Arnold.

MOE. (2001). *quanrizhi yiwu jiaoyu putong gaoji zhongxue yingyu kecheng biaozhuan (shiyangao) (English Curriculum Standards for Full-time Compulsory Education and Senior Secondary School [trial version]).* Beijing: Beijing Normal University Press.

Moon, R. (1998). *The English Exception: International Perspectives on the Initial Education and Training of Teachers.* London: Universities Council for the Education of Teachers.

Morgan, B. (1997). Identity and intonation: Linking dynamic processes in an ESL classroom. *TESOL Quarterly, 31*(3), 431–450.

Morris, P. (1996). *The Hong Kong School Curriculum: Development, Issues and Policies* (2 ed.). Hong Kong: Hong Kong University Press.

Morris, P. (1997). School knowledge, the state, and the market: An analysis of the Hong Kong secondary school curriculum. *Journal of Curriculum Studies, 29*(3), 329–349.

Munby, J. (1978). *Communicative Syllabus Design.* Cambridge: Cambridge University Press.

Nespor, J. (1987). The role of beliefs in the practice of teaching. *Journal of Curriculum Studies, 19*, 317–328.

Neuman, W. L. (2003). *Social Research Methods: Qualitative and Quantitative Approaches* (5 ed.). Boston: Allyn and Bacon.

Ng, C. and Tang, E. (1997). *Can teachers cope with ELT boom in China – A Shanghai perspective?* Paper presented at the TESOL 1997, Orlando, FL.

Nisbett, R. E. and Ross, L. (1980). *Human Interferences: Strategies and Shortcomings of Social Judgement.* Englewood Cliffs, NJ: Prentice Hall.

Nunan, D. (1989). *Designing Tasks for the Communicative Classroom.* Cambridge: Cambridge University Press.

Nunan, D. (1999). *Second Language Teaching and Learning.* Boston, MA: Heinle and Heinle Publishers.

Nunan, D. (2003). The impact of English as a global language on educational policies and practices in the Asia-Pacific region. *TESOL Quarterly, 37*(4), 589–613.

Oakes, J., Wells, A. S. and Yonezawa, S. (2000). Change agentry and the quest for equity: Lessons from detracking schools. In A. Hargreaves (ed.), *The Sharp Edge of Educational Change: Teaching, Leading, and the Realities of Reform* (pp. 72–96). London; New York: Routledge.

Olson, J. (1981). Teacher influence in the classroom: A context for understanding curriculum translation. Elsevier scientific publishing company, Amsterdam. *Instructional Science, 10,* 259–275.

Omaggio, A. C. (1986). *Teaching Language in Context: Proficiency-Oriented Instruction.* Boston, MA: Heinle and Heinle.

Osborn, M., McNess, E., Broadfoot, P., Pollard, A. and Triggs, P. (2000). *What Teachers Do: Changing Policy and Practice in Primary Education.* London; New York: Continuum.

Paine, L. (1990). The teacher as virtuoso: A Chinese model for teaching. *Teachers College Record, 92*(1), 48–81.

Paine, L. (1997). Chinese teachers as mirrors of reform possibilities. In W. K. Cummings and P. G. Altbach (Eds.), *The Challenge of Eastern Asian Education* (pp. 65–83). Albany: State University of New York Press.

Pajares, M. F. (1992). Teachers' beliefs and educational research: Cleaning up a messy construct. *Review of Educational Research, 62,* 307–332.

Patton, M. Q. (1990). *Qualitative Evaluation and Research Methods.* Newbury Park, CA: Sage Publications.

Patton, M. Q. (2002). *Qualitative Research and Evaluation Methods* (3 ed.). Thousand Oaks, CA: Sage Publications.

Payne, G. and Payne, J. (2004). *Key Concepts in Social Research.* London: Sage.

Pehkonen, E. and Törner, G. (1999). Teachers' professional development: What are the key change factors for mathematics teacher? *European Journal of Teacher Education, 22*(2/3), 259–274.

Penner, J. (1991a). *Conflicts with beliefs, pedagogy, and structure: Foreign involvement in pedagogical change of English as a foreign language in the PRC.* Unpublished manuscript, Vancouver: University of British Columbia.

Penner, J. (1991b). *Opening the door with the English key-foreign involvement in EFL teacher education in China: An annotated bibliography.* Unpublished manuscript, Vancouver: University of British Columbia.

Pennington, M. (1989). Faculty development for language programs. In R. Johnson (ed.), *The Second Language Curriculum* (pp. 91–110). Cambridge: Cambridge University Press.

Pennycook, A. (1994). *The Cultural Politics of English as an International Language.* London: Longman.

Pennycook, A. (2000). The social politics and the cultural politics of language classrooms. In J. K. Hall and W. G. Eggington (Eds.), *The Sociopolitics of English Language Teaching* (pp. 89–103). Clevedon: Multilingual Matters.

PEP (2001). *Yin Yu Ke Cheng Biao Zhun (English Curriculum Standards).* Beijing: People's Education Press.

Phillipson, R. (1992). *Linguistic Imperialism.* Oxford: Oxford University Press.

Pintrich, P. (1990). Implications of psychological research on student learning and college teaching for teacher education. In W. Houston (ed.), *Handbook of Research on Teacher Education* (pp. 826–857). New York: Macmillan.

Pollard, A. (ed.) (1994). *Changing English Primary Schools: The Impact of the Education Reform Act at Key Stage One.* London; New York: Continuum.

Pollard, A., Triggs, P., Broadfoot, W. P., McNess, E. and Osborn, M. (2000). *What Pupils Say: Changing Policy and Practice in Primary Education.* London; New York: Continuum.

Potter, J. (1997). Discourse analysis as a way of analysing naturally occurring talk. In D. Silverman (ed.), *Qualitative Research: Theory, Method and Practice* (pp. 144–160). London: Sage Publications.

Poulson, L., Avramidis, E., Fox, R., Medwekk, J. and Wray, D. (2001). The theoretical beliefs of effective teachers of literacy in primary schools: An exploratory study of orientations to reading and writing. *Research Papers in Education, 16*(3), 271–292.

Prabhu, N. S. (1987). *Second Language Pedagogy.* Oxford: Oxford University Press.

Prabhu, N. S. (1990). There is no best method. Why? *TESOL Quarterly, 24*(2), 161–176.

Price, R. F. (1979). *Education in Modern China.* London: Routledge and Kegan Paul.

Putnam, R. T. and Borko, H. (1997). Teacher learning: Implications of new views of cognition. In G. Biddle and I. F. Goodson (ed.), *International Handbook of Teachers and Teaching* (Vol. 2, pp. 1223–1296). Dordrecht: Kluwer Academic Publishers.

Rao, Z. H. (1996). Reconciling communicative approaches to the teaching of English with traditional Chinese methods. *Research in the Teaching of English, 30* (pp. 458–471).

Rao, Z. H. (1999). Modern vs traditional. *Forum, 37*(3), 27.

Richards, J. (1985). *The Context of Language Teaching.* London: Cambridge University Press.

Richards, J. (1990). Beyond methods. In J. Richards (ed.), *The Language Teaching Matrix* (pp. 35–49). Cambridge: Cambridge University Press.

Richards, J. (1996). Teachers' maxims in language teaching. *TESOL Quarterly, 30*(2), 281–296.

Richards, J. (2002). Accuracy and fluency revisited. In E. Hinke and S. Fotos (Eds.), *New Perspectives on Grammar Teaching in Second Language Classrooms* (pp. 35–50). Mahwah, NJ: Lawrence Erlbaum.

Richards, J., Gipe, J. and Thompson, B. (1987). Teacher's beliefs about good reading instruction. *Reading Psychology, 8*(1), 1–6.

Richards, J. and Nunan, D. (1990). *Second Language Teacher Education.* Cambridge: Cambridge University Press.

Richards, J., Platt, J. and Weber, H. (1985). *Longman Dictionary of Applied Linguistics.* London: Longman.

Richards, J. and Rodgers, T. (1986). *Approaches and Methods in Language Teaching: A Description and Analysis.* Cambridge: Cambridge University Press.

Richards, J. and Rodgers, T. (2001). *Approaches and Methods in Language Teaching* (2 ed.). Cambridge: Cambridge University Press.

Richardson, V. (1994). The consideration of teachers' beliefs. In V. Richardson (ed.), *Teacher Change and the Staff Development Process: A Case in Reading Instruction* (pp. 90–108). New York: Teachers College Press.

Richardson, V. (1996). The role of attitude and beliefs in learning to teach. In J. Sikual (ed.), *Handbook of Research on Teacher Education* (pp. 102–119). New York: Macmillan.

Richardson, V., Anders, P., Tidwell, D. and Lloyd, C. (1991). The relationship between teachers' beliefs and practices in reading comprehension instruction. *American Educational Research Journal, 28*(3), 559–586.

Rivers, W. M. (1968). *Teaching Foreign Language Skills.* Chicago: The University of Chicago Press.

Roberts, J. (1998). *Language Teacher Education.* London: Arnold.

Rodgers, T. S. (2001). *Language teaching methodology.* Retrieved 26 October 2002, from http://www.cal.org/ericcll/digest/rodgers.html

Rogers, E. M. and Shoemaker, F. F. (1971). *Communication of Innovations.* New York: Free Press.

Rogoff, B. (1990). *Apprenticeship in Thinking.* Cambridge: Cambridge University Press.

Romaine, S. (1994). *Language in Society: An Introduction to Sociolinguistics.* Oxford: Oxford University Press.

Ronald, W. (2002). *An Introduction to Sociolinguistics* (4 ed.). Malden, MA: Blackwell Publishers.

Ross, H. A. (1993). *China Learns English: Language Teaching and Social Change in the People's Republic.* New Haven; London: Yale University Press.

Rossman, G. B. and Rallis, S. F. (2003). *Learning in the Field: An Introduction to Qualitative Research.* Thousand Oaks, CA: Sage Publications.

Roy, P. and Hord, S. (2004). Innovation configurations chart: A measured course toward change. *JSD, 25*(2), 54–58.

Rust, F. (1994). The first year of teaching: It's not what they expected. *Teaching and Teacher Education, 10,* 205–217.

Sarason, S. B. (1993). *You Are Thinking of Teaching? Opportunities, Problems, Realities.* San Francisco, CA: Jossey-Bass.

Savignon, S. (1983). *Communicative Competence: Theory and Classroom Practice.* Reading, MA: Addison-Wesley.

Savignon, S. (1991). Communicative language teaching: State of the art. *TESOL Quarterly, 25*(2), 261–277.

Schön, D. A. (1983). *The Reflective Practitioner.* London: Basic Books.

Schubert, W. and Lopez, A. (1994). Students in curriculum experiences. In T. N. Postethwaite (ed.), *The International Encyclopaedia of Education.* New York: Pergamon.

Schwandt, T. A. (1997). *Qualitative Inquiry: A Dictionary of Terms.* Thousand Oaks, CA: Sage Publications.

Scovel, T. (1995). *English teaching in China.* Unpublished manuscript, for the United States Information Agency.

Searle, J. R. (1969). *Speech Acts: An Essay in the Philosophy of Language.* Cambridge: Cambridge University Press.

Sergeant, S. (1999). Call innovation in the ELT curriculum. In C. Goh (ed.), *Exploring Change in English Language Teaching* (pp. 75–85). Oxford: Macmillan Heinemann.

Shavelson, R. J. and Stern, P. (1981). Research on teachers' pedagogical thoughts, judgments, decisions, and behavior. *Review of Educational Research, 51*(4), 455–498.

Shaw, K. L., Davis, N. T. and McCarty, J. (1991). A cognitive framework for teacher change. In Underhill, A. E. (ed.), *Proceedings of PME-NA 13* (Vol. 12, pp. 161–167). Blacksburg, VA, Virginia, Tech.

Shen, L-X. and Gao, Y-H. (2004). *Fengkuang yingyu duiyu xuexizhe de yiyi* (What 'Crazy English' means to Chinese students). In Y-H Gao (ed.) *Zhongguo daxuesheng yingyu xuexi shehui xinli: Xuexi dongji yu ziwo rentong yanjiu* (The social psychology of English learning by Chinese college students: Motivation and learners' self-identities) (pp.190–201). Beijing: Foreign Language Teaching and Research Press.

Shu, D. F. (2004). *FLT in China: Problems and Suggested Solutions*. Shanghai: Shanghai Foreign Language Education Press.

Skehan, P. (1994). Second language acquisition strategies, interlanguage development and task-based learning. In M. Bygate, A. Tonkyn and E. Williams (Eds.), *Grammar and the Language Teacher* (pp. 175–199). Hemel Hempstead: Prentice Hall.

Skehan, P. (1995). A framework for the implementation of task-based instruction. *Applied Linguistics, 17*(1), 38–62.

Skehan, P. (1996). Second language acquisition and research and task-based instruction. In J. Willis and D. Willis (Eds.), *Challenge and Change in Language Teaching* (pp. 17–30). Oxford: Heinemann English Language Teaching.

Skehan, P. (2003). Task-based instruction. *Language Teaching, 36*, 1–14.

Skinner, B. F. (1957). *Verbal Behavior*. New York: Appleton-Century-Crofts.

Snyder, J., Bolin, F. and Zumwalt, K. (1992). Curriculum implementation. In P. W. Jackson (ed.), *Handbook of Research on Curriculum* (pp. 402–435). New York: Macmillan.

Soars, L. and Soars, J. (2000). *New Headway Elementary: Teacher's Book*. Oxford: Oxford University Press.

Sparks, G. M. (1984). *In-service education: the process of teacher change*. Paper presented at the Annual Meeting of the American Educational Research Association, New Orleans, LA.

Steinberg, D. D. (1993). *An Introduction to Psycholinguistics*. London: Longman.

Steinberg, D. D. (2001). *Psycholinguistics: Language, Mind and World* (2 ed.). Harlow: Longman.

Stenhouse, L. (1975). *An Introduction to Curriculum Research and Development*. London: Heinemann.

Stern, H. H. (1983). *Fundamental Concepts of Language Teaching*. Oxford: Oxford University Press.

Stigler, J. W. (1998). Video surveys: New data for the improvement of classroom instruction. In S. G. Garis and H. M. Wellman (Eds.), *Global Prospects for Education: Development, Culture, and Schooling* (pp. 129–168). Washington, DC: American Psychological Association.

Stoll, L. and Fink, D. (1996) *Changing Our Schools*. Buckingham and Bristol, PA: Open University Press.

Sutton, S. A. (2000). *DC-education working document*. Retrieved 26 October 2001, from http://www.ischool.washington.edu/sasutton/dced/Pedagogy_SS_1.html

Tanaka, Y. (1996). *The comprehension and acquisition of relative clauses by Japanese high school students through formal instruction*. Unpublished PhD dissertation, Temple University, Tokyo.

Tang, D. and Absalom, D. (1998). Teaching across culture: Consideration for Western EFL teaching in China. *Hong Kong Journal of Applied Linguistics, 3*(2), 117–132.

Tang, J. (1986). San shier nian lai de zhong xue ying yu jiao cai (Thirty-two years of secondary school English teaching materials). In Curriculum Materials and Methodology Association (ed.), *Zhong Xue Wai Yu Jiao Cai He Jiao Fa (Foreign Language Materials and Methodology for Secondary Schools)* (pp. 49–60). Beijing: People's Education Press.

Tang, L. X. (1983). *TEFL in China: Methods and Techniques*. Shanghai: Shanghai Foreign Languages Press.

Taylor, P. H. and Richards, C. (1979). *An Introduction to Curriculum Studies*. Windsor, UK: The NFER Publishing Company.

Thornbury, S. (1998). Comments on Marianne Celce-Murcia, Zoltan Dörnyei and Sarah Thurrells' 'Direct approaches in L2 instruction: A turning point in communicative language teaching?' A reader reacts. *TESOL Quarterly, 32*(1), 109–116.

Tollefson, J. W. (2000). Policy and ideology in the spread of English. In J. K. Hall and W. G. Eggington (Eds.), *The Sociopolitics of English Language Teaching* (pp. 7–21). Clevedon: Multilingual Matters.

Tong, A. S. Y. (2005). *Task-based learning in English language in Hong Kong secondary schools*. Unpublished PhD, The University of Hong Kong.

Tong, A. S. Y., Adamson, B. and Che, M. M. W. (2000). Task in English and Chinese language. In Adamson, D., Kwan, T. and Chan, K. (eds.), *Changing the Curriculum: The Impact of Reform on Primary Schooling in Hong Kong*. Hong Kong: Hong Kong University Press.

Tsui, A. B. M. (2003). *Understanding Expertise in Teaching: Case Studies of Second Language Teachers*. Cambridge: Cambridge University Press.

Tsui, K. T. and Cheng, Y. C. (2000). A framework of curriculum effectiveness: Development and research. In K. Tsui (ed.), *School Curriculum Change and Development in Hong Kong* (pp. xvii–xlviii). Hong Kong Institute of Education.

Vygotsky, L. S. (1978). *Mind in Society: The Development of Higher Psychological Process*. Cambridge, MA: Harvard University Press.

Wang, L-B. (2001). When English becomes big business. Paper presented at the International Conference on Globalization, Culture and English Language Education in China and Hong Kong (SAR), the Chinese University of Hong Kong, Hong Kong, 1–4 March.

Wang, Q. (1999). Reflection and suggestions: The foreign language curriculum innovation towards 21st compulsory education. *Zhong Xiao Xue Wai Yu Jiao Xue (Foreign Language Teaching in Schools), 22*(7), 1–4.

Wang, Q. (2007). The National Curriculum changes and their effects on

English language teaching in the People's Republic of China. In Cummins, J. and Davison, C. (eds). *International Handbook of English language teaching, Vol. 1* (pp.87–106) Norwell, MA: Springer.

Wehling, L. and Charters, W. (1969). Dimensions of teacher beliefs about the teaching process. *American Educational Research Journal, 6*(1), 7–29.

Wertsch, J. V. (1985). *Vygotsky and the Social Formation of Mind.* Cambridge, MA: Harvard University Press.

Wertsch, J. V. (1991). *Voices of the Mind: A Sociocultural Approach to Mediated Action.* Cambridge, MA: Harvard University Press.

Wertsch, J. V. (1998). *Mind as Action.* New York: Oxford University Press.

White, R. V. (1988). *The ELT Curriculum: Design, Innovation and Management.* New York: Basil Blackwell.

Whorf, B. (1956). Science and linguistics. In J. B. Carroll (ed.), *Language, Thought, and Reality: Selected Writings of Benjamin Lee Whorf* (pp. 227–231). Cambridge: Technology Press of Massachusetts Institute of Technology.

Widdowson, H. (1978). *Teaching Language as Communication.* Oxford: Oxford University Press.

Widdowson, H. (1979). The communicative approach and its applications. In H. Widdowson (ed.), *Explorations in Applied Linguistics* (pp. 251–264). Oxford: Oxford University Press.

Widdowson, H. (1990). *Aspects of Language Teaching.* Oxford: Oxford University Press.

Widdowson, H. (1998). Context, community, and authentic language. *TESOL Quarterly, 32*(4), 705–715.

Wideen, M. (1994). *The Struggle for Change: The Story of One School.* Bristol, PA: Falmer Press.

Wilkins, D. A. (1976). *Notional Syllabuses.* Oxford: Oxford University Press.

Williams, M. and Burden, R. (1997). *Psychology for Language Learners: A Social Constructivist Approach.* Cambridge: Cambridge University Press.

Willis, J. (1996). A flexible framework for task-based learning. In J. Willis and D. Willis (Eds.), *Challenge and Change in Language Teaching* (pp. 52–62). Oxford: Heinemann.

Winch, C. and Gingell, J. (1999). *Key Concepts in the Philosophy of Education.* London: Routledge.

Wolcott, H. F. (1994). *Transforming Qualitative Data: Description, Analysis, and Interpretation.* Thousand Oaks, CA: Sage.

Wong, K. Y. E. (2001). *Learner preferences of task types: A case study in a medium-medium secondary school in Hong Kong.* Unpublished MEd dissertation, The University of Hong Kong.

Woods, D. (1996). *Teacher Cognition in Language Teaching: Beliefs, Decision-Making and Classroom Practice.* Cambridge: Cambridge University Press.

Wu, Y. A. (2001). English language teaching in China: Trends and challenges. *TESOL Quarterly, 35*(1), 191–194.

Wyss, R. (2002). *Bringing learners up-to-date on CLT classroom approaches.* Retrieved 27 December 2002, from http://www.eltnewsletter.com/back/January2002/art842002.htm

Xie, Y. (2004). Curriculum situation and strategies: The case study on the curriculum implementation of English in primary schools. *Curriculum, Teaching Materials and Method, 24*(2), 60–66.

Yin, R. K. (1994). *Case Study Research: Design and Methods* (2 ed.). Thousand Oaks, CA: Sage.

Yu, C. (1984). Cultural principles underlying English teaching in China. *Language Learning and Communication, 3*(1), 29–40.

Yu, L. M. (2001). Communicative language in China: Progress and resistance. *TESOL Quarterly, 35*(1), 194–198.

Yung, H. W. B. (2000). *Teachers' beliefs and their teaching of practical work in a school-based assessment scheme.* Unpublished PhD thesis, The University of Hong Kong.

Zhang, J. Z. (2001). Analysis of the 3rd National Competition of High Quality English Lessons (Junior Middle Schools). *Zhong Xiao Xue Wai Yu Jiao Xue (Foreign Language Teaching in Schools), 24*(7), 20–23.

Zhang, Y. F. (2005). *The implementation of the task-based approach in primary school English language teaching in Mainland China.* Unpublished PhD thesis, The University of Hong Kong.

Zheng, X. M. (2005). *Pedagogy and pragmatism: secondary English language teaching in the People's Republic of China.* Unpublished PhD thesis, The University of Hong Kong.

Zheng, X. M. and Adamson, B. (2003). The pedagogy of a secondary school teacher of English in the People's Republic of China: Challenging the stereotypes. *Regional English Language Center Journal, 34*(3), 323–327.

Zhu, X. Y. (2003). *The development of pedagogical content knowledge in novice secondary school teachers of English in the People's Republic of China.* Unpublished PhD thesis, The University of Hong Kong.

Index